Ezumezu

Jonathan O. Chimakonam

Ezumezu

A System of Logic for African Philosophy and Studies

Springer

Jonathan O. Chimakonam
Department of Philosophy
University of Calabar
Calabar, Nigeria

ISBN 978-3-030-11074-1   ISBN 978-3-030-11075-8   (eBook)
https://doi.org/10.1007/978-3-030-11075-8

Library of Congress Control Number: 2019933294

© The Editor(s) (if applicable) and The Author(s), under exclusive license to Springer Nature Switzerland AG, part of Springer Nature 2019
This work is subject to copyright. All rights are solely and exclusively licensed by the Publisher, whether the whole or part of the material is concerned, specifically the rights of translation, reprinting, reuse of illustrations, recitation, broadcasting, reproduction on microfilms or in any other physical way, and transmission or information storage and retrieval, electronic adaptation, computer software, or by similar or dissimilar methodology now known or hereafter developed.
The use of general descriptive names, registered names, trademarks, service marks, etc. in this publication does not imply, even in the absence of a specific statement, that such names are exempt from the relevant protective laws and regulations and therefore free for general use.
The publisher, the authors, and the editors are safe to assume that the advice and information in this book are believed to be true and accurate at the date of publication. Neither the publisher nor the authors or the editors give a warranty, express or implied, with respect to the material contained herein or for any errors or omissions that may have been made. The publisher remains neutral with regard to jurisdictional claims in published maps and institutional affiliations.

This Springer imprint is published by the registered company Springer Nature Switzerland AG.
The registered company address is: Gewerbestrasse 11, 6330 Cham, Switzerland

To the distant, anonymous African logicians, who are now remembered only as ancestors—that your good name and honour desecrated in the colonial times may now be restored.

To my peers, who toil from an impossible historical position in the fields of African philosophy and studies—that our successors may come to know that we did original stuffs.

To all my teachers from childhood, we wrote this book together.

To all my students, past and present, for all that you taught me.

And finally, to my HP Pavilion g6 Notebook computer, 6 years in loyal service without disappointments, this is your last completed book before your scheduled retirement—I don't know what humans might think about this, but I feel you deserve this dedication.

Foreword

I read this brilliant and groundbreaking book in the manner the author wanted me to read it: as an exercise of my own self-education. As I imagine it, Jonathan O. Chimakonam's idea, in having invited me to write the foreword, was to test the type, the limits and the possibilities of a possible dialogue between two scholars, separated by conventional criteria, but converging on similar intellectual disquietudes vis-a-vis conventional professional wisdom, and additionally to envisage how much mutual enrichment can be derived from such an exchange. On the one hand, several degrees of separation stand between the two of us; Chimakonam is a Nigerian philosopher, while I am a Portuguese sociologist with philosophical background. Chimakonam deals with the most intricate and complex meanders of professional philosophy, logic and thought systems, while I have done extensive empirical research in Latin America and Africa with social groups involved in struggles against capitalism, colonialism and patriarchy and anchor my theoretical and epistemological work on such a sociological experience. Chimakonam's mother tongue is the Igbo language and he writes in English, while my mother tongue is Portuguese and I write in Portuguese and English. We think and write from different standpoints. While Chimakonam writes on the basis of the extremely painful memory and lived experience of colonialism and the massive epistemicide and genocide committed by it, I write from the standpoint of active solidarity with the people that fought against colonialism and of the immense damage caused by European colonialism not only upon the colonised peoples and cultures but also upon the European peoples and cultures.

On the other hand, we converge to a large extent on our critique of Eurocentrism and struggle with the task of establishing the conditions under which a post-Eurocentric nonderivative scholarship can emerge. A derivative scholarship is derivative whenever it excels in deconstructive exercises but lacks the creativity and originality necessary to ground new intellectual paradigms. We also converge on the idea that there is no global social justice without global cognitive justice. From different perspectives, we also converge on developing epistemologies of the south, understanding by south not a geographic south (a south populated by so many "little Europes", to use Edward Said's catchy term) but rather an epistemic one.

I have written extensively on the epistemologies of the south, a long journey that started in the mid-1980s with an internal critique of positivism as the dominant epistemological understanding of modern science since the late nineteenth century (1992; 1995; 2007) and evolved toward an external critique of both positivism and anti-positivism and the formulation of the epistemologies of the south, as a learning process focused on the epistemes that throughout the modern era have provided the grounding for the resistance against Western capitalism, colonialism and patriarchy and the epistemologies that legitimated it: the epistemologies of the north (2014, 2018).

I consider Chimakonam's book as the most convincing and powerful formulation of a philosophy of the south that I have read in many years and which emerges from the African historical and existential contexts and cultures. Since we are talking about ancient or pre-colonial thought systems, the idea of emergence must be taken with a grain of salt. It strictly means a more consistent and updated formulation of a given thought system and its expanded credibility before wider publics, beyond the contexts and cultures that originated them. Rooted in other non-Western contexts and cultures, other philosophies of the south have gained broader attention in recent years, such as Chinese, Indian, indigenous, Islamic philosophies of the south. Moreover, this epistemic impulse has extended to different fields of scholarship, from literary studies to sociology and theology.

I have learned a lot from this impressive book. The most salient features of this book are the following. The possibility and nature of African philosophy has been widely discussed since mid-twentieth century. As one might expect, some (the universalists) have taken the position that there is only one, universal philosophy, the one born in Greece, developed in modern Europe and today subscribed to by professional philosophers in the Euro-American world and elsewhere, while others (the relativists) have defended that philosophising, like any other intellectual activity, is a culture-sensitive and context-sensitive activity and that accordingly there is room for an African philosophy as well as for other non-Western philosophies. As happens in other parts of the world, the African philosophers have been divided on this issue. The first position has been criticised for condemning philosophising by African philosophers to a derivative activity, a transliteration or copycat philosophy. In turn, the second position has been criticised for condemning the noble task of philosophising to a cacophony of different ghettoised and incommensurable *lucubrations* or ethnophilosophy, all of them unintelligible beyond the confines of their respective contexts. For reasons that I cannot go into in this foreword, Africa is probably the continent in which this divide has been experienced as a dichotomic dilemma with more existential anxiety or perplexity. The most remarkable feature of Chimakonam's stance is that it confronts this dilemma head on and proves it to be a false one by finding a logical grounding on which original ideas can sprout from, something that has been missing all along and never before done in the field which changes the entire narrative in African philosophy. According to him, African philosophy can dare to be original and creative vis-a-vis the Aristotelian and Platonic tradition without condemning itself to the identity ghetto. African philosophy is context- and culture-sensitive in such a way that makes it an original and creative contribution to the worldwide search for the ultimate meaning of life. Understood in this way, it is a universalisable endeavour like other philosophies stemming from other contexts and cultures.

Such a way of conceptualising African philosophy is a very demanding task, and Chimakonam does not shy away from it. According to him, the originality and creativity of a given philosophy are grounded on a specific method and its underlying logic. It is impossible to think of a genuine African philosophy while subscribing to the Aristotelian bivalence logic that underlies Western philosophy. Africa has at its disposal another logic which, however ostracised by the colonialists and Western philosophers, is very much anchored in the African thought systems and in the existential and historical contexts and cultures present on the continent. In an astounding intellectual tour de force conducted in the most consistent and rigorous way, Chimakonam offers Ezumezu as the prototype of an African logic, a variant of a trivalence logic. In a subliminal invitation to a decentring exercise, particularly for those whose centre has been built with Greek concepts and terms, the journey into Ezumezu logic abounds in Igbo-African words and concepts. As the argumentation proceeds, it becomes more and more convincing that this logic may indeed be universally used since its contextual and cultural roots do not condition all the possible options it generates. Two additional reasons seem to strengthen this conviction. The first one is that Ezumezu has striking similarities with the logic systems underlying indigenous peoples' and East Asian or Indian philosophies. The more we know about them, the more evident it becomes that the Aristotelian logic, in spite of its efficiency in many areas of social life, is in its bud as particular as many other non-Western or non-Aristotelian logic systems. Expressed in sociological terms, it is a localism that managed to get globalised in the modern era, thanks not so much to the force of its idea but rather to the idea of force of capitalism and colonialism that found in the Aristotelian logic an instrument well fitted to its expansionary endeavour.

The second reason is that in an increasingly polarised world, with unprecedented social inequalities and resilient racial, gender and religious discriminations, in a world seemingly heading for a dystopic future characterised by new feudal castles of opulence surrounded by multitudes of oppressed peoples, the call for third or intermediate values, for context- and culture-sensitive notions of truth/falsehood and for the unending alternation of conjunctive and disjunctive intermediation between polar variables or realities seems to promise a better chance for a democratic and peaceful social life. For these two reasons, the abstract universalism of Western-centric philosophy may be morphing into a monolithic, monocultural particularism that is unwillingly opening the space for the emergence of a bottom-up, cosmopolitan universalism made of the differently universalisable vocations or impulses of many intellectual and philosophical traditions. Upon such a new universalism, the aspiration for an intercultural philosophy will have a better chance.

In this lies my totally unconditional agreement with Chimakonam. Indeed, I have been claiming that there are epistemologies of the south only because there are epistemologies of the north and as long as the latter insist on being the only valid epistemologies in spite of the growing evidence to the contrary. Along the same lines, I have been defending that, rather than focusing exclusively on the task of deconstructing the Western intellectual supremacy (as in the deconstruction brought about by the decolonising studies), we must grant equal attention to the credible presentation of knowledges and epistemologies otherwise (the constructive task undertaken by the call for the epistemologies of the south).

As to my self-education, after a deep immersion in the fascinating intellectual landscape offered by this book, I come to the conclusion that I need to dedicate much more work to the methodological and pedagogical dimensions of the epistemologies of the south and of the social sciences grounded upon them. It is true that in my most recent work, I have dedicated myself to such dimensions (2017, 2018); but in light of Chimakonam's book, I concede that much more is needed. I dare to say that, as concerns pedagogy, the same applies to Chimakonam. Chapter 11 dedicated to the topic reads like the first chapter of a new hopefully upcoming book on Ezumezu pedagogy and curriculum.

I think I have given enough reasons to encourage a close reading of this fascinating book. Its readers will eagerly follow the exciting new paths and explore the immense vistas it opens. It will be a demanding task, but the rewards will by far compensate the effort.

Professor of Sociology at the
University of Coimbra, Portugal,
Distinguished Legal Scholar at the
University of Wisconsin-Madison,
Madison, WI, USA

Boaventura de Sousa Santos

References

Santos, Boaventura de Sousa. 1992. A discourse on the sciences. *Review* XV, 1, Winter: 9–47.
———. 1995. *Toward a new common sense: Law, science and politics in the paradigmatic transition*. New York: Routledge. Second edition titled *Toward New Legal Common Sense*. London Cambridge University Press, 2003.
———. 2007. (ed.) *Cognitive justice in a global world: Prudent knowledge for a decent life*. Lanham: Lexington.
———. 2014. *Epistemologies of the south. Justice against Epistemicide*. New York: Routledge.
———. 2017. *Decolonising the University. The challenge of deep cognitive justice*. Newcastle upon Tyne: Cambridge Scholars Publishing.
———. 2018. *The end of the cognitive empire: The coming of age of the epistemologies of the south*. Durham: Duke University Press.

Preface

Without method, difference in philosophical thinking cannot be established. Without difference, unity of ideas cannot be asserted. Two variables, A and B, were first different before they became similar. No two different though similar variables are identical. Universality is something obtained or created from diversity and not the other way round. In other words, diversity is necessary for universality. It is from the particulars that the universal is created. The idea that philosophy is one big intellectual culture tracing its genealogy to ancient Greece, found commonly in Western intellectual history, is false.

This falsehood was born in the legacies of Plato and Aristotle. Unfortunately, it is upon these two ancient philosophers that many a Western philosopher has based his thought and is now attempting to impose the same on all other cultures. Alfred North Whitehead has accurately judged the legion after the golden age of Greek philosophy to be footnotes to Plato and, I dare add, to Aristotle. Karl Popper, that unfazed enigma, has also spoken of the spell which Plato has cast on the later generation of Western thinkers. It is not unpremeditated that Western philosophers now build a wall around their thought, refusing to engage or converse with those they regard as outsiders. They do this not out of fear that such might contaminate or dilute the value of their philosophy but for an ingrained bias and motivation to discount the humanity and rationality of other peoples.

I have called this type of effort "conceptual envelopment"[1] which is dangerous and myopic. Soon, without outside interaction, their philosophical canons would become too old for modern life and too outdated to undergird modern policy. This is already happening as philosophy's value in the Western academy has depreciated to something of a decorative urn. In policy formulation and implementation, the philosopher in the West is isolated farther away from the circle of influence. The conceptual accumulation of Western philosophy is becoming poorer by the day. Indeed, its contemporary actors are still deeply influenced by Plato and Aristotle in

---

[1] See Chimakonam, O. Jonathan. 2015. Conversational philosophy as a new school of thought in African philosophy: a conversation with Bruce Janz on the concept of "philosophical space". *Confluence: Journal of World Philosophies* 3: 9–40.

their conceptual framing that it seems that they think for a different generation and epoch. As a result, some disciplines in the social sciences which are in tune with modern demands are taking up responsibilities of philosophers in the society, while the Western philosopher dazed out there by the delusion of the impregnability of the legacies of Plato and Aristotle, holds tightly to the umbilical cord that connects him to Plato and thus remands himself in perpetual intellectual stagnation.

The world is now moving on from Western canons of thought which Aristotle formalised in the traditional laws of thought. It may still be necessary to look left and right before one crosses the road because it is either the bus or the individual; if it is the bus, then it is the bus, and if it is the individual, then it is the individual. But we can no longer insist that it cannot be both the bus and the individual because we have since found a way to grant both. It means we may now cross the road without having to look left and right. When we tour the cities of the world today and we see overhead or underground crossings, we must ask, what logic or laws of thought explain these? It is definitely not the principle of identity, contradiction and excluded middle with which Aristotle has monopolised and shaped thought for several hundreds of years. The overhead and underground crossings are just two examples of what an alternative thought model like the African system of logic can yield. Albert Einstein has in the twentieth century made a bold statement with his theory of relativity and demonstrated that the dominance of Aristotle's logic may be nearing its end. More than 100 years later, the Western philosopher is refusing to loosen his grip on the cord connecting him to that Prometheus system of thought.

The danger, however, is not only about Western philosophy's lack of flexibility but its use of its position of influence to prevent other emerging traditions of thought, notably the Asian and the African, from forging ahead. This has been possible so far because actors in Asian and African philosophical traditions remain desperate to converse with Western philosophers. They have come up with the battle to first affirm themselves, a battle, quite unfortunately, that has appeared to be an endless one. Western philosophy has found a way to remand these two traditions in a circus of trying to prove a point or endear itself to the Western mind, something both traditions have failed to impress on. It is this desperation to engage with Western philosophy by the epistemologies of the South that has continued to confer a position of importance to an otherwise moribund system of thought in the West.

It is also this quest to impress the West that has trapped reason in the African place, preventing it from reaching full expression and manifestation. The problems which have for nearly a century beleaguered Africa have their common source in Western logic which has proved inadequate in Africa. With this alien logic undergirding every form of life from education to policy to institutions in Africa, it was difficult to raise and train a capable generation that can think critically, creatively and originally. The result is the preponderance of mediocrity, lack of enlightenment and a dangerous culture of imitation.

I here offer a system of logic for African philosophy and sundry disciplines in African studies. Christened Ezumezu logic, it is only a prototype of African logic meaning that another similar system that can axiomatise the conception of reality in Africa is possible. Logic is not a property of one race; we must wake up from this false impression. It is a tool any people can fashion and use in ways that aid them better in the advancement of knowledge. Whoever has logic has idea. It is almost impossible to create a new idea if one has no logic. It is now time for Africa to rise up and systematise its own logic in order to manifest its own natural creative originality. An alien logic inhibits the original expression of reason in a culture which is what has stagnated Africa's development since colonialism displaced African logic with Western logic.

My primary aim for writing this book is to unveil Ezumezu as an Africa-inspired and compatible system of logic with its structure laid out as philosophy of logic, methodology and a formal system. It is my second aim to demonstrate how this logic grounds theories in African philosophy and studies, and, finally, it is my third aim to show how to solve what I think is the foundational problem of Africa, that is, the operation of colonial curriculum of education based of Western logic foundation. I will develop what can be called a theory of curriculum transformation that involves the twin strategies of decolonisation and Africanisation on the basis of a system of African logic.

On the whole, this is a technical book presented in a style that encourages reading. The ideas presented in this book are tools which African scholars, teachers, policy-makers and intellectuals generally can utilise in various ways and in different areas of African studies to liberate the mind of Africa and teach the African child to learn to think professionally. It has taken me nearly a decade to complete this book and bring it up to its current form. A lot of challenges threatened this book during the last 10 years, and some nearly ended it. The first original draft of the five chapters of this book was lost in 2009. It was wholly handwritten, and I wanted to complete the book before taking the manuscript for typing. I had no computer and could not even type as of then. Somehow, in 2010, I managed to find the mental strength to begin again. It was a journey of intrusive research which made me read some of the interesting books you could think of in the ontology and cosmology of various African cultures. I had been frustrated at some point and elated at some others. I cannot count how many times in the last decade I gave up on this project, but somehow, and quite miraculously, there was always a fresh hope that spurred me on—"someone has to write this book," I would say to myself.

Now that the book is finally written, who would read it? This question began to torment me soon after I finished the last chapter. I would gaze into space and see nothingness. I would attempt to think about it and come up with total darkness. Who would read my book? Suddenly, I realised that the right question ought to have been, who should read my book and why? I believe that everyone should read this book. Those in other parts of the Global South might find inspiration in it to rise up and do something different. Those in the global north might be re-educated to see the world from a different perspective. As for those in Africa, the teacher should read this book because he is the most important warrior that leads the line in the battle to reclaim Africa. The policy-maker and the government person should read this book because he fashions the tools of war which the teacher uses. The African scholar and the intellectual should read this book because, most times, they are the ones that can shape minds and reshape them if needs be. Finally, the African students should read this book because they are the future. If the past is lost, we can still hope to recover the future. If the future has strayed, we can still hope to redirect its steps. This book compels the reader to think more than it allows him to feel, and the power to re-create Africa and place it on the path of new creative and inventive beginning will come from thinking.

Calabar, Nigeria   Jonathan O. Chimakonam

Acknowledgements

Some chapters of this book have been adapted from my previously published essays. Here, those essays have been variously modified and improved upon. Some new sections have been added, while a good number of old ones have been removed. Different passages have been rewritten in light of new insights to give this book a coherent structure and a fresh perspective. The original publishers of those essays are here acknowledged and appreciated for graciously granting the copyright permission to reuse them in part or in full in this book. Those essays include:

Chimakonam, O. Jonathan. 2015. The criteria question in African philosophy: Escape from the horns of jingoism and Afrocentrism. In *Atuolu Omalu: Some unanswered questions in contemporary African philosophy*, ed. Jonathan O. Chimakonam, 101–123. Lanham: University Press of America.

———. 2017. The question of African logic: Beyond apologia and polemics. In *The Palgrave handbook of African philosophy*, eds. Adeshina Afolayan and Toyin Falola, 106–128. New York: Palgrave Macmillan.

———. 2018a. The journey of reason in African philosophy. In *Ka Osi So Onye: African philosophy in the postmodern era,* eds. Jonathan O. Chimakonam and Edwin Etieyibo, 1–20. Delaware: Vernon Press.

———. 2018b. Can individual autonomy and rights be defended in Afro-communitarianism? *Filosofia Theoretica: Journal of African Philosophy, Culture and Religions* 7:2.

———. 2018c. The philosophy of African logic: A consideration of Ezumezu paradigm. In *Philosophical perceptions on logic and order,* ed. Jeremy Horne, 96–121. Hershey PA: IGI Global.

———. 2018d. Ezumezu as a methodological reconstruction in African philosophy. In *Ka Osi So Onye: African philosophy in the postmodern era,* eds. Jonathan O. Chimakonam and Edwin Etieyibo, 125–148. Delaware: Vernon Press.

My appreciation also goes to members of The Conversational School of Philosophy (CSP) in different countries—a forum for developing and promoting African philosophy and intellectual history, for leading a new resurgence in original philosophical research in Africa. I thank in a special way all authors I have cited and drawn inspiration from, most especially Boaventura Santos, C. S. Momoh, Meinrad Hebga, Leopold Senghor and Innocent Asouzu, to name but a few.

General Introduction

Ezumezu logic, as my theory is called, is an African culture-inspired system. It is an alternative and universalisable system of logic which can be applied in all relevant contexts anywhere in the world. It is not a unique, African culture-bound or closed system. In a way, it is fuzzy with three-pronged valuation in which greater power rests on the intermediate value.

There are three suppositions that necessitate this book: first, the intellectual history of our world was not only written by Eurocentric scholars from the global north; it was also written in a way that edited out or misrepresented or subordinated epistemic visions from the global south which amounts to epistemic marginalisation. Second, this epistemic marginalisation cannot be redressed by open criticisms that draw attention to the problem alone. Third, there is need, and an urgent one for that matter, to rewrite that falsified history not only in hindsight but, most importantly, in foresight, and logic as the foundation of thought, is where to begin.

To rewrite or make corrections to the world intellectual history in hindsight, i.e. in the case of Africa, reclaiming intellectual legacies which the West has plagiarised and identifying, promoting and putting into history those that the West has edited out and properly presenting those that the West has misrepresented or subordinated are projects for the historian and are certainly not my concern here. My aim in this book is to relay and systematise the foundation of thought in Africa which the West through colonial brainwash, missionary manipulation and postcolonial subliminal activities eroded in order to shine the light and show the way for African intellectuals in the new millennium to contribute to world intellectual history and civilisation as Africans.

Since the colonial times, many African intellectuals have made remarkable additions to the world knowledge economy but are not recognised as contributions from Africa because their African authors have used methods that are grounded in Aristotelian logic regarded as a Western rational framework. So, whatever these Africans created were not new; they proceeded from methods set up by Westerners and are traceable to the logical foundation laid by the West. They become footnotes to Western originality and are therefore quickly swallowed up in the Western intellectual legacy. With this condition, the fate of Africans appear to have been sealed—

a sort of "intellectual entrapment"—they will never, not in a hundred years, not in a thousand years and certainly not in a million years, make original contribution to world history and civilisation insofar as they continue to use Western-developed approaches and intellectual framework in their research; anything they create would be another effort in Western intellectual hegemony.

Unfortunately, few African intellectuals see the reality of the intellectual entrapment of the African. In the intellectual endeavour, there are those called researchers and another small cell called thinkers. Intellectuals in the former group are those that revisit old ideas and attempt to study and make additions to them, whereas intellectuals in the latter group are those that create new ideas. Usually, members of the latter group are few and far between in any society and generation, but they are the reason behind revolutions in thought and monumental developments in our world and civilisation. The intellectual entrapment of the African was orchestrated to prevent the emergence of the "African thinker" and through a carefully planned education system—from school to religious institutions to the social spaces—either destroy the creative originality in him and leave him, at best, a researcher using Western logical framework or put him through the conforming Western education system that brings him out at the other end, a Western thinker whose merit would be denied by racism anyways. It is a double bind of a sort. Either way, the African intellectual is trapped.

Realising this entrapment is as difficult as breaking out of it. To the first, how on earth would you, on your own, realise that you have been miseducated? You need proper education to realise that you have been miseducated, but all around you, in the schools, the religious houses, the social organisations that you belong to and the social spaces that you operate in daily, are the same structure of education that miseducated you. So, one is daily being further miseducated. His trusted friends, teachers, personalities and even popular intellectuals that he holds at high esteem and would listen to are mostly miseducated folk. How on earth is the African intellectual going to realise that he has been miseducated? To the second, assuming one is rarely lucky to run into someone who was properly educated or who by some miracle properly educated or re-educated himself, and this fellow opens his eyes to his intellectual entrapment, what is he really going to do in an African world where most of his relations, friends, colleagues, peers and even the strangers that he meets from time to time are victims of miseducation? This is the authentic African predicament. Two things are involved: any careless attempt to demonstrate his new light of reason would pit him against the convention of his society and make him a social outcast. If he does not want this grim reality, he would have to live a life of a lie from then on or find a way to liberate his people.

But how can an African who has yanked off his orientation of miseducation help others to achieve the same mental emancipation? This, to me, is probably the most difficult responsibility facing the emancipated African. His woes are compounded in the fact that this responsibility is a pan-African task. One cannot liberate brothers and sisters in, say, South Africa and leave those in Nigeria or the Congo, etc. The problem of the emancipated African intellectual is further compounded by the fact that he had to contend with the innocent ignorance of patriotic Africans and the toxic ignorance of the évoléus. Recall the story of Moses who having understood what the Egyptians were doing to the Israelites aided the latter to kill an Egyptian aggressor only for him to watch those he helped report him to the authorities. In the same way, the greatest animadversions an emancipated African intellectual experience as one who is attempting to bring many more Africans to the light of reason of their mental entrapment come from fellow African intellectuals. On a personal note, a good number of fellow African intellectuals have now made it their life's duty to undermine my scholarship and destroy my name at various academic conferences. These crop of people suffer the subtle effect of what Boaventura de Sousa Santos discusses as the postcolonial mindset.

The postcolonial for Santos is not an era after colonialism; it is a continuation of colonialism in subtle and, perhaps, more dangerous psychological forms. As he put it, "[C]olonialism also creates a problem for us in relation to postcolonialism; that is to say, there may be some naïveté in thinking that postcolonialism refers to a postcolonial period when, in fact, postcolonialism claims that colonialism did not end with the end of historical colonialism. There are other ways through which occupation continues, not necessarily through foreign occupation, tutelage and the prohibition of a state formation" [2016: 18]. Santos makes a keen observation in the above when he indicated that indigenous intellectuals who have been tutored or brainwashed in colonial institutions—whether secular or religious—are now doing the work of miseducating their own peoples for the colonial officials. These people are native warriors fighting the cause of the foreign invader unbeknownst to them. They are usually very proud of their colonial miseducation and struggle to show it off at any opportunity. Jurgen Hengelbrock[1], a German intercultural philosopher, reports of his shock upon visiting Africa for the first time and finding the so-called African intellectuals struggling to flaunt their European education and formation rather than show their African originality. He further bemoans the fact that even the European lifestyles they exhibit are in their worst forms.

The above observation points to the problem of the évoléus or the deracinés in Africa of the postcolonial. This is a situation where the colonised African is tutored to reject his African culture as uncivilised and accept that of the colonial Europe as ideal. He goes through life continuously losing touch with his African roots while struggling to ape the West and never truly becoming a European. These jinxed intellectual warriors become leaders or teachers in African villages and urban centres conforming those children who submit to them and destroying the psychology of those who do not. In my days in the secondary school, I had quite unpleasant encounters with some of them. One of our teachers taught us about the nine planets in the galaxy at the end of which I asked: "is it not possible that there may be more planets that have not yet been discovered?" Our teacher called me a bush man, asked me which zoo I came from, for thinking that way, for daring to assume that my little uncivilised mind could rival the divine genius of Western scientists who have searched the entire galaxy and found only nine planets. Usually, your classmates

---

[1] See Jurgen Hengelbrock. 2002. You cannot free yourself from Hegel: An encounter with Heinz Kimmerle. Intercultural communication. www.galerie-inter.de/kimmerle

laugh and join the teacher in ridiculing you. In this way, the psychology of the African child is wounded and will continue to be wounded throughout his schooling days until and unless he submits to the pattern of thinking the évoléus of a teacher imposes on him. Thus, many more Africans are stripped of their creative originality and conformed even before they get to secondary school level because the curriculum of education which they are subjected to is colonial and allows no room for independent and freethinking. In the end, they become professors of knowledge without ever creating any theories or something new in their fields.

The greatest evil of colonialism therefore was not that it suppressed the colonised and stole their resources but that it created a system that could use the native peoples to continue the process of suppression, subordination and intellectual entrapment of peoples thought to have gained their political independence.

My thinking is that Asian and African philosophers should rather find a new consciousness and begin to build new bridges to engage and converse with one another. When it is time for Western thinkers to break out of their walled confines, they will do so and perhaps limp behind as a lesson in humility. For ages, Western philosophers have compelled the rest of the world to accept what Meinrad Hebga calls the dogma of one universal philosophy, something Bruce Janz has described as a pretension of Western philosophy. This can no longer be accepted. But as we cannot talk of a different philosophic tradition without first sorting out its method, nor can we sort out the issue of method without first mapping out its background logic, it is time to take the walk of courage and begin formulating the formal and linguistic rules of our new logic.

For centuries, descendants of Aristotle have cowed us from engaging in new logic projects. They have caricatured and invented names to demoralise us, and they have succeeded in this ploy of making logic a sacred ground, but not anymore. First, Immanuel Kant declared that Aristotle's logic was a completed science to which no one can add any other new idea. Then, the modern logicians who came after treated the traditional laws as Holy Grail. But without going beyond these laws, either to contract or relax them, no new system can be formulated. At least, Rudolf Carnap acknowledges this challenge but grants that new systems of logic are possible insofar as their linguistic rules and formal structures are clearly presented. In the intervening century, tampering with these traditional laws became almost a crime in world philosophy.

But my hunch is that a people cannot lay claim to their own philosophic tradition without formulating its method(s), and every method needs a logic to ground it. In philosophy, method is everything, and there is no one universal method that is adequate for all situations. For this, one thoughtful Nigerian logician Udo Etuk (2002: 102) exhorts that, "[T]he point is important and seems so very obvious, yet so many miss it. Philosophy is a universal discipline only in the sense that the quest for the understanding of life is something that every human group undertakes. But *how* they undertake the quest, and *what* solutions they come up with are bound to differ from people to people." These varying ways speak directly to method and method takes us to logic. Until we realise this truth, we may not be able to free ourselves from the spell of Plato and untie ourselves from the umbilical cord of Aristotle. This project of an alternative logic that could be called African which I pursue in this book has been long overdue and long coming. The efforts which have produced this book started accumulating since 2008 and passed through different phases of experiences, some of which were quite challenging and discouraging. But these experiences have all come together to justify the thesis of this book as, perhaps, the one most urgent book for the African intellectual or, indeed, all those who suspect they may have been miseducated or brainwashed with the colonial curriculum to read.

This book is organised into two parts. Part one consists of Chaps. 1, 2, 3, 4 and 5, while part two comprises of Chaps. 6, 7, 8, 9, 10 and 11. In part one, I laid out the background for the project of African logic and in part two constructed the system of a prototype African logic. In Chap. 1, I discussed how reason manifests in African philosophy. In Chap. 2, I argued for a logic-based foundation for African philosophy and studies. My Chap. 3 focussed on addressing some problematics in African logic, while in Chap. 4, I identified and discussed the schools of thought in African logic and the individual contributions of African logicians. In Chap. 5, I took up the lingering question of method and the need for villagisation of knowledge. These prepared the ground for part two where I unveiled Ezumezu as a prototype African logic. In Chap. 6, I unveiled Ezumezu as philosophy of logic and in Chap. 7, I discussed it as methodology. In Chap. 8, I developed Ezumezu as a formal system. Having completed the structural constructions and system building, I engaged with substantive issues that concern the application of Ezumezu logic in the remaining chapters. In Chap. 9, I showed how Ezumezu logic grounds some theories in African philosophy. In Chap. 10, I offered clarifications and justifications for the system of Ezumezu logic, and finally, in Chap. 11, I applied Ezumezu logic in constructing a theory of curriculum transformation that embeds the burning issues of decolonisation and Africanisation of education curriculum in Africa. It may be important to observe that what stands as Chap. 11 of this work which some colleagues who read the draft manuscript described as exciting and thought-provoking was not originally part of the idea of this book. It was actually supposed to be the general conclusion of the book. But upon completion, I discovered that it was too lengthy for a conclusion and that it can actually stand as a chapter. The section that now stands at the general conclusion was the last passage of Chap. 11 on completion. I had to write a proper conclusion for what eventually became Chap. 11 of this book.

In sum, the objective of this book does not end in stimulating intellectuals in the Global South to shake off the manacles of Plato and Aristotle; it stretches into actually laying the logical foundation for this process. There are many reasons that make this endeavour worthwhile, for example, Africans were suppressed under the weight of enslavement and colonial misrule, and, as a result, did not make too many original and inventive contributions to the modern civilisation at the time. The explanation which the European iconoclasts gave was that it was because they lacked capacity for logical thinking. It is, therefore, imperative to silence the witch that cried at night, whether it was the cause of the death of the child in the morning or not. It may thus be stated that until scholars in the Global South and specifically Africa systematise their logic to drive their intellectual activities, the witch who cried the other night might continue to cry, night after night.

Overall, I conceive this book as the "gamechanger" for two main reasons. First, the nagging issue about the methodology of African philosophy has led to different people proposing all kinds of theories most of which, by their structure, should properly belong to Western philosophy. I deem this as fundamentally a question about background logic on which the methods of the discipline should rest. Thus, suffice it to say that with the formulation of Ezumezu, it would now be easy to separate discourses that qualify as African philosophy and those that do not. In other words, if a discourse cannot be grounded in Ezumezu logic, it is probably a discourse in Western philosophy and it would not matter who authored it, where it is authored or what title it is given.

Second, the nagging questions about criteria for African philosophy have led to different scholars mopping up all kinds of things most of which should be in anthropology, sociology or ethnology under the tag of African philosophy and have inspired many charlatans to confer on themselves the title of African philosophers. Ultimately, we must be courageous to ask, what makes a discourse African philosophy? And, what makes an individual an African philosopher? In the first case, we have to look out for the background logic from which the critical questions are generated and ask ourselves whether it has been properly formulated to map the ontological orientation in African worldview? If this has been done, then we have to check to see if the methods of the discipline have been grounded in the logic. Once the report is affirmative, then such a discourse is an exercise in African philosophy. To the second, and this is crucial, any philosopher that does not understand the logic that undergirds his field is no philosopher to begin with. On the strength of the preceding therefore, it may now be said with authority that no student of African philosophy can be considered as properly trained if he has no firm grasp of the logic of the discipline. In formulating Ezumezu logic, I have not simulated any form of genius; I have merely done what Aristotle did some three centuries B.C. for the world intellectual history, only that in this case, I completed the project he began by formulating a logical model covering the remaining sphere of human thinking (the complementary inferential mode, future contingents and issues arising in the structure of modern physics) which Aristotle did not cover in his programme, logic being a field of ideas rather than a rising structure.

By extension, this logic may now ground ideas not only in African philosophy and studies but in different other fields of research, including the sciences where practitioners desire to carve an intellectual niche for Africa. This is in keeping with a programme I call Africa Intellectual Revolution (AIR). Right from the 1960s when the Great Debate on whether African philosophy exists or does not dominates the intellectual space of the continent to the 1980s when a period of disillusionment set in amongst the debaters, and from the 1990s into the millennium years when system-building became fashionable, the story of African philosophy has been one of a linear progression consisting of metaphysical, epistemological and, most popularly, ethical discussions and postulations. Instead of raising the next, if not predictable line of question, I have in this book attempted a change of course into logic for a breath of fresh air. This is because, until we get the logic of our thoughts right, we, as workers in the field of African philosophy and studies, may lose our vision in the darkness of metaphysics, our direction in the forest of epistemology and our minds in the fantasies of ethics. As African philosophy like other epistemologies of the south, in the words of Santos (2018), comes of age, a time of change has come, and the logical and methodological revolutions mapped out in this innocuous book will eventually, I hope, have far-reaching implications in all areas of scholarship in Africa, including the sciences.

References

Etuk, Udo. 2002. The possibility of African logic. In *The third way in African philosophy*, ed. Olusegun Oladipo, 98–116. Ibadan: Hope Publications.
Hengelbrock, Jurgen. You cannot free yourself from Hegel: An encounter with Heinz Kimmerle. Intercultural communication. www.galerie-inter.de/kimmerle. Retrieved May 3 2017.
Santos, Boaventura de Sousa. 2016. Epistemologies of the south and the future. *European South* 1: 17–29.

Endorsements

In an astounding intellectual tour de force conducted in the most consistent and rigorous way, Chimakonam offers Ezumezu as the prototype of an African logic, a variant of a trivalence logic. In a subliminal invitation to a decentring exercise, particularly for those whose centre has been built with Greek concepts and terms, the journey into Ezumezu logic abounds in Igbo-African words and concepts. I consider Chimakonam's book as the most convincing and powerful formulation of a philosophy of the south that I have read in many years and which emerges from the African historical and existential contexts and cultures.

Boaventura de Sousa Santos
Professor of Sociology at the University of Coimbra, Portugal,
Distinguished Legal Scholar at the University of Wisconsin-Madison, USA
Author of *The End of the Cognitive Empire: The Coming of Age of the Epistemologies of the South*. Durham: Duke University Press, 2018

I agree to the challenge that "an African cannot truly be an African without their language, culture and the logic that underlies them", the prototype of which Chimakonam has systematised in this book and christened Ezumezu logic. I have looked for the meaning of *ezumezu*, an Igbo term that signifies *power* in terms of linguistic geometry, by translating it (using GENO-ASCII Code) into its numerical equivalent: *ezumezu* ~ (E+Z+U+M+E+Z+U) = (5+26+21+13+5+26+21) = 117. In combination with *chi*, an Igbo term that signifies some fundamental ideas, one of which is *okwu* or its closest English translation *word* ~ (3+8+9) = 20, one gets *chi-ezumezu* ~ (20+117) = 137, which is cognate with *word power* ~ (W+O+R+D)+(P+O+W+E+R) = (23+15+18+4)+(16+15+23+5+18) = (60+77) = 137. This is a fundamental physical constant of the Big Bang Theory of the creation of the universe. It is, therefore, appropriate, as the author has done, to anchor the logic of African philosophy and studies on *okwu* or *word* which he has put forward as the primordial raw material for thought. As the Igbo would say, ike di na okwu ~ (4+9+14+1+15+11+23+21) = 123, meaning "there is power in the word" and where the numerical value 123 could mean first, second and always. This is a clear indication that *okwu* ~ (15+11+23+21) = 70 is more powerful than *logos* ~

(12+15+7+15+19) = 68 which is also shown by their numerical equivalents generated using the GENO-ASCII Code; hence, the author urges a paradigm shift from the Greek-inspired logocentricism to the Africa-inspired okwucentricism. This book brings forth the originality of the African mind and should be read by all who are unbiased in their pursuit of knowledge.

Alexander O.E. Animalu, FAS, NNOM
Professor Emeritus of Physics, Department of Physics and Astronomy
University of Nigeria, Nsukka
Author of *Geno-ASCII Code for Translation of Alphabets into Natural Number Equivalents and Geometry*

An important feature of this book is that it demonstrates what a system of African logic looks like and thereby makes some advancement on African philosophical logic or philosophy of logic as well as methodology. By doing this, it contributes to the ongoing discussions about African logic as well as to the decolonisation and Africanisation of philosophy projects.

Edwin Etieyibo
Associate Professor, Department of Philosophy, University of the Witwatersrand, Johannesburg
Author of *African Philosophy and Proverbs: The Case of Logic in Urhobo Proverbs*

Contents

Part I Background to African Logic

1 The Manifestation of Reason in African Philosophy 3
  1.1 Introduction 3
  1.2 Postmodern Thinking as a New Logic 5
  1.3 The Influence of Logos on the Postmodern 10
  1.4 The Emergence of Okwu as an Unbranded Index for Thought 13
  1.5 Conclusion 17
  References 18

2 In Search of a Logic-Based Foundation for African Philosophy and Studies 21
  2.1 Introduction 21
  2.2 Paulin J. Hountondji 23
  2.3 H. Odera Oruka 25
  2.4 T. Uzodinma Nwala and Sophie B. Oluwole 27
  2.5 Chukwudum B. Okolo 27
  2.6 Peter Bodunrin 28
  2.7 Kwasi Wiredu 30
  2.8 John Mbiti, Ifeanyi Menkiti and Innocent Onyewuenyi 32
  2.9 Uduma O. Uduma 33
  2.10 The Logic-Based Criterion 34
  2.11 Conclusion 36
  References 36

3 Some Problematics in African Logic 39
  3.1 Introduction 39
  3.2 Problematising the Categories of Non-classical, Non-standard and Non-western 41
  3.3 The Problematic of the idea of African Logic 44
  3.4 African Logic and the Relative-Universal Problematic 47

		3.5	The Problematic of Regional Logics	50
		3.6	Conclusion	52
		References		53
4	**The Schools of Thought in African Logic**			55
	4.1	Introduction		55
	4.2	The Apologists		56
	4.3	The Polemicists		64
	4.4	The System Builders		66
	4.5	Conclusion		73
	References			73
5	**African Logic and the Question of Method: Towards Villagisation of Knowledge**			77
	5.1	Introduction		77
	5.2	The Issues of Scope and Methodology		79
	5.3	The Pretensions of European Philosophy		80
	5.4	African Philosophy and the Question of Method		83
	5.5	The Need for Villagisation of Knowledge		85
	5.6	Conclusion		88
	References			89

Part II Unveiling Ezumezu as a System of African Logic

6	**Ezumezu as Philosophy of Logic**			93
	6.1	Introduction		93
	6.2	Towards a Conception of African Logic		95
	6.3	Some Notations and Principles of Ezumezu System		96
		6.3.1	Trivalence	97
		6.3.2	Sub-contrary Valuations	98
		6.3.3	The Modes	99
		6.3.4	Context Principle	99
		6.3.5	The Three Supplementary Laws of Thought	100
		6.3.6	The Wedged-Implication (Conditional)	101
	6.4	On Principles of Consent		101
		6.4.1	Permissibility Principle	102
		6.4.2	Ohakarasi Principle	102
		6.4.3	Unification Principle	103
		6.4.4	Thesis of Regimented Ontology	104
	6.5	The Philosophy of Ezumezu Logic		105
		6.5.1	The Issue of the Third Value, Scope of the Laws	106
		6.5.2	Between Logical Bivalence and Trivalence: Unveiling the Essential Tension	108
	6.6	Conclusion		111
	References			112

7	**Ezumezu as Methodology**	115
	7.1 Introduction	115
	7.2 Unfolding the Three Pillars of Thought in Ezumezu Methodology	116
	7.3 The Two Inferential Methods in Ezumezu Logic	117
	7.4 Further Justification of the Ezumezu Methodology: The Context-dependence of Value (CdV)	119
	7.5 The Centrality of the Concept of Nmeko for Theorisations in African Philosophy and Studies	123
	7.6 Ezumezu and Methodological Anarchy	124
	7.7 Conclusion	128
	References	129
8	**Ezumezu as a Formal System**	131
	8.1 Introduction	131
	8.2 The Universe of Discourse in Ezumezu Logic	133
	8.3 Elementary Syntactic and Semantic Mappings in Ezumezu Logic	135
	8.4 Discussion of the Three Supplementary Laws of Thought	137
	8.4.1 The Law of Njikọka	139
	8.4.2 Law of Nmekọka	139
	8.4.3 Law of Ọnọna-etiti	140
	8.5 The Two Theses in Ezumezu Logic	141
	8.6 The Formal Structure of Ezumezu Logic	143
	8.7 Conclusion: Insights and Controversies	146
	References	148
9	**How Ezumezu Logic Grounds Some Theories in African Philosophy with a Special Focus on Afro-Communitarianism**	151
	9.1 Introduction: How Logic Grounds Theories	151
	9.2 How Ezumezu Logic Grounds Some Theories in African Philosophy	153
	9.3 On the Accusation of Transliteration and Copycat Philosophy	163
	9.4 Conclusion	165
	References	165
10	**Justifying the System of Ezumezu Logic: An Analysis of the Problematic Structure of 'q na abughi q'**	167
	10.1 Introduction	167
	10.2 Clarification of the Concept of African Logic	169
	10.3 Justifying the System of Ezumezu Logic	171
	10.4 Investigating the Structure 'q na abughi q'	175
	10.5 Conclusion	177
	References	178

11 Decolonisation, Africanisation and Transformation: Why We Need 'That' African Contribution to World History and Civilisation 181
   11.1 Introduction 181
   11.2 A Theory of Curriculum Transformation in Africa: From Decolonisation to Africanisation 182
       11.2.1 Interpretation 186
   11.3 Why We Need 'That' African Contribution to World History and Civilisation 186
   11.4 How Slavery and Colonialism Destroyed African Epistemologies and How Postcolonialism is Sustaining that Epistemic Destruction 201
   11.5 Conclusion 204
   References 204

General Conclusion 207

Index 211

About the Author

Jonathan O. Chimakonam PhD, is a senior lecturer at the University of Calabar, Nigeria, and a research fellow at the University of Pretoria, South Africa. He is a research associate at the University of Johannesburg. His teaching and research interests cover the areas of African philosophy, logic, environmental ethics and postmodern/postcolonial thought. He aims to break new grounds in African philosophy by formulating a system that unveils new concepts and opens new vistas for thought (conversational philosophy), a method that represents a new approach to philosophising in African and intercultural philosophies (conversational thinking) and a system of logic that grounds them both (Ezumezu). His articles have appeared in refereed and accredited international journals. He is editor of some books including the award-winning *Existence and Consolation: Reinventing Ontology, Gnosis, and Values in African Philosophy* (by Ada Agada), Minnesota, Paragon House, 2015 (CHOICE Outstanding Academic Title Award, 2015); *Atuolu Omalu: Some Unanswered Questions in Contemporary African Philosophy* (Lanham, University Press of America, 2015); *African Philosophy and Environmental Conservation* (London, Routledge, 2017); *African Philosophy and the Epistemic Marginalization of Women* (London, Routledge, 2018, with Louise du Toit); *Ka Osi So Onye: African Philosophy in the Postmodern Era* (Delaware, Vernon Press, 2018, with Edwin Etieyibo); and *The Death Penalty from an African Perspective* (Delaware, Vernon Press, 2017, with Fainos Mangena). He is the convener of the professional African philosophy society, The Conversational School of Philosophy (CSP), and the founding editor of *Filosofia Theoretica: Journal of African Philosophy, Culture and Religions*. He is winner of Jens Jacobsen Research prize for Outstanding Research in Philosophy by the International Society for Universal Dialogue. He is African philosophy area editor in the Internet Encyclopedia of Philosophy. Jonathan is working on a new manuscript in African philosophy.

Part I
Background to African Logic

Chapter 1
The Manifestation of Reason in African Philosophy

Abstract I argue that the manifestation of reason in Africa's intellectual space has been logocentric since colonial times which is detrimental to the development of the African idea. I propose a transition from logocentricism to okwucentricism as a reconstruction of the identity of reason in African philosophy. To do this, we are compelled to ask: what constitutes the foundation of African philosophy and by extension, the sundry disciplines in African studies? It is this innocent question that can lead us into the ultimate justification for the study of African philosophy as a distinct tradition. I argue that we do not study African philosophy to prove a point (that we can philosophise exactly as the Westerners do) or defend a territory (that we have a unique and culture-bound system)—this would be myopic to say the least. I contend that when we take up a handful of literature in African philosophy these days, hardly do we find anymore reason for their creation besides proving a point and a defence of some territory. I show that the purpose of the study of African philosophy has to be narrowed down to the use of reason in resolving social, political, economic and environmental challenges facing the continent and the management of its interaction with other peoples of the world—things that are acutely phenomenological rather than perverse encounters.

1.1 Introduction

When we are settled on the point that there is African philosophy and that we are African philosophers, we must then ask: what constitutes the foundation of African philosophy and by extension, the sundry disciplines in African studies? It is this innocent question that can lead us into the ultimate justification for the study of African philosophy as a distinct tradition. Certainly, we do not study African philosophy to prove a point (that we can philosophise exactly as the Westerners do) or defend a territory (that we have a unique and culture-bound system)—this would be myopic to say the least. Unfortunately, when we take up a handful of literature in African philosophy these days, hardly do we find anymore reason for their creation besides proving a point and a defence of some territory. To the first, we must point accusing fingers to the members of the so-called universalist school who in their eagerness to ape the West committed African philosophy to mere commentary on Western philosophy. And to the second, we must chastise the ethnophilosophers who in their short-sightedness demobilised African philosophy by cutting it off from any universalisable traits and remanded it in cultural excavations and in a fixated precolonial originary.

Clearly, the purpose of the study of African philosophy has to be narrowed down to the use of reason in resolving social, political, economic and environmental challenges facing the continent and the management of its interaction with other peoples of the world—things that are acutely phenomenological rather than empty debates. This is why Chukwudum. B. Okolo (1993: 12) defines African philosophy as a "critical thinking on the African and his experience of reality." It is the biting pains of issues worrying the continent that should creditably compel us to engage reason in finding ways to survive as a people and with other peoples, to resolve our problems and to progress like the rest of the world. It is in these that we must locate the value for the study of African philosophy and this value has to be more pragmatic than sentimental. But the attempts to locate this value cannot be successful without the clarification of the methods of African philosophical tradition and the logic that grounds them all.

Some say philosophers must philosophise for philosophy's own sake; others say that the ultimate value of philosophy is to be found in its pure abstract form. I beg to disagree. So long as one sees philosophising as a form of game for pastime, so long is one correct in one's views that its value lies in its abstract form alone. But when the activity of philosophising is viewed from a more phenomenological angle, its ultimate value can be nothing else besides practical. For it is the lot of philosophy as Jacques Derrida (1994) observes to honour its debts and duties to the cultural settings in which its questions arise.

In the above sense, we must conceive the focus of this book which is on the logic of African philosophy to be pragmatic. Talk about distinct philosophical traditions or distinct ways of knowing or the epistemologies of the south which Boaventura de Sousa Santos (2016a, 2018) writes so copiously on, borders on alternative epistemic perspectives have their bases on alternative logics even though they easily come across as postmodern. Postmodernism when studied closely is an intellectual movement that upholds alternative logics. When understood as a movement that seeks to unmask the pretensions of Western absolutistic, and all-embracing cloak of reason, that all valid *epistemes* are upheld by Western-developed Aristotelian logic; the illusions of metaphysics, that there is a common foundation for all thought; and the idea of the "unity of sciences" in which a common method is prescribed for knowledge, then we grasp the alternative nature of the logic that grounds postmodernism. Hence, to the extent that postmodernism embraces relativity of knowledge with specific appeal to the uniqueness of different circumstances and affirms the validity and possibility of many methods; and acknowledges that reality has multiple ongoing interpretations which speak to specific contexts, to such extent is it pragmatic. I evoke the term pragmatism in a simple sense of what is practical.

In this chapter, I will show the manifestation of reason in the portions of history of African philosophy as palpable logocentricism which is an offshoot of the stranglehold of modernism. To dethrone logocentricism, I make a cautious advocacy for a postmodern mindview. I call it cautious because I am of the view that modernism's logocentricism could survive in a postmodern mindview in the form of what I call logomania.[1] To avert this, I propose okwucentricism as a new philosophical, but by no means, an absolute centre and a necessary replacement but not displacement narrative to logocentricism. On the basis of the latter, I shall explain the new direction for reason in African philosophy as a mode of conversations in an arena of unities. The authentication of unities in a field of knowledge as I shall strive to accomplish in this chapter will be a prognostic, pointing towards an African or alternative logic that will ground our brave claim to the postmodern modification or villagisation of knowledge.

1.2 Postmodern Thinking as a New Logic

The march of postmodern thinking is primarily a movement from the Aristotelian hegemonic logic to more liberal alternatives like the African logic. As soon as the Enlightenment birthed modernism, the emergence of postmodernism became inevitable. Modernism is like a church warden passing around the offering box and compelling everyone to toss in their wills; definitely a time will come when they will want it back. Such a time is the rise of postmodern thinking whether in architecture, literature or philosophy. Jean-François Lyotard has conceived the postmodern as "incredulity toward metanarrative" (1984). Yes, the postmodern challenges convention. It is the liberalisation of reason and the radicalisation of doubt towards universals, of philosophy freely questioning itself and questioning its answers about the objective. It is the recognition of the particular and the relative. It is an affront on the Aristotelian legacy. One way of interpreting Lyotard's conception is to say that it sees the postmodern as an expression of doubt or sceptical attitude towards universal pigeonholing of reason. This, in my view does not still tell the whole story about postmodernism. The problem is the widespread mistake of conceiving modernism and postmodernism as world-views. Those who mistake the modern and the postmodern as world-views tend to see them as humans' attitudes to the world while those who correctly conceive them as mindviews see them as intellectual revolutions in their own right. Postmodernism like modernism is more than an attitude, it is movement of logics. Those who tended to view it as an attitude have ended with the mistake of treating the postmodern as a continuation or a rupture or a strain on modernism.

A mindview as I conceive it is the intellectual scope of thought, its processes and approaches relative to any individual or society or age (2015a: 475). What this tells us is that the way an individual thinks conventionally about realities constitutes his mindview; the way individuals in a society or age think on average constitutes the psychographic analysis of that society's mindview; now any radical shift from the

---

[1] I conceive this as intellectual intoxication and unconscious addiction to logos.

conventional mindview of an age constitutes an intellectual revolution. Modernism for instance was a radical shift from the way the medieval thought and so is postmodernism a radical shift from the conventional way of thinking in modern age which pays obeisance to the ancestorship of Aristotle. I would therefore wish to conceive the postmodern as a form of intellectual revolution in the way humans think in the liberal age.

Thus both the modern age and postmodern age are not world-views. They are rather mindviews. Doctrinally, whereas world-view is the state of the world as it impresses itself on the human mind, mindview on the other hand, is the state of the mind as it conceives the world. There is a Kantian Copernican revolution here at play. Whereas traditional epistemology holds that reality impresses itself on the human mind at perception, Immanuel Kant proposes (in the style of the switch between Ptolemaic and Copernican astronomical models) that it was the human mind using its categories that structures the world at perception. The history of philosophy and of human ideas, it is safe to say, has hitherto being constructed on the world-view model explained above. Here I wish to state the error of such a model and propose a switch to mindview model.[2] It is the philosopher, the individual for that matter that philosophises and offers his views of the world. There is nothing like the objective view of the world. It is therefore the authority of this individual that should take pre-eminence over whatever anyone imagines is the authority of the world as an inanimate 'other'. It is the individual philosopher that we hold responsible for the truth or falsity of his views. No one ever approaches the world for this interaction. Indeed, there is no way we can know the world's view about itself. The world holds no learned opinion. And so we must depend exclusively on the opinions of the individual philosophers (who alone hold learned opinions of the world) who structure the world differently with their minds.[3]

Whilst Kant could be said to be the first to articulate the mindview model explained above, my version veers away from the main implications of his. Kant wants us to believe that every human mind has categories, and that these categories function in exactly the same way in every individual. While I agree with the existence of the categories I disagree with his conclusion that every individual applies them in exact same way. This is what I will call 'Kant's *robotification* of humanity.' From common sense perspective it is silly to suggest that all humans think alike; we know this to be false. It was obvious from the temperament of *Critique of Pure Reason* (1991a) that Kant wanted by all means to restore the Cartesian 'self'

---

[2] One of the reviewers drew my attention to the fact that a world-view could be a passive mindview. I do not agree with this but I see the point. Whereas I conceive world-view as the state of the world as it impresses itself on the human mind, mindview on the other hand, is the state of the mind as it conceives the world. Notwithstanding the difference, it may be apt to also point out that they share important similarity i.e., they (the two visions of the world) both have connections with the human mind except that in the former, the mind is passive and in the latter, it is active. I would not subscribe to one being a version of the other since that will trivialise the 'vision of the world' which each attempts to capture.

[3] This position may be regarded as individualistic in light of the on-going discussions on individual-community relationship in Afro-communitarianism. See. Menkiti (1984), Gyekye (1992).

1.2 Postmodern Thinking as a New Logic

which David Hume's scepticism had seriously vitiated and thus preserve the modern mindview. Evidently, when we want something desperately, we usually run into errors of omission. This was Kant's shortcoming as he omitted the apparent fact that the categories of the mind are under constant influence of the human passion such that it is almost difficult for two individuals, using the categories of their minds to structure the world in exact same way. In this consists my defence of the postmodern as an intellectual revolution.

It can be argued that from the beginning of human civilisation some 10,000 BC, to the AD 1560, the pattern of human thought in general albeit progressive remained largely in the same direction until the arrival of the Renaissance (new beginning) followed by the Enlightenment age (1650–1800). Kant (1991a) however reports that the foremost intellectual revolution occurred in the Ancient Greece when men like Archimedes and Euclid by their studies in mathematics revolutionised human thinking about quantity and space some 300 B.C. Kant stated that they had done so by building on the earlier achievements of the Egyptians under whom mathematics remained merely in a "stage and blind groping after its true aim and destination..." (1991a: 9). This early intellectual revolution which Kant reports notwithstanding its importance, was limited since it changed human thinking only in one field namely, mathematics.

However, a greater intellectual revolution was later to occur in the A.D 1650s by the masterstroke of one man namely Francis Bacon. After the revolution in the way humans think about quantity and space some 300 B.C, Kant writes that "[A] much longer period elapsed before physics entered on the highway of science...the wise BACON gave a new direction to physical studies...here, too, as in the case of mathematics, we find evidence of a rapid intellectual revolution" (1991a: 10). I think that what makes this latter revolution greater than the earlier is that Bacon had seamlessly orchestrated a break away from how humans think about reality in general irrespective of field, i.e. from a dominant supernatural outlook; he had introduced a scientific mindview, and from the direction of faith; he had introduced the direction of reason—two radical changes to the construction of human thinking on an entirely new path known as the Age of modernism. The book in which Bacon drew the outline of the modern intellectual revolution is titled the *New Organon*. In it, he made a strong allusion to the power of experiments and inductive reasoning in studying nature. Kant interprets the thesis of *New Organon* as saying:

> Reason must approach nature with the view, indeed, of receiving information from it, not, however, in the character of a pupil, who listens to all that his master chooses to tell him, but in that of a judge, who compels the witnesses to reply to those questions which he himself thinks fit to propose. To this single idea must the revolution be ascribed by which, after groping in the dark for so many centuries, natural science was at length conducted into the path of certain progress". (1991a: 10–11)

Bacon obviously had been aided by the return of freedom of inquiry in the Enlightenment. In describing the Enlightenment Kant (1991b) in his *Political Writings* explains that it was a new age when men found courage to use their own reason. Thus he declares "The motto of enlightenment is therefore: *Sapere aude!*

Have courage to use your *own* understanding!."[4] One important fact about Kant's statement above is the acknowledgement that the Enlightenment is the age of 'reason'. But does this mean that before the Enlightenment, humans never used their reason? Definitely not! Let me explain what is meant here by identifying two prominent events that characterise the age of Enlightenment and set it apart from the world before it. First, the approach used in interpreting the world prior to A.D 1650 was dominantly supernaturalism, Enlightenment introduced scientific/empirical approach. Second, the principle that guided inquiry about truth was faith in the ages before. But with the emergence of Enlightenment, faith-based direction was replaced with reason. Thus in the intellectual revolution of the Enlightenment age, human thinking generally about reality was radically transformed in the West such that a new convention came to replace an old convention. Even though it was possible to see a handful of people like Hypatia, Copernicus and Galileo who thought rationally and acted empirically in the Dark Ages, it was easy to see that they behaved unconventionally, hence, Hypatia was stoned to death in A.D 415 (Wider 1986) and Galileo faced the inquisition in 1633 A.D. (Scruton 1995: 27).

On the whole, what came out of the radical shift in human thinking in the Enlightenment was a new consciousness called modernism. This consciousness was further streamlined and entrenched philosophically by Rene Descartes in his *Discourse on Method* (1968) and scientifically by Isaac Newton in his *The Mathematical Principles of Natural Philosophy* (1999). In their separate efforts, the two established an intellectual unity for knowledge in both method and doctrine called the 'universal'. Truth, from then onwards, acquired a universal stature. Whatever that is true and credible must be universally so and knowable to all inquiring 'selves'. Credible methods of philosophy and science are therefore held to be only the ones that are capable of yielding universally objective truths. In this, the intellectual revolution from the Dark Ages to the Modern age was completed.

Problem however arose many years later when David Hume in his *An Enquiry concerning Human Understanding* (2014) brought the Enlightenment to a sudden end with his scepticism about the ability of the 'self' to objectively comprehend reality. Hume apparently protracted the sceptical method which Descartes had employed to arrive at his *cogito*. The result of that was the dis-centring of the Cartesian 'self' from the modern mindview. But Kant (1991a) stepped in to rescue modernity by arguing that knowledge depends on the structure of the mind or what he calls the categories. Humans comprehend reality because categories exist within their minds that actively generate perception and these categories, for Kant, are universally the same in every human. Thus, the implication is that all humans perceive the world in the same way, all things being equal. This was in a way, a restoration of the Cartesian 'self' and the objectivity and universality of truth. Even though Kant's efforts gave birth to the question, 'How do we know if the perception generated by the mind truly corresponds to reality?', which his work did not sufficiently address and which eventually led to the postmodern agitations, he had on the whole given modernism a lifeline by preserving a belief in objective and universal truth.

---

[4] Some translations would use 'reason' in place of 'understanding.'

1.2 Postmodern Thinking as a New Logic

It was Friedrich Nietzsche who finally orchestrated the transition from modern to postmodern mindview in human thought. In his *Beyond Good and Evil* (2002) he demolished the modern mindview by rejecting Kant's theory of categories, which are supposedly shared by all people, and declares that truth is nothing more than an illusion. For him, every individual constructs his own world and what is true for him is what he perceives to be so. With this, Nietzsche brought to an end the reign of the 'self' which was enthroned by Descartes and re-enforced by Kant. Postmodern thinkers took this lead and began exploring other issues in textual interpretation and language.

What I want to demonstrate in this section above all else, are (1) that modernism and postmodernism are mindviews and not world-views, (2) that the postmodern is a shift or a break away from the modern age and not some sort of a rupture or a strain or even a continuation of modernism, (3) that this break away amounts to an intellectual revolution—a radical transition in the conventional way of thinking. This shift is revolutionary because it changes the way humanity on average looks at reality. If modernism for example says: 'I am because we are', postmodernism says: 'we are because I am'.

Apparently, the modern mindview which holds that truth is objective and universally knowable by everyone is a myth. It is a carry-over from the mindview of the Dark Ages addicted to control and domination. Thus modernism did not completely exculpate itself from some of the demons of the Dark Ages. Yet, it is a break from it in that domination and control were in the modern age conferred on rule of law unlike in the Dark Ages where the Pope or the Emperor was the law. The law in the modern age is depersonalised. Individuals could now plead their cases before a dispassionate law. A fact that provided an opening for the rise of postmodern thinking; individuals could now legitimately take back from the state what they had been compelled to submit to it. In this way, the postmodern is threatening to overrun the modern in our twenty-first century world especially in the area of liberalism rather than in what Ludwig von Rochau (1853) calls "realpolitik", i.e. a system of politics or principles based on practical rather than moral or ideological considerations (Bew 2014). Often, these days, the main legitimate index for policies and serious decisions is becoming the individual liberties and rights rather than state interest and exigencies. Increasingly, policy initiatives and decisions that tend to overlook individual liberties and rights in favour of state exigency as it used to be in the nineteenth and twentieth centuries are now being demonised in some corners of the globe. It is perhaps in the sciences that postmodernism still struggles. In philosophy, there is now a massive stand-off between modernism and postmodernism intensified by pressures from philosophies or epistemologies of the south. Indeed, there are signs that in no distant time, as different philosophical traditions gather momentum, modernism might be overrun in philosophy which might mark the beginning of the end to the influence of Plato, Aristotle, Descartes and Kant in the emerging systems of thought in philosophy.

1.3   The Influence of Logos on the Postmodern

The journey of reason in African philosophy so far, has been marred by logocentricism and logophilia.[5] To begin with, logos is a Greco-European concept for word, speech or reason and from this concept, logic was derived. There is probably no other concept in the entire history of Western philosophy that has been instrumentalised and perhaps also abused as logos has been. It has been identified as God, as son of God, as soul, as mind, as logic, as being, as life, as word, as speech and ultimately as reason to name the most regularly used. The questions are: how can one concept mean all of these? And why is logos unhindered even in translations? What has happened to W. V. O. Quine's indeterminacy of translation; Hans-Georg Gadamer's impossibility of interpretation; and above all, the consistent attributes of theory of meaning and of definition in philosophy of language and semantics? Why does logos seem to defy all limitations of language? It is not my intention to attempt to answer these questions here. Rather I intend only to highlight the foundational problem that could be associated with logos. Logos in its fluid, charming and changing nature could be a philosophical sham. The inspiration behind its philosophical adoption and usage appears to be the fabled philosopher's stone of the alchemist that can do everything including turning all metals into gold.

In the mainstream intellectual history, logos has become a weapon of discrimination, domination and subjugation. In what Jacques Derrida (1978) characterised as the divide between the 'self' and the 'other', logos has become the identity of the 'self' in discriminating against the 'other'. And in what Paul Ricouer (1974) designated as the hermeneutics of suspicion and distrust, logos has stood out as the foremost instrument of colonial domination. And in what the likes of Georg Hegel (1975), David Hume (Popkin 1977), Immanuel Kant (Popkin 1977), Lucien Levy-Bruhl (1947) and V. H. Verwoerd (Eze 2010: 33) variously characterised as forms of racial superiority of Europeans over Africans, logos has acted not only as the identity of Europeans but as the justification of racial subjugation.

In the history of philosophy, Lucius Outlaw (2003: 165–166) has carefully observed how logos has birthed logocentricism in the works of Plato and Aristotle and was sustained in the modern time in the works of Descartes and Kant. It was however, Michel Foucault (1972: 228) who drew the conclusion that the over commitment to reason in contemporary philosophy initiated in the works of Descartes and Kant has now led to what he called "logophilia". According to Foucault, there is no other philosophical tradition where actors treat the manifestation of reason in their culture as synonymous with the universal as they do in Western thought. There is a sense that Foucault almost attributes a feeling of arrogance and supremacy to this. This for him is worrisome and he has no better word for describing this delusion of Western mind than "logophilia" (1972: 228–229). There is a sense in which Foucault's views about logophilia here connects with my idea of "conceptual

---

[5] Michel Foucault (1972: 228) coins the term "logophilia" to ridicule a sense of over commitment to logos or reason in the history of Western philosophy.

envelopment" (2015b: 38–39). And I explained that any philosophical place would be guilty of "conceptual envelopment" when it treats its accumulated concepts as if they were privileged philosophical paraphernalia produced by minds that tower above all others—minds that are sufficient unto themselves and lacks nothing that it can learn from others, nor do others have anything to teach them. This is corroborated in Santos (2016b):

> The problem is that after five centuries of 'teaching' the world, the global North seems to have lost the capacity to learn from the experiences of the world. In other words, it looks as if colonialism has disabled the global North from learning in non-colonial terms, that is, in terms that allow for the existence of histories other than the 'universal' history of the West. This condition is reflected in all the intellectual work produced in the global North, Western, Eurocentric critical theory included. A sense of exhaustion haunts the Occidental, Eurocentric critical tradition. It manifests itself in a peculiar and diffuse uneasiness expressed in multiple ways: irrelevance, inadequacy, impotence, stagnation, paralysis. Such uneasiness is all the more disquieting because we are living in a world in which there is so much to be criticised,…(2016b: 19–20)

Indeed, Santos could not have captured it better; the global north is intellectually exhausted and fatigued. In another work, I clearly pointed accusing finger at Western philosophy and cautioned on the basis of this that:

> European or, broadly speaking, Western philosophy is facing the danger of coming out moribund and second best in the Global Expansion of Thought. Historically, the journey of reason has stalled in Western philosophy, when in the centuries following the 18th century, actors engrossed themselves in the error of supposing that reason has reached its highest manifestation in Greek-born Western thought; that beyond Western thought, there is no and never will again be a better manifestation of philosophical reason. In the glory of this delusion, actors almost unanimously and, without any form of logical justification, embraced the assumption that any claim to a manifestation of reason in any world at all, actual or possible, must not lack Western authenticity. (2015a: 475)

I contend therefore that while logocentricism draws a line between one philosophy tradition (Western) and others such as African philosophy, logophilia draws a line between one set of philosophers (Westerners) and others such as African philosophers. I would like to stretch my argument further.

The modern mindview described above rides on the crest of logocentricism and logophilia in that it strengthens the impression that Greco-European logos is not only universal but absolute. It is important to observe here that after centuries of exportation of European cultural particular as the universal model, the Eurocentric idea of the universal has become twisted and now comes across in different knowledge industries as absolute. In this connection, Tsenay Serequeberhan writes that:

> In the name of the universality of values, European colonialism violently universalized its own singular particularity and annihilated the historicity of the colonized. In this context, Western philosophy—in the guise of a disinterested, universalistic, transcendental, speculative discourse—served the indispensable function of being the ultimate *veracious buttress* of European conquest. (1991: 4–5)

Bruce Janz corroborates the assertion above. For him:

> While this tension may exist everywhere, it becomes an existential issue within African philosophy precisely because Western thought has taken on the position of universality of

> its own local form of reason. In other words, the Western pretension is that the development of universal reason and the reflection on particular issues within the West are identical. African philosophy cannot afford this pretension (short of simply asserting it).... (2009: 66)

This pretension of European philosophy that was entrenched in the works of Plato and Aristotle became orthodoxy in modern time. The manifestation of reason in European philosophy became not just another particular manifestation but as Janz observes, identical with the universal structure of reason. Other philosophical traditions would now obtain stamp of authenticity by identifying with the Greco-European logos which is the embodiment of Aristotle's logic of non-contradiction. This is what Serequeberhan in the above referred to as "the ultimate *veracious buttress* of European conquest". This conquest is a domination and a subjugation of African mind by European mind in which the former must completely ape the latter or lose authenticity. Robert Bernasconi (1997: 188) aptly captures this implication in what he calls the "double bind" problem stated thus: "either African philosophy is so similar to Western philosophy that it makes no distinctive contribution and effectively disappears; or it is so different that its credentials to be genuine philosophy will always be in doubt". Needless to point out that this double bind also applies to the African philosopher in that one can argue that the African philosopher cannot be identified by the work he does because they are not different from the ones done by the Western philosophers or that his work are so different from those of Western philosophers that one begins to doubt the philosophical rigour of African discourses. These are some of the mean manifestations of logocentricism and logophilia in the modern mindview.

Indeed, it will appear as though the worst has been identified, and that the postmodern holds the promise of a constructive remedy, but this is not so. African philosophers must be careful and approach postmodernism with suspicion; otherwise they may inadvertently and yet innocently dip African mind in a worse menace of the manifestation of logos. Something I characterise as 'logomania'. By logomania I mean the mindless adoption of the Greco-European logos by epistemologies of the south in their different constitution of cultural and philosophical particulars. The Greco-European logos would now be the basis and the ultimate principle of different philosophical traditions. Even if these philosophical particulars find voice in the postmodern affirmation of their places, they also lose the same in the echo of the Greco-European logos that structures such particular voices. Thus logomania as I conceive it is not just an addiction to the Greco-European logos by the otherness of philosophy such as African philosophy but an unconscious addiction to that effect. The breaking of the hegemony of the Greco-European logos in modernism appears to redistribute this hegemony in postmodernism. This is because, so long as philosophical thinking in African philosophy, and in different philosophical places is structured by the ideas and logical principles of Plato and Aristotle, to that extent are logocentricism and logophilia dominant and subsistent. In fact, with the increasing discrimination in the views of some schools and in the thoughts of many African philosophers, one cannot but agree that the journey of reason in African philosophy has been logocentric.

It has been argued by Alfred North Whitehead in *Process and Reality* (1978: 39) that the whole history of European philosophy consists of a series of footnotes to Plato. Innocent Asouzu (2011) on his part singles out Aristotle's influence on Western metaphysics as that which has done the greatest damage to world philosophies. This cannot be unconnected with the fact that logic is what shapes thoughts. He accuses Aristotle of being essentialist and of having introduced the essentialism that balkanises philosophy and humanity alike. Thus so long as the African or the Asian or the Polynesian or the native South American philosopher builds his theories on the framework of Plato's philosophical legacies and Aristotle's logical legacies, to that extent do they continue to affirm the hegemony of the Greco-European logos in their various philosophical places. So, even if they claimed to have arrived at the postmodern condition, it is not their cultural voices that echo; it is rather that of the European particular. In this way, postmodernism in philosophy could well mean post-European modernism in intercultural philosophy. By this I mean a sort of the mindview of European modernism redistributed to various world philosophies and African philosophy in particular.

From the foregoing, one could see that the influence of the Greco-European logos may well continue in postmodern philosophy. This assures different philosophical traditions and especially African philosophy, what we may describe in the words of W. E. Du Dois (1989) as the seventh son of world philosophies, that logocentricism and logophilia would not simply go away at the deconstruction and reconstruction in African philosophy as Outlaw hopes; but that reconstruction has to be exhaustive and methodological in order to weed off the last but most dangerous remnant of logos to wit: logomania. To accomplish this, African philosophers must desist from constructing African philosophy strictly on the bases of the philosophical frameworks of Plato and Aristotle's logic in particular.

1.4 The Emergence of Okwu as an Unbranded Index for Thought

If, as I have done in the preceding section, one discourages the philosophical frameworks of Plato and Aristotle as methodological preconditions for doing African philosophy, what alternative would be offered? Before I attempt this question, it should be made clear here that what I oppose is logos because it skews the journey of reason in African philosophy; I do not oppose the need for a philosophical centre. Logos is more Eurocentric than philosophical and as such promotes epistemic injustice and lacks the merit to occupy the world philosophical centre. Logos is ontologically branded and has dragged reason off course in its journey in African philosophy. Here, I offer in its place an unbranded entity called 'okwu'. Okwu is an Igbo-African concept which has no cognates among English words. It is not 'word' rather; it is that raw material from which words are formed. Its meaning is definite. It does not imply or connote anything else. It carries no further figurative interpretation. If there be other languages that have a meaning for okwu, it can easily be translated without a loss or an addition of meaning. This, I think makes the Igbo concept 'okwu' the more definite and stable than its near equivalents in other languages. Take for example, the English concept 'word'; if we colloquially describe word as a unit in a language, it could also in the same English language mean 'message' as in send a word; 'speech' as in give a word of advice; 'information' as in break word, etc., needless to mention the Greek translation logos which carries a baggage of meanings. This is however, not the case with okwu. Unlike the English concept 'word', okwu is not a unit in the syntax of a sentence. The Igbo term for word is 'mkpuru-okwu' (meaning 'the first fruit of okwu' or that which is derived from okwu). Thus okwu precedes 'word'. It is the very ancestor of word, and it is raw, formless and shapeless. I do not know many languages in the world that have a cognate for this wonderful concept. Historians of language have reported that in the beginning of human evolution, there was only one language spoken in the world, precisely in Africa where the first humans lived. In the words of John McWhorther:

> Like animals and plants, the world's languages are the result of a long "natural history," which began with a single first language spoken in Africa. As human populations migrated to new places on the planet, each group's version of the language changed in different ways, until there were several languages where there was once one. Eventually, there were thousands. (2004: iii)

From the foregoing, one might be tempted to suppose that the Igbo (an African language) that gifts us with 'okwu' is historically disposed to be that first language. Jerome Okonkwo (2012), one of the leading Igbo philosophers of language has done some work to accentuate this supposition. But that would be a discussion for another place.

Returning to our focus; one major inhibition of logos is that it is essentialist. It dichotomises reality into what is acceptable and unacceptable; approvable and unapprovable; superior and inferior. When a philosophy sets out with this biased cleavage, it inexorably comes short of producing a true picture of reality (metaphysics); or truth (epistemology); or value (ethics). The journey of reason in African philosophy has severely been affected by this Western influence. Indeed, the logocentric posture of reason has been the lot of European philosophy. Anyone in doubt need only look at the concatenation of conflicting theories of being, truth and value in European philosophy. Unfortunately, the strong influence of Plato and Aristotle in African philosophy today has tended to project African philosophy as essentialist where the so-called universalists claim superiority over the particlarists and vice versa. In this way, the journey of reason in African philosophy became logocentric. Some African philosophers who now follow Outlaw to advocate deconstruction have this menace of essentialism in mind. For example, Jay van Hook writes:

> To the extent that African philosophy is prepared to move beyond deconstruction, it should feel free to draw from its own varied traditions and from whatever other philosophical traditions may prove useful in particular cases. In other words, and in a very general sense, African philosophy might well cash in its *essentialist* framework for an *existentialist* one—not in the sense of mimicking Kierkegaard, Sartre, or Heidegger, but in the basic sense of

1.4 The Emergence of Okwu as an Unbranded Index for Thought

attending to the existential situation(s) in which African communities find themselves. (2002: 92)

Unlike logos, okwu is not essentialist because it is not an active principle; it is simply a raw material for thought. It has neither the capacity to polarise nor the propensity to dichotomise and discriminate as logos. It is not thought; it only has a sense and that sense is fixed. In the hands of a philosopher, okwu is like clay, formless and shapeless. It falls to the philosopher of any persuasion to turn it into thought. The place of okwu as a philosophical centre from which thoughts could be developed can be appreciated when we observe that it is from okwu that words are formed. A collection of words make a sentence and sentences with elementary linguistic (syntactic and semantic) rules make a language. If we press further, we would observe that languages often have cultural bases and that these bases are sometimes geographic. People in these various geographies who own and speak these languages are human beings participating in humanity whose common index is their development of intelligent cultures. Without an intelligent culture, it seems impossible that a people can develop a language. Thus language becomes one way of manifesting humanity's shared rationality. In other words, rationality is not an attribute standing on its own to which one may argue that a philosophy tradition has it and some others don't; or that some philosophers have it and some others don't. Rationality is embedded in human languages.

Because philosophers are those who produce thoughts when they structure the world with their mind's categories, language with all of its appurtenances and rules becomes the motor through which they communicate their thoughts. Now, whether these thoughts are intelligible or not, it is language that tells us so. Even the philosopher in his private ruminations uses language to make sense of his reflections. Indeed, every philosopher thinks in a language. There is nothing like non-language form of thinking. Thinking is linguistic; for the mind of the philosopher or whatever faculty that does the thinking speaks the language of the philosopher. In fact, when the thinking faculty speaks, we call it thinking or reflection. So, it is correct to say that rationality is embedded in language and every language is rational because it takes an intelligent culture to develop a language in the first place. My thinking is that reason is not a collectivist expression of all *selfs*. It is not even the identity or an attribute of the individual self; it is rather, self expression. Self expression is a linguistic activity and any entity capable of this manifests rationality. Similarly, any culture that is intelligent enough to develop language is rational. Indeed, the enigmatic nature of human language can only be de-emphasised but never overemphasised. This is why many a linguist places it at the centre of some of the greatest evolutionary accomplishments. Tecumseh Fitch for one writes that:

> Language, more than anything else, is what makes us human: the unique power of language to represent and share unbounded thoughts is critical to all human societies, and has played a central role in the rise of our species in the last million years from a minor and peripheral member of the sub-Saharan African ecological community to the dominant species on the planet today. Despite intensive searching, it appears that no communication system of equivalent power exists elsewhere in the animal kingdom. The evolution of human language is thus one of the most significant and interesting evolutionary events that has occurred in the last 5–10 million years, and indeed during the entire history of life on Earth. (2010: 1)

The significance of okwu in the entire linguistic matrix as the very ancestor of language notwithstanding, my interest here seems to glide also, towards the importance of language in philosophical inquiry. The excerpt by Fitch above leaves no one in doubt as to the power of language not only in civilisation but also in thought. I have in a passage above suggested that thinking in itself is linguistic. Indeed, there is no language that is spoken or written that was not first spoken or written in the mind of the speaker or the writer. Thus in any mind in which language can be formulated, spoken and written, in such a mind also can be found rationality. I strongly think that language and rationality are buried into each other. The existence of one cannot be separated from the other. We know what they are individually but cannot effectively set them apart without serious ripples. I would like to describe this inseparability of language and rationality as 'structural *ratiosusuism*'. Derived from two root words '*ratio*' (Latin) meaning reckoning, reason or having the ability to reason or state of being rational; as well as '*asusu*' (Igbo) meaning language. Thus *ratio* + *asusu*, gives birth to the concept *ratiosusuism*. By structural *ratiosusuism* I mean a structure of two inseparable units in which language is the manifestation of rationality and rationality is the form of language. This makes thinking linguistic and portrays language whether in speech or writing as a manifestation of rationality.

Granted that thinking is linguistic as I said above and okwu aggregates to language, it seems plausible to conclude that okwu is the definitive raw material for thought. That was what the philosopher needed; that is what he needs and shall ever need. Gottlob Frege in his "The Thought: A Logical Inquiry" (1956: 292) has explained that the sense of a sentence is what we call *thought*—something "for which the question of truth arises in general". This sense is the immaterial component of language that expresses it. In his words:

> Without wishing to give a definition, I call a thought something for which the question of truth arises. So I ascribe what is false to a thought just as much as what is true.' So I can say: the thought is the sense of the sentence without wishing to say as well that the sense of every sentence is a thought. The thought, in itself immaterial, clothes itself in the material garment of a sentence and thereby becomes comprehensible to us. We say a sentence expresses a thought. (1956: 292)

Frege also made similar point when in his "Sense and Reference" he drew the distinction among sign, referent and sense in a language (1948). Indeed, how remarkable is it to discover that without language, philosophers may never be able to think because thinking is linguistic! And this thing called language, were it to be decomposed from macro to micro would simply leave a mountain of words; if words are dissolved, they will turn into a linguistic molten called okwu; and it is from okwu that words are formed. And by okwu I do not mean any specific terms or concepts, those would be okwu already structured by some sets of linguistic rules. Okwu is in a raw state, formless and shapeless and like clay only moulded into specific words or terms or concepts following some linguistic rules as to be used to form sentences in a language. In other words, okwu does not translate to 'word' in English language. So, 'word' is not a cognate for okwu. Okwu has no cognates; it is and will remain okwu. It is the primary philosophical material. The philosopher never truly needed logos and all the conflicting list of baggage it carries. As a matter of fact, by its numerous contrasting meanings, logos is inimical to philosophy and much more so to African philosophy.

What I offer here replaces (not displaces) logos as the definitive philosophical centre. Thus from logocentrism we might begin to talk about okwucentricism. The difference in terms of reverse discourse is that while the former displaces, dichotomises, bifurcates and polarises the world of philosophy and humanity, the latter in replacing the former seeks to unify same. So, okwucentricism is not a displacement narrative—it is a unifying narrative. The reason and logic that emerge from it do not discriminate against the other; they recognise the right of the other. Okwu does not equate a particular manifestation of reason with the universal or treat one as absolute; it confers equality on all, recognises the validity of their differing contexts and awards the character of universal to all as a common attribute. Reason that emerges from okwu is not absolute and none of its contextual manifestations is capable of being elevated to an absolute instance. Perhaps one sterling difference between logos and okwu when construed as reason is that whereas the voice of logos is a monologue that of okwu is a polylogue. While logos dictates to what it scornfully regards as the 'other', okwu converses with all selfs. Okwu leaves equal room for different cocks to crow, logos denies that other cocks can crow. This is the genuine advantage okwu has over logos when understood as reason.

Okwucentricism thus overcomes the discrimination of logocentrism and becomes a manifestation of rationality that affirms differentiation and recognises the homogeny of common indices. It demonstrates the capacity to return the journey of reason in African philosophy to proper course where creativity and originality replace transliteration/copycatism and imitation/commentating philosophy, the latter being the consequences of logocentrism in African philosophy.

The recognition that philosophies and philosophers command equal pedestal from their different places which okwucentricism fosters might be a good postmodern beginning for African philosophy. In this chapter, I have identified logocentrism as characterising the journey of reason in African philosophy so far, and made an advocacy for an okwucentric shift. Okwucentricism therefore aims at reconstituting the broken philosophical village, only this time into villages and at returning philosophers to such villages wherein they would turn from logos-inspired monologue and begin conversing. In elevating okwu as the primordial index for language, and language as the ultimate motor for communicating thought, one of the recent developments in African philosophy called conversational thinking as a mode of philosophical inquiry emphasises exchange between protestants and contestants in the arena of unities, and thus holds a great promise for the future journey of reason in African philosophy.

1.5 Conclusion

I have in the above advocated the centring of the Igbo-African okwu and the discentring of the Greco-European logos. I have also shown that rationality could be language-embedded which paves way for de-absolutisation and consequent contextualisation of reason. In contextual manifestation of reason, the goal ceases to be which philosophy or philosopher is superior and becomes pure and simple: the production of new thoughts. The recognition of okwu as a philosophical centre inevitably presents conversational thinking as one of the veritable modes of any philosophical inquiry and African philosophy in particular. To converse in any way at all, one needs language. More so, philosophical conversation, the type I espouse needs language to flourish. Okwu as I have presented above is the primary resource for language.

Finally, I have in this chapter identified the journey of reason so far in African philosophy as being largely logocentric. And on the basis of this discovery, I attempted to chart a course for okwucentricism in which contextual manifestation of reason and recognition of the same disbands the philosophical city and reconstitutes it into philosophical villages where conversations rather than monologues direct philosophical inquiry with the aim of achieving villagisation of knowledge. I, therefore, project philosophical conversation whether between philosophical traditions (in the form of comparative, intercultural and cross-cultural philosophies) or between philosophers or philosophers and non-philosophers as a veritable way of unveiling reality (metaphysics), truth (epistemology) and value (ethics). This mode of inquiry can successfully apply where philosophy is conceived as constituting villages rather than just a village or which is worse, a city; and where reality is conceived as an arena of unities rather than just a pillar of growing unity. In the arena of unities, philosophers generally and African philosophers in particular think of reality or truth or value as consisting of different structures whose common index is reason contextually embedded in different languages of conversation. To converse in an arena of unities requires open-mindedness, tolerance, critical balance, non-veneration of authority, mutual respect and constructive disposition towards truth. It is a rainbow reflection and a true beauty of philosophy. These villages are not run by any dictator; they are contexts for the manifestation of okwu-driven reason or jackets of alternative logics. Also, the philosophical city is run by 'emperor' logos whose voice is a monologue. It discriminates and bifurcates. It holds no other cultures in any regard and considers the other as not worth conversing with. So, it speaks or rather dictates to the other. The voice of logos is therefore a voice of monologue but the voice of okwu is that of polylogue. In the mode of philosophical inquiry I advocate, it will be called the voice of conversation. In the remainder of this book I will make conversational thinking my main method of discourse.

References

Asouzu, Innocent. 2011. *Ibuanyidanda and the philosophy of essence*. 50th inaugural lecture of the University of Calabar, May, 18. Calabar: University of Calabar Press.
Bernasconi, Robert. 1997. African philosophy's challenge to continental philosophy. In *Postcolonial African philosophy: A critical reader*, ed. Emmanuel C. Eze, 183–196. Cambridge, MA: Blackwell Publishers.
Bew, John. 2014. *Real realpolitik: A history*. Washington, DC: The Library of Congress.

References

Chimakonam, O. Jonathan. 2015a. Transforming the African philosophical place through conversations: An inquiry into the Global Expansion of Thought (GET). *South African Journal of Philosophy* 34 (4): 462–479. https://doi.org/10.1080/02580136.2015.1104795.

———. 2015b. Conversational philosophy as a new school of thought in African philosophy: A conversation with Bruce Janz on the concept of "philosophical space". *Confluence: Journal of World Philosophies* 3: 9–40.

Derrida, Jacques. 1967/1978. *Writing and difference*. Trans. A. Bass. Chicago: University of Chicago Press.

———. 1994. Of the humanities and the philosophical discipline: The right to philosophy from the cosmopolitan point of view (the example of an international institution). SurfacesIV(310), Folio1, Montreal. https://www.ufmg.br/derrida/wpcontent/uploads/downloads/2010/05/08-Derrida-Jacques-Of-the-Humanities-and-Philosophical-Disciplines.pdf. Retrieved 3 Nov 2015.

Descartes, Rene. 1968. *Discourse on method and the meditations*. Trans. F. E. Sutcliffe. London: Penguin.

Du Bois, W.E.B. 1903/1989. *The souls of black folk*. New York: Bantam Classic edition.

Eze, O. Michael. 2010. *Intellectual history in contemporary South Africa*. New York: Palgrave and Macmillan.

Fitch, Tecumseh. 2010. *The evolution of language*. Cambridge: Cambridge University press.

Foucault, Michel. 1972. The discourse on language. In *The archaeology of knowledge and the discourse on language*. New York: Harper & Row.

Frege, Gottlob. 1948. Sense and reference. *The Philosophical Review* 57 (3): 209–230.

———. 1956. The thought: A logical inquiry. *Mind, New Series* 65 (259): 289–311.

Gyekye, Kwame. 1992. Person and community in African thought. In *Person and community: Ghanaian philosophical studies, 1*, ed. Kwasi Wiredu and Kwame Gyekye, 101–122. Washington, DC: Council for Research in Values and Philosophy.

Hegel, W.F. Georg. 1975. *Lectures on the philosophy of world history*. Trans. H. B. Nisbet. Cambridge: Cambridge University Press.

Hook, Van, and M. Jay. 2002. The universalist thesis revisited: What direction for African philosophy in the new millennium? In *Thought and practice in African philosophy*, ed. Gail Presbey, D. Smith, P. Abuya, and O. Nyarwath, 87–93. Nairobi: Konrad Adenauer Stiftung.

Hume, David. 2014. *An enquiry concerning human understanding*. Text derived from the Harvard Classics 37: P.F. Collier & Son. eBooks@Adelaide The University of Adelaide Library.

Janz, Bruce. 2009. *Philosophy in an African place*. Lanham: Lexington Books.

Kant. Immanuel. 1934/1991a. *Critique of pure reason*. Trans. J. M. D. Mieklejohn. London: Everyman's Library.

———. 1784/1991b. An answer to the question: What is enlightenment? In *Kant: Political writings,* ed. Hans Reiss ed. 2nd edn. Trans. H. B. Nisbet. Cambridge: Cambridge University Press.

Levy-Brhul, Lucien. 1947. *Primitive mentality*. Paris: University of France Press.

Lyotard, Jean-François. 1984. *The postmodern condition: A report on knowledge*. Manchester: Manchester University Press.

McWhorther, John. 2004. *The story of human language*. Part 1. The Teaching Company Limited Partnership.

Menkiti, Ifeanyi. 1984. Person and community in African traditional thought. In African philosophy: An introduction, 3rd edn., Richard Wright, 41–55. Lanham: University Press of America.

Newton, Isaac. 1687/1999. *The mathematical principles of natural philosophy*. California: University of California Press.

Nietzsche, Friedrich. 2002. *Beyond good and evil*. Trans. Rolf-Peter Horstmann and Judith Norman. Cambridge: Cambridge University Press.

Okolo, B. Chukwudum. 1993. What is African philosophy? A short introduction. Enugu: Cecta.

Okonkwo, Jerome. 2012. *Okwu danahu onu: The basic principle of Igbo philosophy of language*. Inaugural lecture no. 6 of Imo State University, Owerri. Owerri: Imo State University Press.

Outlaw, Lucius. 1987/2003. African philosophy: Deconstructive and reconstructive challenges. In *The African philosophy reader*, ed. P.H. Coetzee and A.P.J. Roux, 2nd ed., 162–191. London: Routledge.

Popkin, Richard. 1977-1978. Hume's racism. *The Philosophical Forum* 9 (2–3): 213–218.
Ricouer, Paul. 1974. In *The conflict of interpretations: Essays in hermeneutics*, ed. Don Ihde. Evanston: Northwestern University Press.
Rochau, August Ludwig. 1853. *Grundsätze der realpolitik angewendet auf die staatlichen Zustände Deutschlands*. Stuttgart: Karl Göpel.
Santos, Boaventura de Sousa. 2016a. *Epistemologies of the south: Justice against epistemicide*. New York: Routledge.
———. 2016b. Epistemologies of the south and the future. *European South* 1: 17–29.
———. 2018. *The end of the cognitive empire: The coming of age of epistemologies of the south*. Durham: Duke University Press.
Scruton, R. 1995. *A short history of modern philosophy, from Descartes to Wittgenstein*. 2nd ed. London: Routledge.
Serequeberhan, Tsenay. 1991. African philosophy: The point in question. In *African philosophy: The essential reading*, ed. Tsenay Serequeberhan, 3–28. New York: Paragon House.
Whitehead, Alfred North. 1978. *Process and reality*. New York: Free Press.
Wider, Kathleen. 1986. Women philosophers in the ancient Greek world: Donning the mantle. *Hypatia* 1 (1): 21–62.

Chapter 2
In Search of a Logic-Based Foundation for African Philosophy and Studies

Abstract In this chapter, I hold a conversation with some egg-heads in African philosophy who directly or indirectly offered explanation(s) that attempted to answer the question about the criterion or the Africanness of philosophy. The criterion question asks two simple but challenging questions in African philosophy and they are: what makes a discourse, philosophy? And what makes a philosophy, African? I posit a logic-based criterion for African philosophy and studies. I show that understanding what makes a discourse African is foundational to the project of African studies as a whole if without this much, we may not be able to differentiate our project from those of the Westerners and the Easterners. I contend that all traditions might be universal but they were first particulars rooted in different systems of logic. The universal in this sense is a collection of particulars with distinct methodical and logical nuances.

2.1 Introduction

I believe that understanding what makes a discourse African is foundational to the project of African studies as a whole if without this much, we may not be able to differentiate our project from those of the Westerners and the Easterners. All these various traditions might be universal but they were first particulars. The universal in this sense is a collection of particulars.

I believe that the universal is logical insofar as it does not destroy the identity of its constituent particulars and this is the type of universal I subscribe to, not the absolutising type that denies the viability of the particulars. I doubt that a walled particular can be logical, but I have no doubt whatsoever that a particular can be universal and this is the type of particular I subscribe to, not the walled, border-sensitive and exclusivist type. In a letter to Maurice Thorez in 1956, Aime Cesaire (2010: 152) wrote the following immortal words: "I am not burying myself in a narrow particularism. But neither do I want to lose myself in an emaciated universalism. There are two ways to lose oneself: walled segregation in the particular or dilution in the "universal."" This is the summary of my goal in this chapter: to show as much as possible the difference and similarity between African philosophical tradition and non-African philosophical traditions.

In this chapter, I will hold a conversation with some egg-heads in African philosophy who directly or indirectly offered explanation(s) that attempted to answer the question about the criterion or the Africanness of philosophy. This conversation in search of a foundation for African philosophy is inspired by Uduma O. Uduma's essay entitled "The Question of the 'African' in African Philosophy: In search of a Criterion for the Africanness of a Philosophy". In this essay, Uduma coined what he calls "the Africanness" of a philosophy question which consists in the ultimate criterion for African philosophy. In other words, what makes a philosophy, African? He was not the first to dwell on the Africanness issue in African philosophy when broadly conceived but he was the first, to my knowledge, to christen it as such. Before Uduma framed the question into a proper metaphilosophical concern in African philosophy, old campaigners like John Mbiti, Paulin Hountondji, Ifeanyi Menkiti, Odera Oruka, Peter Bodunrin, Kwasi Wiredu, Chukwudum B. Okolo, Sophie Oluwole, Innocent Onyewuenyi, etc., have all dwelt on it with some going more in-depth than others. I have also dwelt partly on this question before in an essay entitled "The Criteria Question in African Philosophy: Escape from the Horns of Jingoism and Afrocentrism". Incidentally, my treatment of the issue was not exhaustive as I did not mention the likes of Bodunrin, Wiredu, Oluwole and even Uduma himself who will now be discussed here.

The criterion question asks two simple but challenging questions in African philosophy and they are: what makes a discourse, philosophy? And what makes a philosophy, African? Until we answer these questions satisfactorily, we may be exposed to the error of pilling a lot of things that are sociological, anthropological, archaeological and even psychological, etc., under the canopy of African philosophy as Egyptologists and ethnophilosophers desperate to prove a point do. The two questions above speak to a lot of things including, and most specifically, method and logic. To the first, a discourse is philosophy if it is critical and rigorous in approach. The claim is that method is essential to understanding why a body of knowledge may be described as a philosophy, and is also cardinal in sorting it into a philosophy of a given tradition or the other. So, the question of a criterion is in a way, a question of method and the latter is a logical concern. Until African philosophers map out their methods and the logic that grounds them, the charges of transliteration and copying of ideas in Western philosophy will persist and may even seem accurate.

Jurgen Hengelbrock and Heinz Kimmerle are two of the Western philosophers who made the charges of transliteration and copycat against African philosophers apparent. Their hunch is that if African philosophers discuss problems already exhausted in Western philosophy and show no observable difference in their approach when compared to those of Western philosophers, then, it is not the case that what they do can be described as a different tradition of philosophy. They further question the rigour of aspects of African philosophy that deal with atavistic ideas and seem to conclude that African philosophers have a long way to go in terms of elevating and mapping the boundaries of their discourse. In this chapter, I am not so much interested in answering the charge of lack of rigour embedded in Hengelbrock's and Kimmerle's submission as I am in addressing the Africanness of a philosophy or the originality question implicated in their criticism. The Africanness question like the criterion question, speaks directly to method, that is; how may we do philosophy in order for it to become African or, what approach can we possibly adopt in doing philosophy that would qualify what we do as original African philosophy tradition?

The preceding question is partly at the centre of Godwin Sogolo's book *Foundations of African philosophy: A definitive analysis of conceptual issues in African thought*. Sogolo argues that to construct a true African philosophic tradition, African philosophers "should be more self-asserting and start their search from within an indigenous cultural base" (1993: xx). Sogolo further explains that the foundation of African philosophic tradition should not be constructed by "domesticating alien ideas" as some attempt to do. Even though Sogolo did not specifically mention an index that one can appeal to as consisting this foundation, he identifies the raw materials for constructing such a foundation. In this chapter, I have identified a number of African philosophers who have offered opinions as to what could represent this foundation or criterion for determining the Africanness of philosophy.

This encounter with some notable actors on the issue of the Africanness of a philosophy question is scheduled here not for the sake of argument but because it is necessary to the project of contemporary African philosophy. Like I stated earlier, I had elsewhere taken up this concern but not as the central concern of that work. Although I do not intend to change my line of argument in the essay referred to, I shall have to deepen and strengthen it in light of the theses of the philosophers mentioned above. I shall employ the method of conversational thinking in analysing the thoughts of thinkers relevant to the Africanness of a philosophy concern. The goal shall be to demonstrate the inherent inadequacy of their thoughts. And on the basis of that, offer a better criterion for African philosophy.

I shall begin with the conversation on the Africanness of a philosophy and end with a discussion on why we need a foundation for African philosophic tradition. This conversation therefore is with the actors already listed and in particular, with that of Uduma O. Uduma. I shall like to begin with Paulin Hountondji.

2.2 Paulin J. Hountondji

In the first edition of his monumental work *African philosophy: Myth and reality* (1983), Paulin Hountondji declared: "By 'African philosophy' I mean a set of texts, specifically the set of texts written by Africans and described as philosophical by their authors themselves" (Hountondji 1996: 33). This can be called the "geographic origin" criterion and which has persisted in some of Hountondji's earlier writings. Following scathing criticisms from different quarters especially from Yai O. Babalola, a man he describes as one of his harshest critics (Hountondji 1996: xi), Hountondji amended his position in the preface to the second edition of his book (1996). The new position reads: "By 'African philosophy' I mean the set of philosophical texts produced (whether orally or in writing) by Africans" (Hountondji 1996: xii). Thus, the ultimate criterion for African philosophy as far as Hountondji is concerned is that the philosophical work be a written or oral production by an African. The 'African' from his usage merely refers to the geographical origin of the author (to give a work the stamp of African authenticity) whose production must be analytic, and reflect the pattern of critical individual discourse to qualify a work as philosophy (Hountondji 1996: 62–70). Evidently, Hountondji's criterion was primarily posited to answer the dicey question that members of his school (universalist) faced, to wit: how can a work be philosophy and African at the same time? But even as he ties up the bag from one end, it bursts from another.

This geographic origin (criterion) presented by Hountondji stands on a quick sand. If any philosophical discourse produced by an African whether it has anything to do with Africa or not (Hountondji 1996: 65) qualifies as African philosophy; would Hountondji wish this to be a universal standard by which different philosophical traditions are identified? If yes, then different philosophical traditions such as the Western, the Oriental, the African, etc., would simply be racial philosophies which only members can perform. Even this queer proposal is against the position of the universalists. This proposal which is a direct implication of Hountondji's criterion would not only be abstruse but more seriously would eclipse the universality of thought. The talk of philosophical reason being the crest on which philosophy as a common human heritage rides, would become nonsensical. This is because; every philosophical tradition would become essentially culture-bound, strictly unique and substantially different from others for the implication of Hountondji's position to hold. The thesis that philosophical reason in its particular manifestations in philosophical places is continuously in motion striving for the universal would crumble. But we know, even if intuitively, that philosophical reason is at the centre of the philosophical endeavour which means that Hountondji could not have been more in error.

Hountondji may have laid out his arguments with good intentions but my position is that the geographic origin criterion false-started and does not support his probably other well-argued thoughts. Hountondji spent a great deal of time arguing that why ethnophilosophy must be replaced with a rigorous individual discourse that is in tune with universal appurtenances of philosophy is because it unwittingly commits Africans to the hands of the Europeans who taunt them as pre-logical. However, his criterion that African philosophy can only be produced by Africans directly commits Hountondji to the same position he tries to flee from. I have elsewhere referred to this as Hountondji's dilemma.[1] Thus I establish the inadequacy of Hountondji's geographic origin criterion.

---

[1] I have technically called this the Hountondji's dilemma. Cf. Jonathan O. Chimakonam (2015a). Preface. In Atuolu omalu: Some unanswered questions in contemporary African philosophy, ed. Jonathan O. Chimakonam, xiii. University Press of America: Lanham.

2.3 H. Odera Oruka

Odera Oruka the illustrious Kenyan philosopher did better than Hountondji by my own estimation on what constitutes the criteria for African philosophy. He started by distinguishing two senses of philosophy as a universal disciple. While one makes reference to topics discussed by all the philosophers in the world regardless of their background, the other refers to the body of knowledge whose truth can be proved by methods which are independent of any personal, national or racial values and feelings (Oruka 1975: 45). Thus for him philosophy must be a discipline which employs principles that are objectively granted, or else that are rationally (logically) warrantable. And these principles, he maintains, if true, are true regardless of the person or place from which they originate (Oruka 1975: 46). Adopting the second sense, Oruka went ahead to argue that though, this being the universal idea of philosophy; it is consistent with the idea of African philosophy as with other traditions in philosophy. This is due to the fact that every tradition in philosophy is philosophy primarily, because it has the universal characteristics.

However, Oruka had to distinguish between African philosophy in a unique sense which he says is debased and mythical and African philosophy in a simple sense which is the authentic African philosophy (Oruka 1975: 47). He therefore presents the criteria of authentic African philosophy as follows:

> Now it is possible and necessary that the concern for African philosophy is a demand for African philosophy not in the unique sense, but only in the simple sense. Here a piece of African philosophy would deserve to be described as 'African philosophy' simply in the sense that either (i) it is a work of an African thinker or philosopher (regardless of its subject-matter); or (ii) that it is a work dealing with a specific African issue, formulated by an indigenous African thinker, or by a thinker versed in African cultural and intellectual life. (Oruka 1975: 50)

This may be called "the many-option criteria," since Oruka presented them as disjuncts in which any could suffice. Thus Oruka added one other criterion to the one provided by Hountondji to make his two although with more options. But had Oruka married them with a conjunction, it would have made his postulation a lot stronger than that of Hountondji rather; he carefully chose a disjunction probably not to discredit a fellow universalist. So, by implication, either Hountondji's or his criterion would suffice in making a discourse African philosophy. What however places Oruka's criterion on a higher pedestal is the admission that any such discourse that treats African issue or even non-African issues whether produced by an African or a non-African would qualify as African philosophy.

Consider the sense of Oruka's definition of universal philosophy which gives him the leverage to agree that African philosophy is consistent with it. This definition consists of two clauses namely: (i) "the truth of philosophy can be proved by methods which are independent of any personal, national or racial values and feelings" (ii) that "philosophy is a discipline which employs principles that are objectively granted or else that are rationally (logically) warrantable" (Oruka 1975: 46).

Then two paragraphs down the same page where he tries to show that this universalist thesis is consistent with African philosophy, he states:

> That philosophy is universal does not mean that all the philosophers must have similar interests and employ similar *methods* in philosophy. Neither does it mean that all the rationally warrantable or objectively granted principles or methods must be identical or that they must establish similar truth. (Oruka 1975: 46)

What was Oruka thinking when he penned down those words? He referred to it (possible methodological and logical nuances), we all do so, although unconsciously. In this situation, it is hardly the case that Oruka did not at least, have the feeling that he was referring to different methods and logic traditions for different philosophical traditions. He seems to be aware because in the universal definition he offered earlier, the word "logically" was enclosed in a parenthesis between "rationally" and "warrantable". So he must have intentionally omitted it when he evoked the same definition later to justify African philosophy. Obviously, he must have been shy to imply that a logic system that can be described as African must exist not only to shape inquiries in African philosophy and studies but to ground their methods.

But he boldly acknowledged immediately that "Two separate philosophical methods, both being rational, can be opposed to one another, similarly two methods of philosophical inquiry, both using rationally granted or warrantable principles, can come to dissimilar truth" (Oruka 1975: 46). It does not require a logician to understand the logical implications of these statements.

On the whole, Oruka's criteria which describe African philosophy as that discourse produced by an African or a non-African versed in African cultural and intellectual life whether on African or non-African topic is still not adequate. The inadequacy becomes obvious when one engages Oruka in a conversation. To start with, Oruka's criteria are captured in a number of disjuncts: (a) That African philosophy is that discourse produced by an African (b) or that it is that discourse produced by a non-African who is versed in the African cultural and intellectual life (c) or that African philosophy is any discourse on any choice African issue (d) or that African philosophy is any discourse on any choice non-African issue. Granted the above, here is the shocker: When a non-African versed in the African intellectual life produces any philosophical discourse whose theme falls on non-African issue, at least, one of Oruka's criteria says that such a discourse qualifies as African philosophy. But we know this to be ridiculous as for example, when Edwin W. Smith who was versed in African cultural and intellectual life produced a work say on theology, Oruka's criterion says such qualifies as African philosophy simply because the producer Edwin W. Smith, though a non-African; though, his subject was not on a specific African issue, was nonetheless versed in Africa's cultural and intellectual life. The question therefore is: what is the connection between his proficiency in African culture and his work on theology that should confer on the latter the status of African philosophy? In this therefore consists the weakness and inadequacy of Oruka's criteria for African philosophy as discussed above.

Evidently, what makes a discourse African philosophy transcends geography and authorship of a thought. Until the actors in African philosophy project are able to put their house in order concerning the standard of their philosophical practice, we may not have a clear vision of the philosophy we profess as African.

2.4 T. Uzodinma Nwala and Sophie B. Oluwole

Some have argued that what makes a discourse African philosophy is that it has a stamp of African authenticity. Put differently, any work that is called African philosophy must carry African identity. This identity is to be found in African culture or world-view, as such, a work of African philosophy is expected to project this world-view irrespective of how it is structured. Uzodinma Nwala and Sophie Oluwole are the major exponents of this African authenticity criterion. As Nwala explains, African philosophy refers to the collection of basic beliefs or world-view about the universe and man which a society holds in light of the existing social environment (Nwala 1985: 4–6). Nwala suggests that it is the world-view of the African that gives any thought espoused as African philosophy its authenticity or identity. Oluwole was more pungent when she states:

> This task appears at first sight simple and straightforward. A literary piece from Africa is naturally African by the very token that it originated from Africa. But even if this were so, there is still the need to identify, characterize and if possible, rationally justify such works as constituting a literary tradition with specific features which make the group a distinctive cultural phenomenon probably different from some other well known cultural types. (1989: 209)

What Oluwole tries to highlight in the above is the important place of cultural identity of any discourse to be regarded as African philosophy which alone gives it the African authenticity. The problem with the African authenticity criterion is that it easily leads to ethnographic studies and descriptive work. Above all, it leaves a very broad and disorganised scope for African philosophy. Virtually any work in African sociology, anthropology, literature, religion, etc., would by dint of this criterion establish themselves as works in African philosophy.

2.5 Chukwudum B. Okolo

What I am about to discuss here can be called 'the African experience' criterion. C. B. Okolo (1993) is clear on the point that African philosophy is that discipline that focuses on the African and his experience of reality. He explains that African philosophy, like other philosophical traditions is a critical, creative and rational inquiry. Okolo also explains that the goal of philosophy irrespective of which tradition is to employ reason to attend to the issues that arise from human experiences.

Thus for African philosophy, there should be a focus on the experiences of the African in his world. Little wonder Okolo (1983: 8) declares that African philosophy is "a path to a systematic coherent discovery and disclosure of the African as a being-in-the-African-world. Through this knowledge and disclosure of himself and his world by critical reflection, the African grasps reality..." Okolo further explains that like philosophers in other traditions, the African philosopher can also study his experiences of reality in parts, from the lens of the branches of philosophy. To this end, he divides African philosophy into various branches. For lack of space, I will not go into that discussion here.

The point made is that for Okolo, what makes a discourse African philosophy is its focus on the African experiences. It is not clear what may constitute these experiences but one is apt to judge that Okolo refers to social, political, economic and environmental issues that characterise life in Africa. However, one may raise an objection that people from different corners of the world often share experiences but Okolo must be focusing not just on peculiar experiences but on the nuances that characterise those common experiences as well. People all over the world may experience something in common but there are always small differences in the ways they occur from place to place. These little nuances may mean that, if such experiences are problems, their solutions may vary. This is why Okolo suggests that due to the variation in experiences which people in different parts of the world have, the African philosopher may have to take note not only of the *what* of the subject-matter of African philosophy but of the *how* of its method as well. This is because, different experiences, if they are problems could require different approaches.

2.6 Peter Bodunrin

Peter Bodunrin in a sense framed his criteria in form of questions. He believes the answers to the questions shall constitute the criteria for African philosophy. He was not completely satisfied with the out-of-the-blue prescription Hountondji had given. He felt it was too simplistic. There should be clearer reasons and deeper suggestions as to why a piece of literature qualifies as African philosophy. That it has to be an oral or written production of an African as Hountondji states was not very informative and convincing. In Bodunrin's words therefore:

> Recent discussions and further reflections on the matter have convinced me that the different positions as to the nature of African philosophy held by various contemporary Africans reflect different understanding of the meaning of philosophy itself. I now think that our not wholly terminological dispute as to what is and what is not to count as African philosophy cannot be settled without answering some important questions. Some of these questions are: what exactly are African philosophers trying to do, namely, what challenges are they trying to meet? What is the proper answer to these challenges? In other words, what would constitute an appropriate answer to the problems African philosophers are trying to solve? What is the difference between a piece of philosophical discourse and discourse in some other discipline? What is it for a given idea or philosophy to be correctly definable as African philosophy? I shall attempt in this paper to answer these and related questions. (Bodunrin 1991: 65–66)

The problem is that Bodunrin never really answered these questions in ways that will bring out his views as to the criteria a discourse would have to meet before it qualifies as African philosophy. But in analysing the position of the philosophic sagacity later on Bodunrin stated what some like Uduma (2014, 138) have taken to be a statement of his criterion thus: any group of philosophers engaged with some philosophical exercise are doing African philosophy only because the participants are Africans or are working in Africa and are interested in a philosophical problem (howbeit universal) from an African point of view (Bodunrin 1991: 72).

From the foregoing and according to Uduma, Bodunrin in the above made a minor adjustment to Hountondji's criterion. He was able to split the geographic criterion into two components to wit; origin and location. While Hountondji's criterion is that of geographical origin in which an actor is required to be an African that of Bodunrin is geographical location in which an actor is merely required to be working within the African context and on problems that are African and universal. This was an improvement if you like on Hountondji's criterion thought to be too strict by some. By Bodunrin's criterion, a non-African may now be able to produce African philosophy. This was not so different from one of Oruka's criteria already discussed and just as Oruka's proposal; it has its own flaw. According to Uduma:

> The major merit of Bodunrin's position lies in his recognition that non-African philosophers can do African philosophy but his insistence that such non-African philosophers must be working in Africa is illegitimate and not persuasive. (Uduma 2014: 138)

I am inclined to agreeing with Uduma on that point except that I will like to bring in Oruka's demand for such non-African being at least, versed in African cultural and intellectual life which requires such an actor to have lived for a reasonable number of years in Africa. Additionally, I shall like to state that in no definite terms would the questions raised by Bodunrin lead to a clear articulation of the criteria for African philosophy, little wonder his answers failed to lay to rest the criteria puzzle. A probing conversation would readily unfold the impotency of those questions. To begin with, we may have to sum up his questions in two simple ones: what is the problem that an African philosopher/philosophy aims to solve? And what is the correct answer to this question? So in the main, there is only one question namely; what is the correct answer to the question about the problem that an African philosopher/philosophy aims to solve? Essentially, I think this question is incorrectly framed by Bodunrin and as such is potentially misleading.

The idea of a correct answer or in his words a proper answer is misleading. It is difficult if not clearly impossible to conceive one proper answer to that question. Would you say that African philosophy is one that aims to solve African problems? Or the one that aims to demonstrate the manifestation of philosophical reason from the African place whether or not it grapples with any specific African issue? Or the one that aims to enthrone the native African as its producer? Or the one that aims to locate any producer within Africa? These four answers representing many more that could be articulated are without doubt proper to Bodunrin's question depending on the inclination of the African philosopher. But are these answers sufficient to the question about what makes a given philosophical tradition different from another, (by far the truly proper question to be asked)? The answer is no! To locate the criteria of African philosophy, correct questions are not those framed at the micro level because the criteria question is not a micro question; it is rather a macro question. It is macro because it seeks to show the difference between various philosophical traditions. One cannot find this thin membrane within a designate philosophical place which is what most actors like Bodunrin have been doing, but at a comparative philosophical space. It should therefore be noted that the value of philosophy as a questioning discipline lies not just on the importance of questions but more accurately, on the importance of "correct" questions. Incorrect questions are likely going to lead to incorrect answers at which behest the tools of philosophy would be vanquished.

2.7 Kwasi Wiredu

Kwasi Wiredu was primarily concerned with understanding the African orientation to philosophy and the nature of African philosophy (1980, 1991). To begin with, Wiredu rejects what the ethnophilosophers do, i.e. the discussions of the pristine values, maxims, proverbs and sundry ideas in African cultures as deserving of the title African philosophy. These cultural corpuses consist of "the accumulated wisdom of what might be called the collective mind of our societies, handed down through traditions both verbal and behavioural, including aspects of art, ritual and ceremonial" (1980: 28). Wiredu describes these cultural contents variously as folk philosophies which consist mainly of what elders said or are said to have said and are generally pre-scientific. The authentic African philosophy for him cannot be found in these.

Even though, Wiredu subscribes to the cultural origins of philosophies, he separates philosophy as an individual discourse from ethnological materials. As critical, rigorous and rational individual inquiry, process appears to be central to what might qualify as African philosophy in Wiredu's reckoning. Whether one researches into the traditional world-view or introduces new ideas, "[T]here is the need to record, reconstruct, and interpret, and above all to correct false interpretations. But it should be clear also that there is need, possibly more urgent, to fashion philosophies based upon contemporary African experience with its many-sidedness" (1980: 36). Until such a time when architects of African philosophy abide by these processes, Wiredu insists that what they produce does not deserve to be called African philosophy.

Also, Wiredu seems to suggest elsewhere that definition holds the key to the discovery of the criterion for what counts as African philosophy. He set off analysing and exposing the weaknesses inherent in the articulations of his contemporaries notably Hountondji. His submission afterwards is that a proper definition of African philosophy must take into consideration process and issues such as (a) universal philosophical tools, because those are what make a discourse philosophy (b) African cultures and languages, because philosophy is culture relative (c) and exchanges among individual African philosophers, because, that is the proper mode of philosophical engagement (Wiredu 1991: 105). It is the stern warning of Wiredu that:

2.7 Kwasi Wiredu

> Any attempt on the part of a contemporary African philosopher to define African philosophy that does not take account of this process is out of touch with reality. But for him to take account of it is not just to take notice of it; it is for him to take a position with respect to it. For in this matter, he would not be merely trying to describe a phenomenon existing entirely independently of himself, but, rather, seeking to define the principles of his own practice. (Wiredu 1991: 105)

The above quote places emphasis on prescriptive individual discourse and universal orientation as the veritable mode African philosophy must take. With this mode at the foreground, Wiredu identifies three options in ascending order each of which might be considered as a criterion for African philosophy. The first 'option' as he calls it is collecting, interpreting, and retelling those of our traditional proverbs, maxims, conceptions, folktales, etc., that bear on the fundamental issues of human existence. But he says that this option would be chiefly reactionary, backward looking and incapable of leading to modernity. The second option is to learn and disseminate and even possibly make original contributions to the philosophies of the Westerners. Again, he says that this would lead to the African ignoring his culture and committing himself to colonial mentality. This option which he describes as 'uncritical Westernism' for him would be unintelligent. The third option which can be described as the 'process criterion' and which is the option he favours is captured in the following words:

> For a body of thought to be legitimately associated with a given race, people, region or nation, it is sufficient that it should be, or should become, a living tradition therein. It is indifferent whether it is home brewed or borrowed wholly or partially from other peoples. Since we are, as has been repeatedly pointed out, still trying to develop a tradition of modern philosophy, our most important task is not to describe, but to construct and reconstruct. And the real issue regarding African philosophy is how best this may be done. (Wiredu 1991: 106–107)

I shall like to fault part of Wiredu's process criterion. The proper tradition of African philosophy necessarily has to be home-brewed or at worst borrowed partly, on no justification would it be wholly borrowed and still remain African philosophy. In fact, the clause that allows African philosophical tradition to be wholly borrowed from any other tradition leads directly to what he criticised as colonial mentality or uncritical Westernism (Wiredu 1991: 106). However, of the three options given by Wiredu, it is in the third option that he placed greater credibility so I shall converse with him on that. This criterion literally states that for a discourse to qualify as African philosophy, the process for its construction has to represent an African orientation to philosophy. We know from his earlier discussion that this process necessarily includes rigorous individual-based exercise that is universally applicable; which takes cognizance of African culture since for him philosophy is culture relative (Wiredu 1991: 106). What Wiredu fails to clarify however, is the model of this construction. He fails to observe that model is very important in constructing philosophical traditions. If not, Georg Hegel's *Lectures on the philosophy of world history* or Immanuel Kant's *anthropology from a pragmatic point of view* or Lucien Levy Bruhl's *Primitive mentality* or even William Anton Amo's writings where he did some constructions about Africa would qualify as African philosophy. It is not just construction or reconstruction that settles the matter, model is central. Wiredu probably noticed this lacuna in his criterion which is why he ended it by saying, "And the real issue regarding African philosophy is how best this may be done" (Wiredu 1991: 106–107). It is his inability to supply a clear answer to that question that vitiates his process criterion for African philosophy.

2.8 John Mbiti, Ifeanyi Menkiti and Innocent Onyewuenyi

John Mbiti (1969) explains that the African ontological formation is communal and that an individual is intertwined in a relationship with others. This relationship for him characterises what might be called a communitarian order in which the community is prior to the individual. The individual depends on the community and must submit to it in order for him to thrive. The African world-view therefore is communal and strives to protect individual interests by protecting the communal interest. To make sense of African cultures, religions or even its intellectual history and philosophy, Mbiti seems to suggest that a communitarian view point is critical. This applies in everything including in what constitutes the criterion for African philosophy.

Ifeanyi Menkiti (1984) shares the communitarian view with Mbiti who indeed inspired his theory of radical communitarianism. In this theory, Menkiti claims that the community precedes the individual. In fact, he paints a picture that shows that the community subsumes and dominates the individual. The individual according to him, "is defined by reference to the environing community" (1984: 171). The community is pre-eminent and shapes the lives of the individuals in it. Reality is constructed through the lens of the community and so is philosophy, religion and sundry spheres of knowledge. To understand African cultures or lifeworld, Menkiti seems to claim that the communal perspective is critical. One of the major implications of Menkiti's radical communitarianism is that a communitarian approach to knowledge formation is imperative for a discourse to become authentic African philosophy.

Like Mbiti and Menkiti, Innocent Onyewuenyi (1991) also represents a group of African philosophers who hold fast to what they think is a model of thought common to all Africans south of the Sahara. They are convinced that the communitarian ontology is the bastion of African thought. Mbiti, Menkiti and Onyewuenyi are not alone in this view. William Abraham, Henry Olela, Mogobe Ramose, Olusegun Oladipo, T. Uzodinma Nwala, are some other actors who share this view which Kwasi Wiredu ridiculed as an exercise in "community thought" (Wiredu 1980: 14). Paulin Hountondji also lambasted them for been naïve in their inclination towards consensus or what he calls 'the myth of unanimity' (Hountondji 1996: 60–61).

Notwithstanding the criticisms, most members of this school remain adamant. They variously defend their position and insist that any discourse that is not constructed on top of this communitarian ontology cannot be said to be African philosophy. For them therefore, the communitarian ontology is the insignia of African thought. It differentiates African philosophy from say, Western philosophy which rides on the crest of individualistic ontology. It is in connection with this that Onyewuenyi articulates the communitarian criterion as follows:

> The discovery of African philosophy has influenced African scholars in writing about African personality or what the French speaking Africans call Negritude. Kwame Nkrumah, Julius Nyerere, Leopold Senghor, Aime Cesaire, Nnamdi Azikiwe, and Chinua Achebe have written prose and verse to celebrate this philosophy—a philosophy of unity and complete encounter of all things and beings, which by reason of the dynamic character of African ontology, has surfaced on the communal structure of our society based on the division of labour and rights; in which man attains growth and recognition by how well he fulfils a function for the over-all well-being of the community. (Onyewuenyi 1991: 44–45)

Thus from the above, a discourse is African philosophy if and only if, it has the communitarian model of thought as its background. The shortcoming of this criterion lies not in its logical vision but in its theoretic framing. The communitarian criterion is articulated to reflect some form of ontological strait-jacket where every variable is determined to serve the centre and for the good of the centre without the justification of critical reasoning. Hence, Wiredu says of this model that it gives the "impression that African philosophy is a monolithic body of argumentative communal beliefs, and nothing else" (Wiredu 1991: 95). Wiredu goes on to suggest that it is a "descriptive, theoretically unreconstructive model" (Wiredu 1991: 103). We shall in this work seek to transcend this level of explication (ontology) in our quest to fathom the true criteria for African philosophy.

2.9 Uduma O. Uduma

Uduma has recently articulated the criterion question as the Africanness of a philosophy question (Uduma 2014: 135). Besides my work where I conceptualised the same problem as the criteria question (Chimakonam 2015b: 102), Uduma's attempt is next in line as the most recent. From the foregoing, the equivalence of the Africanness question and the criteria question can here be established. I have decided to revisit this metaphilosophical exercise because as I explained earlier my former attempt was not digestive. In his essay, Uduma criticised Hountondji, Bodunrin and Oluwole insisting that their criteria were not adequate. He went on to adopt Theophilus Okere's and C. B. Okolo's suggestions which he transformed into a criterion. For Okolo, what makes a philosophy African is its identification with the cultural, historical or existential experience of Africa/ns (Okolo 1993: 33–4). On the other hand, Okere explains that African philosophy refers to a critical reflection either on a given universal phenomenon or a unique problem in Africa through the glasses of an African culture (Okere 1976: 5). It is on the inspiration of these two that Uduma resolved that:

> [w]hat makes a philosophy Western, African or Oriental is neither the geographical origin nor location of the author; rather it is the cultural and geographical content. It is, therefore, the cultural/geographical background/content of a philosophy that makes it African. For

any philosophical work, system, theory or idea to be African, whether it is written by an African or non-African, it must have an African flavor. It must be a product of wonder from or on the African experience and the African world. (Uduma 2014: 143)

Thus I shall like to call Uduma's criterion, "culture-dependent" criterion for the Africanness of a philosophy. There are two points Uduma makes in the above. First, he posits that philosophy is a child of wonder and second, he concludes based on the first that when this wonder resonates from an African cultural background which provides the material object for philosophising, African philosophy is produced. In his words again; "philosophy is a product of human wonder…on their immediate environment. This is what is meant when we say that philosophy is a child of circumstance" (Uduma 2014: 142). To unfold the limitations in Uduma's criterion, I shall hold a brief conversation with him.

If cultural background is the Alchemist's stone that transforms any discourse into philosophy and draws a line between one philosophy tradition and another, Uduma was unable to identify those cultural elements that perform this magic. These cultural elements, if they exist, must be in the form of institutions, ceremonies, rituals, belief systems, and perhaps incantations; would Uduma grant for instance, that a discourse that would qualify as African philosophy must be done through incantations? Yet, this is the far-reaching implication of Uduma's criterion of cultural basis.

As interesting as his criterion sounds, we must note that in philosophy, things are not usually what they seem. It is by the arumaristic[2] power of the method of conversational thinking that cumbrous theses like Uduma's can be compelled to bear witness against itself. That cultural coloration of discourse is what characterises different philosophical traditions sounds too simplistic for comfort. It is not just enough to make this type of big statement which do not have any deeper implications and simply go to sleep believing that the job has been done. Uduma should have been able to tell us exactly which cultural elements colours a discourse into Western, Oriental, and African philosophies, and how? Anyways, his failure to decide this and the weaknesses of other criteria articulated by others before him, form the justification for the logic-based criterion I shall offer presently.

2.10 The Logic-Based Criterion

I reject as unnecessary and irrelevant the Hountondji's criterion that a discourse has to be produced by an African before it would qualify as African philosophy, but I retain Oruka's clause that any discourse can qualify as African philosophy whether it is by an African or non-African; whether it is on African or on non-African issue, and on it erect an important and foundational "logic criterion." We can therefore state the "logic criterion" thus:

---

[2] See Chaps. 7 and 8 for detailed discussion of this notion.

2.10 The Logic-Based Criterion

(i) Any discourse that treats African or non-African issues whether produced by an African or non-African versed in African cultural and intellectual life but is capable of universal application can qualify as African philosophy insofar as it is produced with African culture-inspired methods grounded in the logic of African ontology or the instrument of logic tradition in Africa which is arumaristic in structure.

In suggesting a logic tradition for Africa, I probably have in the words of the dogged Nigerian philosopher Udo Etuk stirred the hornet's nest (Etuk 2002: 99). Some of the universalists would regard this position as unapt and the idea of universal instrument of logic to be inconsistent with African logic or less horrifying, logic tradition in Africa. But my evocation of "African logic" is no different from similarly accepted evocations such as "Indian logic," "Chinese logic," "Arabic logic," "Western logic" to name a few which as far back as 1967 Paul Edwards proudly allocated important places to in the history of logic as treated in his *Encyclopedia of philosophy volume iv* (Edwards 1967: 520–528). My idea of logic tradition in Africa or simply African logic is perfectly consistent with the idea of universal logic no less than the ideas of universal philosophy and philosophy tradition in Africa. It is intellectual cowardice or colonialist stereotype that makes one assume that any time the predicate "African" is evoked in philosophy, a red flag is at once raised to signal the intrusion of ethocentricism. The preponderance of this sort of thinking has become sickening in our time. It is, therefore, arguable that some architects of African philosophy project—universalists included (whilst not denying them their credits) in the time of the debate and soon after, are in the habit of overlooking the definitional or foundational role of logic in any discourse called philosophy. So, it is understandable to expect them to reject the idea of an African logic at one hand and at another demonstrate it in their argumentation. This is however, not unconnected with the terrifying predicate "African" placed in front of "logic". Indeed, Wiredu in commenting on Victor Ocaya's work on logic within the Acholi language even suggested that the idea of African logic should never be considered a reasonable project. He describes the idea of African logic as precipitous and blanket speculation (Wiredu 1991: 101). My own project however, which has been called Ezumezu system is not exactly as those of Ocaya, Chukwuemeka Nze, Etuk, Chris Ijiomah, Ademola Fayemi, Edwin Etieyibo, etc., who attempt to describe what they feel is the structure of logic in their various cultures. Ezumezu does not describe how Africans reason that is similar or different from how the rest of humanity reason; it takes inspiration from the arumaristical model of thought common to African cultures (specifically undergirding the well known communitarian ontology of the African tradition) to devise an alternative system of logic that could drive philosophising in Africa. To drive philosophising in African philosophy, one that would be absolved from the blame of transliteration of Western philosophy, an alternative model of thought is imperative. The concept of the "alternate" has no direct implication to "difference in substance" which is the erroneous basis of the assumptions associated with the concept of "African logic".

2.11 Conclusion

From the foregoing, the Ezumezu system is therefore called African logic because it is developed within the African philosophical tradition and with generous African ontological paraphernalia, to shape and undergird philosophical inquiries in Africa not as polemicists suppose that it points to a unique African way of thinking. Again, this latter attribute of driving philosophical inquiries in Africa does not in any way vitiate its universal applicability. The fear then, that the evocation of "African" reawakens the idea of ethnophilosophy or any sort of unique, pure, culture-bound excavations is therefore unfounded. Thus devising a system of alternative logic model as a foundation for African philosophy is not merely ceremonial but acutely imperative. Godfrey Ozumba in this connection admonishes that "understanding the underlying African logic is sine qua non to understanding the latent philosophic wisdom which is embedded in African philosophic systems" (Ozumba 2015: 184). This foundation is what is required all along to jolt African philosophy out of the vicious circle of metaphilosophical dialogues and onto a path of architectonic growth and progress. Hence, the future direction of African philosophy can successfully be charted only on the wheels of an alternative thought model. In the absence of this alternative thought model, African philosophy can hardly wash itself clean from the blame of transliteration. Already, some Western philosophers like Heinz Kimmerle and Jurgen Hengelbrock according to Ozumba accuse the architects of African philosophy of transliteration of Western thought (Ozumba 2015: 181–184). Ozumba may have doggedly answered the charge of transliteration wherein he described his Western opponents as narrow-minded (2015: 174), the fact however remains, as Ozumba agrees and appears to suggest (2015: 184), that an alternative system of logic is necessary to ground the methods of African philosophy project. C. S. Momoh observed long ago that this was the last piece of the African philosophy jigsaw and challenged African logicians to take up the task of developing a system of logic that would serve as a foundation for African philosophy (Momoh 2000:187). Ezumezu represents the accomplishment of this requirement.

References

Bodunrin, Peter. 1991. The question of African philosophy. In *African philosophy: The essential readings*, ed. Tsenay Serequeberhan, 63–86. New York: Paragon House.
Cesaire, Aime. 1956/2010. Letter to Maurice Thorez, Trans., Chike Jeffers. *Social Text 103* 28 (2): 145–152. https://doi.org/10.1215/01642472-2009-072.
Chimakonam, O. Jonathan. 2015a. Dating and periodization questions in African philosophy. In *Atuolu omalu: Some unanswered questions in contemporary African philosophy*, ed. Jonathan O. Chimakonam, 9–34. Lanham: University Press of America.
———. 2015b. The criteria question in African philosophy: Escape from the horns of jingoism and Afrocentrism. In *Atuolu omalu: Some unanswered questions in contemporary African philosophy*, ed. Jonathan O. Chimakonam, 101–123. Lanham: University Press of America.

References

Edwards, Paul, ed. 1967. *Encyclopedia of philosophy*. Vol. iv. New York: Macmillan Publishing co.
Etuk, Udo. 2002. The possibility of African logic. In *The third way in African philosophy*, ed. Olusegun Oladipo, 98–116. Ibadan: Hope Publications.
Hountondji, Paulin. 1996. *African philosophy: Myth and reality*. Rev. 2nd edn. Bloomington Indianapolis: Indiana University Press.
Mbiti, John. 1969. *African religions and philosophy*. London: Heinemann.
Menkiti, Ifeanyi. 1984. Person and community in African traditional thought. In *African philosophy: An introduction*, ed. Richard Wright, 3rd ed., 41–55. Lanham: University Press of America.
Momoh, S. Campbell. 2000. The logic question in African philosophy. In *The substance of African philosophy*, ed. Campbell Momoh, 2nd ed., 175–192. Auchi: APP Publications.
Nwala, T. Uzodinma. 1985. *Igbo philosophy*. Lagos: Lantern books.
Okere, Theophilus. 1976. The relation between culture and philosophy. *Uche* 2: 4–11.
Okolo, B. Chukwudum. 1993. *What is African philosophy? A short introduction*. Enugu: Cecta.
———. 1983. African Philosophy: A Process Interpretation. *Africana Marburgensia*, xv:2.
Oluwole, B. Sophie, ed. 1989. *Readings in African philosophy*. Lagos: Masstech Publications.
Onyewuenyi, Innocent. 1991. Is there an African philosophy. In *African philosophy: The essential readings*, ed. Tsenay Serequeberhan, 29–46. New York: Paragon House.
Oruka, Odera. 1975. The fundamental principles in the question of African philosophy. *Second Order* 4: 1 44–1 65.
Ozumba, Godfrey. 2015. The transliteration question in African philosophy. In *Atuolu omalu: Some unanswered questions in contemporary African philosophy*, ed. Jonathan O. Chimakonam, 171–185. Lanham: University Press of America.
Sogolo, S. Godwin. 1993. *Foundations of African philosophy: A definitive analysis of conceptual issues in African thought*. Ibadan: University of Ibadan Press.
Uduma, O. Uduma. 2014. The question of the "African" in African philosophy: In search of a criterion for the Africanness of a philosophy. *Filosofia Theoretica: Journal of African Philosophy, Culture and Religions* 3: 1 127–1 146.
Wiredu, Kwasi. 1980. *Philosophy and an African culture*. Cambridge: Cambridge University Press.
———. 1991. On defining African philosophy. In *African philosophy: The essential readings*, ed. Tsenay Serequeberhan, 87–110. New York: Paragon House.

Chapter 3
Some Problematics in African Logic

Abstract I argue that the concern of African logic should really be about constructing systems and criticising the systems. I show that recent discussions have however threatened to veer it off-course. Instead of engaging in robust rigorous conversations, some logicians and philosophers have taken to apologias while others have taken to polemicism both of which have narrowed their visions to a debate about the correctness and incorrectness of the idea of an African logic rather than practical demonstrations. I contend that this diversion has created some problematics in African logic which include: the categorisation of logic into classical or standard and non-classical or non-standard, the problematic of the idea of African logic, the relative-universal problematic and the problematic of regional logics. I show that if the talk about African logic is going to make any meaning, it must be within the scheme of constructing an alternative logic system and not a culture-bound apologias as ethnologicians champion or fruitless animadversions as the polemicists demonstrate.

3.1 Introduction

A host of African philosophers beginning with Meinrad Hebga (1958) have written about African logic but it was C. S. Momoh that provocatively engaged this topic in his paper 'The "Logic" Question in African Philosophy' (2000: 175–192). In the final passage of the work, Momoh made a clarion call which partly informs not only this chapter but this book as whole. In his words:

> …even though it is possible to use existing formal logics and rules of inference to evaluate discourse, reasoning and thoughts in African cultures and world-views, the authentic African logic in artificial language is yet to be developed. African professional philosophers have this gauntlet to pick up. (2000: 187)

I will pick up this gauntlet in subsequent chapters of this book where I unveil Ezumezu as a philosophy of logic, methodology and formal system. What I will do in the present chapter is to re-visit the 'logic question' and show why it is a valid concern in African philosophy.

The idea of (an) African logic falls within the scheme of universal-particular debate. While some say that logic as the instrument of thought is universal and cannot be relative, others are of the view that logic systems are relative or are particular systems that can be universalised. They find support for this claim in the emergence of three-valued, many-valued and even-multi-valued logics. Logic systems therefore are methodological nuances. This latter group (call them the relativists) seeks to fault the premises of the first group (call them the universalists). For the relativists, when the universalists talk of logic as universal they actually mean an absolute conception of logic with laws and principles that apply in all cultures and in all topics irrespective of context. The relativists deny that any logic system has such power. They grant that a logic system, for example the two-valued logic may have more expressive power than, say, three-valued logic or even many-valued logic, but none has an absolute expressive power which can axiomatise statements in all contexts without exceptions.

All logics are alternatives to others and the creation of any alternative logic involves the relaxation of the traditional laws of thought. Support is found in literature where Oliver Reiser (2004) observes that any shift in the three traditional laws of thought presupposes the emergence of an alternative system of logic. It is in this way, I suppose, that the field of logic has witnessed exponential growth in the modern time. It would then be incorrect to continue to put it in a strait-jacket of absolutism as the universalists tend to do. Susan Stebbing has clarified that the "science of logic does not stand still, during the last half-century, greater advances have been made in logic than in the whole preceding period from the time of Aristotle" (1950: ix). It continues to grow not strictly in an architectonic order but possibly also as a field of systems which is what the relativists uphold. In this way, anybody and indeed, any philosophical tradition might create their own system of logic insofar as its laws and principles are clear enough for others to follow. To this end, Rudolf Carnap states that people are free to construct any logic system they wish and according to whatever convention they choose, so long as the logic system is constructed clearly and the syntactical rules and conventions are properly formulated (Harris 1992: 42).

Thus if the talk about African logic is going to make any meaning, it must be within this scheme of constructing an alternative logic system and not a culture-bound enterprise as ethnologicians champion. The relativists want to ignore the scare tactics of the universalists whose opinion it is that such a system is not only impossible but erroneous. So the concern of African logic should really be about constructing a system and criticising the system. Recent discussions have however threatened to veer it off-course. Instead of engaging in robust rigorous conversations, some logicians and philosophers have taken to apologias while others have taken to polemicism both of which have narrowed their visions to a debate about the correctness and incorrectness of the idea of an African logic rather than practical demonstrations. This diversion has created some problematics in African logic which include: the categorisation of logic into classical or standard and non-classical or non-standard, the problematic of the idea of African logic, the relative-universal problematic and the problematic of regional logics. These are some of the problematics in African logic which will be the focus of this chapter.

3.2 Problematising the Categories of Non-classical, Non-standard and Non-western[1]

In the history of logic, obviously dominated by Western scholars, there is a categorisation of the discipline into classical or standard, referring elementarily in this context to the tradition pioneered by the Greek-born Aristotle, and the rest as non-classical or non-standard or non-Western, referring elementarily in this context to the various traditions from different cultures. But this categorisation is problematic because it promotes epistemic lopsidedness that glorifies the Western intellectual legacy and subordinates the intellectual legacies of other cultures. It presented Western peoples as the privileged owners of the instrument of logic and people from other cultures as humble beneficiaries of Western-invented and Western-owned logic. The categorisations, non-classical, non-standard and non-Western therefore were intended to subordinate the nature of logics developed in other cultures and since logic is the foundation of thought, by extension, it subordinates the minds of other peoples in the world.

Beginning with the first category called classical and non-classical, we must ask ourselves, what makes the Western logician feel entitled to designate his logic tradition as classical and those of other cultures as non-classical? Various dictionaries define the adjective classical as qualifying something that pertains to ancient Greek culture standing for an exemplary standard that has a long-established reputation and before the era of relativity theory, etc. It is well known in literature that Western scholarship adopted ancient Greece and have strived, quite pretentiously to present it as the original home of human civilisation. To accomplish this, Western scholars have had to resort to all sorts of unprofessional strategies including falsifying history as Amos Wilson (1993) reports, and plagiarising other intellectual heritages like Egypt as George James (1954) clearly established. Designating ancient Greek intellectual legacy of logic as classical obviously has more to do with the project of Eurocentricism than with mere recognition of excellence.

There may be people out there who would argue that the classical vs. non-classical distinction refers to the eras from Ancient Greece to Isaac Newton/Rene Descartes and from Albert Einstein/Jan Łukasiewicz onwards. But this is not clearly the case. In physics, this same categorisation is maintained but with a curious nuance. Physics before the time of Albert Einstein is called classical but from the time of Einstein onwards, the era of relativity theory is not called non-classical

---

[1] It was my former student Victor Nweke who first drew my attention to this problem. He suggested to me to drop the category non-standard and use non-classical instead, in qualifying African logic, because, for him, the former was obviously too uncomplimentary. I went through this manuscript making the changes before Michael Onyebuchi Eze again frowned at my use of the category non-classical because, for him, it was derogatory and presents African knowledge formation as residual. The old category Western and Non-Western also promotes the same epistemic lopsidedness by forcing African knowledge formation to be defined in reference to the West, so Eze suggested that I use the categories Western and African logics, traditional/old and supplementary laws of thought. I here appreciate Nweke and Eze for spurring me on to problematise this categorisation in logic.

physics. It is given the flamboyant names: quantum or modern physics. The question is why? The logic that underbellies classical physics is called classical logic but curiously, Einstein who thought outside the boxed up Western logical framework was able to arrive at a new scientific protocol which according to J.M Bochenski (1965) the so-called classical logic could not axiomatise. This not only brought to light the inadequacy of classical logic but mocked the acclaimed inviolability of Western intellectual reputation. Little wonder most of Einstein's colleagues fought hard to destroy his theory. Some say it defies commonsense and by commonsense they were referring to the logical protocol of Aristotle, the so-called logic with long-established exemplary standard.

Einstein's theory bored a huge hole under the unverified and sanctimonious assumption that Aristotle's logic is an unimpeachable standard. Classical logic was shown not to be classical after all and this was a big dent on the Western pride and as such, the theory of relativity must be rejected.

A recent article in the well-respected online academic magazine *The Conversation*, written by Richard Gunderman (2015) recounts the bitter unprofessional attack which Einstein suffered in the hands of a fellow physicist Philipp Lenard. Lenard, a German and a fervent advocate of Aryan superiority, sort to destroy Einstein's relativity theory on the grounds of racism and the presumed mental inferiority of non-Westerners. He called Einstein's work on relativity dangerous and pernicious to the field and called on other scientists to reject it. He lamented that what Einstein brings to the field of physics was the despicable 'Jewish spirit'. In one of his racists comments against Einstein, Lenard said "just because a goat is born in a stable does not make it a noble thoroughbred" (Gunderman, 2015). Further, Gunderman states that Lenard's conviction that science, like every other human intellectual achievement has basis in bloodlines characterised his attack and rejection of Einstein's theory. This divisiveness, intellectual racism and subordination of other peoples by Westerners were exactly the inspiration behind the category of classical vs. non-classical logics. When Einstein's theory was confirmed through experiments and became very useful in developing the bombs that defeated the Nazi Germany, many scientists in the West accepted it and claimed it as part of Western intellectual achievement. For this, the era of Einstenian physics was not labelled the derogatory name of non-classical. It is either called quantum or modern physics even though it is grounded in the sort of logic they would describe as non-classical.

I come to the second category called standard and non-standard. Various dictionaries define the adjective standard as an authoritative model granted by general consent, something that represents the basis for comparison, and something that has recognised excellence and established authority. The logic tradition pioneered by the Greek-born Aristotle is given the name standard logic to position it as the bar to which other traditions would have to strive in vain to reach. The contrast non-standard is meant to indicate the subordinated nature of the rest of logic traditions. Just like in the category classical and non-classical, standard and non-standard is a dichotonomous binary that reflects the lopsidedness between one established model and the rest.

3.2 Problematising the Categories of Non-classical, Non-standard and Non-western

But what gives the Western intellectual the authority to legislate that Western logic tradition is standard and those of other traditions are not? On what basis does he make this type of pronouncement? Again, just like in the category classical and non-classical, the Western scholar is haunted by Eurocentricism by which he wants every other intellectual tradition to be defined with reference to the Western order. This will make such traditions residual to the Western tradition. The category standard and non-standard logics is probably one of the worst intellectual categorisations that residualises the otherness as something inferior and below the range of humanity. To think that this category was used to describe logic which is the foundation of all human intellectual endeavours, suggests a carefully orchestrated programme of intellectual subordination of other cultures and peoples by Western scholarship.

Finally, I come to the third category called Western and non-Western. Even though this category looks quite innocuous at face value, and is widely used nowadays in different fields, I have come to realise that it may even be the worst form of racial and cultural categorisation of humanity. This is because, it contains an implicit bias against all other cultures that are defined in reference to the West. Anyone that employs this hideous category accepts quite in error and maybe unbeknownst to him that the West is superior and the rest are residual. To be defined as non-Western victimises the culture or peoples so defined. Non-Western then is a horrendous adjective that deflates the identity of the victim. It is an intellectual tragedy that occurs in the process of identity manifestation that retards and eventually displaces a formed original identity while replacing it with 'nameless restness'. It is also a strategy that not only denies the identity of other cultures but binds them up into the nameless other. To say that a culture or a logic is non-Western is to count it off before it is ever given an opportunity to express itself. Non-Western therefore becomes an adjective for qualifying anything, culture or logic that is below approved standard, a poor model. Non-Western also, and this is very important, represents a model that is an imitation of the original. Because it is not original, it does not have a name. So, it has to be qualified by a pseudonym derived from a model that has an original name, hence, non-Western. There may be no other form of intellectual categorisation that creates a binary in which the one is an authenticated original identity and the other is a forced nameless *disidentified* 'restness' than the category of Western and non-Western. So, whether in logic, philosophy, history, arts, culture, etc., the category non-Western is intellectually subordinating.

Thus to avoid all of this, I have resorted to the simple cultural categorisations such as African, Asian, Chinese, Indian, Western logics to name a few, in this book and I thank Michael Eze for stimulating me to problematise these categorisations in logic. I believe that problematising these racially divisive and subordinating categories for logic is part of the ongoing decolonial project. Colonialism rides on the crest of superior/inferior dichotomy in which the one has authentic existence and the other has inauthentic existence. Colonialism is a script in which both the colonialist and the colonised are characters depicting different roles assigned by the scriptwriter. The problem is that the colonialist also doubles as the scriptwriter who assigns to himself the role of the protagonist and assigns to the colonised the role of the villain. Unfortunately, the protagonist always wins and the villain is always the second best that loses. The project of intellectual decolonisation is thus aimed at re-writing the script of colonialism such that the colonised working on his own stage and script will be the one to assign roles to his characters. But besides this problematic, African logic has other worries which will be my focus in the next section.

3.3 The Problematic of the idea of African Logic

Some scholars in the past like Georg Hegel, Immanuel Kant, David Hume and Emil Ludwig have suggested the non-existence of logos among African peoples.[2] Lucien Levy-Bruhl (1947) resurrected and strengthened some of these despicable conclusions in the twentieth century. Later, Robin Horton (1977) stretched it a bit further when he claimed that the laws of logical reasoning are not present in African languages and cultures, and suggested that Africans lacked the capacity to engage in logical reasoning. For Hegel, in his *Lectures on the philosophy of world history*, Africa has no well-developed culture; it has no history and has made no positive contribution to world civilisation. It is "a land of childhood, removed from the light of self-conscious history and wrapped in the dark mantle of night" (1975: 174). Levy-Bruhl, in his *Primitive Mentality*, tells of the primitives without logical ability which has been construed in literature as part of the giant project of Eurocentricism against Africans. C. M. Okoro sums up the racist Eurocentric vision as follows:

> In these inhuman and ugly treatments of the black race, the Whiteman argued that even if an African is a person without tail, he is a Negro or dark in complexion anyway and darkness connotes for him all that is evil, wicked, monstrous and demonic. It has been written that according to an official legal position in the United States, the Negro is 2/3 of a human being with putative rights that the Whiteman is under no obligation to respect. (2004: 3)

Okoro goes on to disclose that some European anthropologists, in the same mold as Levy-Bruhl, out of their ignorance of African metaphysics were contemptuous of African cultures and underrated the people. For example, he quotes Levy-Bruhl as saying that the primitives are "pre-logical people who always ascribed to invisible and supernatural forces" (2004: 3). This means, among other things, if we take the concept of primitive to apply to Africans as is widely the case in colonial literature, that Africans think and behave in anti-scientific ways. It does therefore imply that such a culture and language which supported this type of thinking would be, to say the least, devoid of logic.

E. E. Evans-Pritchard gives a different interpretation of Levy-Bruhl's assertion of a primitive mentality. In *Theories of primitive religions*, Evans-Pritchard (1965: 81–82) argues, first, that Levy-Bruhl was misunderstood. According to him, by the notion of "pre-logicality," Bruhl simply made allusions to the thought system or

---

[2] See Hegel (1975); Eze (1995); Popkin (1978); Smith (1966).

pattern of primitive peoples which is magical or religious, and hence appearing absurd to the Europeans. Evans-Pritchard tries to explain that Levy-Bruhl did not mean that primitives are incapable of thinking coherently but merely that most of "their beliefs are incompatible with a critical and scientific view of the universe." Second, their thought pattern contains "evident contradictions" in light of Aristotelian logic. This is because some of the laws of thought which guide reasoning in African system of thought might be a little bit more complicated. Third, Evans-Pritchard also argues that Levy-Bruhl was not saying that the primitives are unintelligent but that their beliefs are unintelligible to Europeans. This, he says, does not mean that Europeans cannot follow their reasoning. He claims that primitives reason logically but that the problem is that they reason from different premises, which are too absurd for Europeans to follow in light of Aristotelian logic. Thus Evans-Pritchard declares that primitives "are reasonable but they reason in categories different from ours. They are logical but the principles of their logic are not ours, not those of Aristotelian logic." Further, Evans-Pritchard explains that pre-logical as used by Levy-Bruhl does not mean alogical or anti-logical. When applied to primitive mentality, it simply means that they do not go out of the way, as Europeans do, to avoid contradictions and they do not always present the same logical requirements.

But despite the defence mounted by Evans-Pritchard in favour of Levy-Bruhl, some African thinkers are of the view that the notion of pre-logicality whether ascribed to the so-called primitive people or to the African, to his language or culture is anathema.[3] As C. B. Okolo (1993: 13) put it "[T]hinking as such is a property of all men, of all races and of all times. There is no such thing as a pre-logical stage of human development. Every language has its own inner logic and all races think logically." This changes the complexion of the argument entirely. By this clarification, Okolo is able to show that notwithstanding the fact that Evans-Pritchard has white-washed the degrading position of Levy-Bruhl, to convince us that Levy-Bruhl meant well, the point still remains that the concept of pre-logicality which underbellies whatever Levy-Bruhl said including what he meant and what he did not mean is despicable. And it is this idea above all else that reveals his true intensions.

From the above, it is clear that Evans-Pritchard has a different understanding of the so-called primitive culture. The term primitive as used by Levy-Bruhl and later Evans-Pritchard or by Alexander Goldenweiser or later Harry Barnes could mean the earliest cultural human. It is certainly deployed in the colonial anthropological literature to mean the dark-skinned people of the continent of Africa. The term is prominent in Goldenweiser's *Early civilisation* (1922). Barnes for instance, in *An intellectual and cultural history of the Western world*, argues:

> In discussing the mind of the primitive man we are treading on thin ice and few topics of discussion produce more errors and misrepresentations than the attempt to compare primitive and civilized thinking. These misconceptions arise from two basic fallacies. First, most men living in the twentieth century believe that they are civilized by virtue of this fact alone.

---

[3] For an elaborate criticism of Levy-Bruhl's thesis and the Hortonian position that proceeded from it, see Maurice M. Makumba (2007: 171–175).

> Secondly, it is assumed that primitive man had no rudimentary and undeveloped brain and was originally incapable of complex thinking. (1965: 42).

This latter assumption reflects Hegel's thought concerning the Negro race. Barnes disputes these assumptions saying that "what we (Westerners) have that he (primitive man) does not is a greater accumulation of positive knowledge," where the term "positive knowledge" means the orientation of science and technology. Barnes goes on: "practically speaking, the primitive mentality is dominated by comparative ignorance, and by a type of attitude we call superstitions, from which the civilized and educated man of today is relatively free from" (1965: 42). But Goldenweiser contends that "supernaturalism as a system of ideas is in itself perfectly reasonable (where the term reasonable connotes being logical). When the limitation of knowledge and theoretical naiveté of aboriginal men are taken into consideration the unconscious conclusion or hypothesis reached by him with reference to the world of things and beings are well-nigh inevitable" (1965: 43 emphasis mine).

Thus we can see that in the Western understanding of the nineteenth and twentieth centuries, the Negro people were considered primitive, had no brains for the rigour of logical exercise. As Barnes notes, the primitive man is also seen to lack the mental discipline which comes from some training in logic. This for Barnes means that his imagination is unrestricted. He creates and believes in a great number of mythologies. He therefore tries to control nature by magic—that is, by incantations, prayers, rituals, and festivals. Such intellectual advances as civilised person (i.e. European) has made have been achieved mainly through release from such naiveté. Barnes thus concludes:

> Grant primitive man his premises and he could often draw logical conclusions. He was by no means so absolutely devoid of logic as philosophers like Lucien Levy-Bruhl have imagined...what we call human culture is essentially an extra-organic or super-organic mechanism employed by man to control his life and living: i.e., his environment and himself. Primitive man was unable to exercise a real and direct control over much of his environment because of the undeveloped character of his culture, especially in its technological aspects. Therefore he was compelled to employ symbolic, that is, fictional, rather than factual means to exercise control over his life and surroundings. This symbolic and fictional system of control is what we call supernaturalism. (1965: 43)

Barnes further notes that the primitive person's great mistake, though of course an unavoidable one, lay in his failure to recognise that his control over his environment was infantile. Supernaturalism is outdated since technological progress determines control of human environment in terms of fact instead of fiction (1965: 43).

While the literature on colonial anthropology has been critically unpacked and attacked for denying logical reasoning capacity to Africans, a positive deduction one could make from all the arguments above, contra supernaturalism, is that Africans are capable of logical thinking like other peoples and can develop a different system of logic to ground the methods of their philosophical tradition and that the idea of African logic is sensible. To defend this alternative system, we must resist the lure of exclusiveness that makes culture-bound systems attractive. I affirm the relativity of logic systems but only insofar as such systems are universalisable. To this end, I agree with Bochenski who stresses that the relativity of logics is indubitable. According to him, there are many logic systems and that the two-valued logic is in itself limited:

> All this might be thought pure speculation on the part of logicians, of no importance for the day-to-day business of science. But that is not the case. In 1944 Reichenbach showed that quantum mechanics cannot be axiomatized without contradiction on the basis of "classical logic" (such as that of *Principia Mathematica*) but that it can be axiomatized straightforwardly without contradiction in the framework of Lukasiewicz's three-valued logic. (1965: 78)

Bochenski simply establishes in the above that the relativity of logic systems has gone beyond mere speculation, and that the orthodoxy of the two-valued logic has in the same measure been undermined. Thus, apart from the two-valued logic, we now also necessarily talk of three-valued, many-valued and even multi-valued logics as the case may be. In this consists the theory of relativity of logic systems which makes sense of the idea of African logic. However, the relativity of logic systems does not oppose the universality of such systems. Relative logic systems are relative based on background influence alone; they are universal because they are capable of wider applicability. The discussion of the idea of an African logic falls into this relative-universal scheme.

3.4 African Logic and the Relative-Universal Problematic

To address this problematic, one has to distinguish logic relativity from logic relativism. While the former describes a scenario where a system is culture-inspired in terms of the formulation of some of its principles, the latter describes a scenario where a system is not only culture-inspired but most importantly culture-bound in application of its principles. What is implied is that while the former could be universal in application, the latter could not because it is an ethnic logic. My conception of African logic is in terms of logic relativity rather than logic relativism. Logic relativity further allows us to contrast African logic with say Western logic. Both may be relative and universalisable but their applications of rules of reasoning may have some nuances. In other words, logic is now a generic term to be used in qualifying systems of thought arrangement, judgments and inferences obeying the same rules differently, or different rules in the same way. We may therefore speak of logics instead of logic as used to be the case. The rules or principles of African logic in this way would be different re-conceptualisations of those of Western logic.

Fundamentally, this shift in conception also implies that the question "what is African or Western logic" may not be encompassing in light of the new though overlapping borders of the subjects, since "what is African logic" is related but not the same as "what is Western logic" yet, "what is logic?" appears to encompass them both. However, it is made imperative that in attempting the question "what is logic?," one is expected to point out that logic now has a number of traditions which though being universally applicable in their own right have little nuances on the bases of which we can now talk of logic as relative but not culture-bound. These nuances must be made explicit usually from the perspective of value analysis or reasoning framework to prevent the error of creating a logic tradition that is only different from another in name. Any genuine logic tradition must be influenced by the native intellectual culture and mindview of a given people—a system of which would be an alternative model for thought. It is in connection to this that Carnap endorsed a form of liberal attitude towards the construction of new systems of logic. Ezumezu as a prototype African logic is one such alternative model for thought.

Dale Jacquette makes a bold suggestion concerning the existence of alternative logic traditions since the semantic contents of our logical expressions may vary from culture to culture. He gestures towards the possibility of different logical systems, all of which could be credible in serving the cause of reasoning. As he puts it:

> What makes all of these projects logical, a part or different forms of logic, or distinct logics? A working definition that may be correct if somewhat uninformative as far as it goes is to say that logic in any of its manifestations is the systematic study of principles of correct reasoning. The principles of logic can then be explored formally or informally, and by any of a number of different styles of exposition, some of which may be highly specialized in dealing with very particular areas of reasoning. (2006: 2)

The point being made is that logic as instrument of thought is not exhausted in Western logic—other systems are not only possible but needful. This is contrary to the popular position by some Western scholars who as Joseph Omoregbe suggests (1985) give the impression that logic is absolutistic and is a pride possession of the Western mind. This is also decried by Meinrad Hebga in the following words:

> Even at the interior of a given logical system, we can find propositions true in themselves which do not agree with the totality; or we can find some objectively false that do not harmonize very well with other true propositions. Whence arises the necessity of admitting the existence of polyvalent logics with opposed truths, with intrinsic truths distinct from extrinsic truths which flow from the meeting of the system with empirical data or other systems. (1958: 223)

Ezumezu therefore, becomes an alternative logic system which is capable of purveying methods that rival and or complement those of Western philosophy inspired by the hegemony of Plato and Aristotle. I truly believe that any well-meaning endeavour in African philosophy ought to begin from a premise similar to this. Otherwise, we shall merely be casting the spell of Plato and Aristotle in the African place which go on to terrorise the African mind with logocentricism in its bid to deify the rules formulated by Western iconoclasts.

To the discussion proper, in the debate on African logic, there have emerged two schools namely; the universalists and the relativists. While the former plagued by Eurocentricism insists that logic is universal, their conception of this universal, as I have stated, is absolutistic; the latter has two camps. The first, conceived as 'logic relativity' admits of the universal characteristics and applicability of logic and sees African logic as only culture-inspired but not culture-bound. C. S. Momoh leads this camp. The second, conceived as "logic relativism" is plagued by Afrocentricism and denies the universal property of logic. For this second camp, African logic is a regional logic that is culture-bound. C. O. Ijiomah leads this camp. Keeping logic relativity aside, both the universalists and the camp of logic relativism err at some point. On the one hand, while logic as the instrument of thought necessarily has to be universally applicable, there is a difference between being universal and being absolute. In being universal, the principles of a logic system apply in different cultures and topics but certainly not in all contexts. There have to be some contexts which a logic system will not have the capacity or the expressive power to axiomatise. On the other hand, every logic system is systematised from a certain cultural thought system. It is this specific thought system that shapes the structure of its laws and principles. In other words, such a thought system becomes the cultural inspiration for the logic and to which its structures could be traced. This is what I mean by logic 'relativity' as opposed to relativism. The relativity of logic is not in application but in formulation which does not, in any way, imply that a properly formulated system of logic cannot have universal applicability. It is language that we must all be wary of.

The universalists may therefore be cautioned to be careful with their understanding of the role of language in logic. Language as Gordon Hunnings notes consists of linguistic rules whose ultimate sanction derives from convention and human agreement. He goes on to observe that we misunderstand the very nature of language when we deify these rules (e.g. the traditional three laws of thought) and project on to the world what belongs only to our means of representing it in language (Hunnings, 1975). It is this misunderstanding that leads the universalists to suggest without a second thought that the principles of Western logic are absolute. The truth is, they apply in all cultures but still have some contextual limitations as a result of the dynamism of statement relations in logic. Due to these limitations, it would be incorrect to declare their absolute applicability without some reservations. Take for example, a statement like President Donald Trump will be impeached in May 2019. If stated in May 2018, there is no way of evaluating this statement within the axioms of two-valued logic. The expressive power of the latter is therefore limited in this context. Stephen Korner (1967) explains that the results of modern logical developments have deprived the traditional laws of thought of their privileged position as the supreme principles of all logical truths.

In fact, with the emergence of the theory of the relativity of logics, it is safe to say that all logical systems are relative even the so-called classical logic developed in the West which is erroneously treated as absolute. The universality of the concept of logic is an abstract idea or generic concept to be employed strictly as such and to which different logical traditions participate. What this means is that though different logical traditions are relative for the fact of originating from a particular culture with varying legal nuances, they are nonetheless universal because as instrument of reasoning, they are supposed to cut across cultures. But we must admit that even the universalisable systems suffer limitations in some contexts.

African logic is relative in the positive sense of being African culture-inspired and universal in the sense of being applicable in relevant contexts anywhere in the world. Some understand the idea of logic relativity to mean that the traditional laws of thought apply in some cultures but do not apply in some other cultures. This is the thinking of Polemicists like Makinde who even used the criticisms against the laws of contradiction and excluded-middle as examples. It is on this basis that

Makinde (2007: 44) asserts that "[I]f logic could be relativized in this way, there seems to be no escape from an equally damaging conclusion against the arguments for the so-called prelogical mentality of the African thinkers." Unfortunately, my earlier explanations show that Makinde does not understand the sense in which logic relativity is used. His assumption that it implies that the traditional laws of thought do not apply in some cultures is erroneous and the conclusion he drew from the erroneous premise cannot be true. Logic relativity does not imply that the so-called prelogical mentality is true needless to point out that Makinde's evocation of that infamous line is fallacious.

The relativists do not doubt that the traditional laws of thought apply in all cultures, what they claim is that the traditional laws of thought do not apply in all contexts of logical evaluations. As a result, supplementary laws of thought come in demand for those contexts in which the traditional laws succumb. But even the supplementary laws are limited because no set of laws of thought can actually apply in all contexts of logical evaluations.

Evidently, I do not advocate cultural logics that are border-sensitive and exclusivist. What I promote on the contrary is the reality that logical principles are not essentially strait-jacketed and rigid as supposed by all the proponents of the dogma of absolute logic. Logic is universal but the capacity of its principles varies from culture to culture. When logic has its principles applied differently, it gives birth to methodology which is a theory of methods. This implies that every method of thought represents an application of the principles of logic in a specific way. In some cultures, the formulation of these principles implies absolute identity and absolute difference that are mutually exclusive, an example is the two-valued logic of the Western thought. In others like in the African thought, the formulation of those logical principles implies relative identity and relative difference that are mutually inclusive and as such mitigates absolute identity and absolute difference that are mutually exclusive. This mitigation in essence is a form of complementation because the principles of two-valued logic are observed in African thought albeit not without limitation.

3.5 The Problematic of Regional Logics

One of the strongest arguments against the possibility of African logic is based on analogy. Polemicists like Akin Makinde (2007) and Uduma Oji Uduma (2015) can be credited with this type of argument by analogy. They argue that logic is analogous to mathematics, and since we cannot talk of regional mathematics, it is just as impossible for us to talk of regional logics. As Makinde (2007: 42) put it: "[B]ecause of its assumed universality and applicability in all thoughts, logic, like mathematics, cannot be relativised. As there is no American or African mathematics, there is nothing to be called American or African logic, otherwise it would not [sic] longer be true that the principles of logic are assumed in all rational thought…" On his part, Uduma (2015: 93) claims that "…the philosopher uses the tool of logic to

3.5 The Problematic of Regional Logics

organize reality and render it intelligible; this explains why logic and mathematics work so well together: they are both independent from reality and both are tools that are used to help people make sense of the world." Uduma (2015: 100) goes further "[A]s Etuk even admits, 'it would be just as silly to suggest that there can be an African logic as it would be to urge that there should be British or Indian Mathematics.'" These two excerpts fairly summarise the positions of Makinde and Uduma and constitute the problematic of regional logics.

The problematic of regional logics assumes two technical questions: (1) Is there such a thing as 'African logic'? (2) Or, should we rather talk about 'logic in Africa'? The polemicists, Makinde and Uduma reject the first but accept the second thesis. Their main argument for rejecting the possibility of African logic is presented in the form of analogy already captured in the citations above. They claim that logic is like mathematics and since we cannot have regional mathematics, it follows that we cannot have regional logics. But this is a very bad analogy based on falsehood and not facts. First, logic is not mathematics and, it is not even 'like' mathematics. I reckon that the polemicists assume quite in error, that since the average student of philosophy perceives logic to be tasking just like the average student of science perceives mathematics, then, that means that logic and mathematics are similar. This is a very bad supposition, unpardonable for a layman to think this way, let alone trained logicians like Makinde and Uduma.

But let us assume for a moment that there is a modicum of truth in the supposition that logic is like mathematics, in what sense do they establish this similarity? Neither Makinde nor Uduma elaborated on this. They seemed desperate for a certain outcome that they did not mind utilising any strategy at all. Polythene and paper can both be used to make customer bags for wrapping products. We could say that polythene is like paper in light of the functions they could both perform in this context but we cannot say, on the basis of this contextual instance, that such similarity is sufficient to warrant in any real sense, the blind deduction that what applies to polythene as a bio-non-degradable substance can also apply to paper as a bio-degradable substance. So, in no way would it be plausible to extend a perceived similarity beyond a specific context let alone making strong assertions on that basis. Makinde and Uduma failed to report the context in which they claim similarity for logic and mathematics. That notwithstanding, they went ahead to draw a far-reaching conclusion that regional logics are impossible on the basis of a factual error.

Second, the purposes and ontologies of logic and mathematics are not the same. The primary purpose of logic is to clarify and evaluate thought whereas that of mathematics is to quantify objects. Elementarily, logic deals with realities including actual and possible, and the relationship that can be *stringed* amongst them, but mathematics deals with an aspect of reality, that is number. In the course of writing this book, I searched extensively in extant literature for a detailed treatment of the difference between logic and mathematics and I ran into an online academic forum where logicians shared ideas on this topic. I found the expert views agreeable that I decided to cite one of them to show that logic and mathematics are not the same and are not even similar in any real sense that could warrant the type of deduction Makinde and Uduma made in their argument by analogy. According to Paul Ikeda:

> While all mathematics was derived based upon logical premises, I think they are actually very different tools with very different purposes. In fact, I would say that mathematics and logic are complementary opposites. Simply put, mathematics quantifies while Logic clarifies. Mathematics provides accurate numerical results, but little intuitive understanding of cause and effect. Logic provides a greater understanding of cause and effect, but usually only first order estimates of quantitative results. Mathematics is only useful for matters dealing with numbers, logic is useful for all matters and is basically the creative thought process. (2018, https://www.quora.com/What-is-the-difference-between-logic-and-mathematics)

Going further, Ikeda adds that:

> Logic is prone to errors due to intuitive false premise, while mathematics is prone to errors of intuitive false conclusions. Mathematical formalism is a rigorous step by step process that can only progress forwards. Logic includes deduction (forward) and induction (backwards) processes. Therefore it can solve problems in hindsight such as criminal investigations or trouble shooting problems. It can also solve hidden domains such as reverse engineering and Integrated Circuit. It answers more than how much or how long, but it answers any question, such as why or how it does what it does. The more mathematics that you need to apply to solve a problem, the more complex the solution will become. The more logic that you apply towards solving a problem, the more simple the solution will become. (2018, https://www.quora.com/What-is-the-difference-between-logic-and-mathematics)

From the foregoing, two things stand out: first, the polemicists, Makinde and Uduma used a bad argument from analogy to draw a far-reaching conclusion on the basis of a factual error or a thesis that is not substantiated which is, that logic is like mathematics. Second, I have been able to tap into expert views to show that logic is not like mathematics in any real sense that can warrant the deduction of the type, $p \supset q$, $q \supset r$ therefore, $p \supset r$. Thus, the claim that regional logics are impossible simply because regional mathematics are impossible is not only outlandish, it is also baseless.

3.6 Conclusion

In conclusion, it would be naïve for anyone to expect talk about African logic to go smoothly. In fact, the concept 'African logic' is not only provocative; it appears to raise a red flag by its sound alone. The idea of logic since Aristotle's model became orthodoxy, has stuck in the minds of scholars as a subject which is not only one-standard but which should not have alternatives. My point therefore is that what makes scholars perceive logic from this straw hole is nothing more than a prolonged bad habit. Worse still is that logic is a tool that attempts to streamline people to a particular thinking habit. So, once the Aristotelian model became the convention and people formed the habit of thinking within its framework, it was not difficult to get people to form another habit of thinking that there cannot be any other way of thinking. But just like most bad habits which get broken along the line, this one can also be broken. This book is one of such attempts geared towards providing motivation for breaking the habit of thinking that the Aristotelian logic was, is and will be the only logic model possible.

I have in this chapter addressed some polemical issues which come across in the young discipline of African logic as problematic. Some are issues those who stand opposed to the idea of African logic normally throw up. Others are like cogs in the wheel of African logic. As distant as some of these issues might seem to the heart of the project on African logic, they are, interestingly, quite close to the core of the problem. Until, for example, we recognise and expose the hidden Eurocentric agenda behind the categorisation of logic into classical or standard and non-classical or non-standard, we may not be able to realise the urgency of the project on African logic tradition.

References

Barnes, Harry. 1965. *An intellectual and cultural history of the Western world*, Vol.1., 3rd rev. ed. New York: Dover Publications.
Bochenski, M. Józef. 1965. *The methods of contemporary thought*. Dordrecht/Holland: Reidel Publishing.
Evans-Pritchard, E. Edward. 1965. *Theories of primitive religion*. Oxford: Oxford University Press.
Eze, Emmanuel Chukwudi. 1995. The color of reason: The idea of 'race' in Kant's anthropology. In *Anthropology and the German enlightenment: Perspectives on humanity*, ed. Katherine M. Faull. Lewisburg: Bucknell University Press.
Goldenweiser, Alexander. 1922. *Early civilisation: An introduction to anthropology*. New York: Knopf.
Gunderman, Richard. 2015. When science gets ugly – The story of Philipp Lenard and Albert Einstein. *The Conversation* June 16. http://theconversation.com/when-science-gets-ugly-the-story-of-philipp-lenard-and-albert-einstein-43165. Retrieved 18 Sep 2018.
Harris, James. 1992. *Against relativism: A philosophical defense of method*. Peru: Open Court Publishing Company.
Hebga, Meinrad. 1958. Logic in Africa. *Philosophy Today* 11 (4): 221–229.
Hegel, W. F. Georg. 1975. *Lectures on the philosophy of world history*. Trans. H. B. Nisbet. Cambridge: Cambridge University Press.
Horton, Robin. 1977. Traditional, thought and the emerging African philosophy department: A comment on the current debate. *Second Order: An African Journal of Philosophy* 3 (1): 64–80.
Hunnings, Gordon. 1975. Logic, language and culture. *Second Order: An African Journal of Philosophy* 4 (1): 3–13.
Ikeda, Paul. 2018. *What is the difference between logic and mathematics?* https://www.quora.com/What-is-the-difference-between-logic-and-mathematics. Retrieved 24 Sept 2018.
Jacquette, Dale., ed. 2006. Introduction. In *A companion to philosophical logic*. Malden: Blackwell publishing.
James, George. 1954. *Stolen legacy: Greek philosophy is stolen Egyptian philosophy*. New York: Philosophical Library.
Korner, Stephen. 1967. Laws of thought. In *Encyclopedia of philosophy*, ed. Paul Edwards, vol. iv. New York: Macmillan Publishing co.
Levy-Bruhl, Lucien. 1947. *Primitive mentality*. Paris: University of France Press.

Makinde, Akin, M. 2007. *African Philosophy: The Demise of a Controversy.* Ile-Ife: Obafemi Awolowo University Press.

Makumba, M. Maurice. 2007. *An introduction to African philosophy, past and present.* Nairobi: Paulines Publications Africa.

Momoh, S. Campbell. 2000. Nature, issues and substance of African philosophy. In *The substance of African philosophy*, ed. C.S. Momoh, 1–22. Auchi: APP Publications.

Okolo, B. Chukwudum. 1993. *What is African philosophy? A short introduction.* Enugu: Cecta.

Okoro, C. Michael. 2004. *A course on African philosophy, Book One: Question and debate.* Enugu: Paqon Press.

Omoregbe, Joseph. 1985. African philosophy: Yesterday and today. In *Philosophy in Africa: Trends and perspectives*, ed. Peter Bodunrin, 1–14. Ile Ife: University of Ife Press.

Popkin, Richard. 1978. Hume's racism. *The Philosophical Forum* 9 (2–3): 213–218.

Reiser, Oliver. 1935/2004. Non-Aristotelian logics. *The Monist* 45: 100–117. Reproduced online 20041-10 at: www.vordenker.de/ggphilosophy/reiser_non-aristotelian-logic.pdf. Retrieved 25 Feb 2015.

Smith, Edwin. 1966. *African ideas of God.* London: Edinburgh House Press.

Stebbing, Susan. 1950. *A modern introduction to logic.* London: Methuen and Co.

Uduma, O. Uduma. 2015. The logic question in African philosophy: Between the horns of irredentism and jingoism. In *Atuolu omalu: Some unanswered questions in contemporary African philosophy*, ed. Jonathan O. Chimakonam, 83-100. Lanham: University Press of America.

Wilson, Amos. 1993. *The falsification of Afrikan consciousness: Eurocentric history, psychiatry and the politics of white supremacy.* New York: Afrikan World InfoSystems.

Chapter 4
The Schools of Thought in African Logic

Abstract I identify three schools of thought in the African logic debate namely, the apologists, the polemicists and the system builders. I show that while the first two are haunted by the essentialist ideologies of Afrocentricism and Eurocentricism, it is the last school that is actually doing the correct thing. I highlight the individual positions or contributions from members of each school and show where they failed or succeeded. I conclude by identifying system building, the type I propose to do in Ezumezu logic as the proper direction of African logic project.

4.1 Introduction

Much of the history of thought in Africa, to this day, is a duel between apologists and polemicists. On the one hand are diehard Afrocentricists who would risk "truth" to affirm what they believe is an African agenda. On the other hand are committed Eurocentricists whose skewed epistemic goal is one and one only: to orchestrate an intellectual decimation of African peoples. These two groups, it is safe to say, are intellectual outlaws who play by jungle rules to achieve their off-centred goals. In reality, neither Afrocentricists nor Eurocentricists represent the best interests of Africa and Europe as they claim respectively. The nineteenth and twentieth centuries had the battle ground for these two groups in archaeology, history and philosophy. But from the later part of the twentieth century, as more awareness was drawn to the works of Immanuel Kant, Georg Hegel, and eventually Lucien Levy-Bruhl, the battle ground has being shifting to logic. And it has almost become a myth that whoever controls logos controls the provenance of epistemology.

However, logos, when interpreted as reason is not a tool that has absolute global manifestation as advocates of one-standard logic hold. Reason can also have a particular manifestation insofar as it can be universalised. African logic is not a structure where reason manifests in the particular alone as the apologists would argue but it does make sense to theorise on the system of African logic contrary to the assumption of the polemicists. It is in this regard that I formulate syntactic and semantic rules for a model of African logic called Ezumezu logic.

On the whole, my objective in this chapter is to highlight the danger of off-centeredness which the dispute between the apologists and the polemicists of the idea of an African logic has created and to chart a practical course for African logic that involves system building and on which we can ground the assumptions and methods of African philosophy. I will argue, overall, that while it is significant to further the debate on African logic alongside the need for such a philosophy of logic (*logica utens*), it is even better to begin laying the foundation for African logic as a system of logic (*logica docens*).

Here, I will identify three schools of thought in the African logic debate namely, the apologists, the polemicists and the system builders. I will show that while the first two are haunted by the essentialist ideologies of Afrocentricism and Eurocentricism, it is the last school that is actually doing the correct thing. I will highlight the individual positions or contributions from members of each school and show where they failed or succeeded. I will conclude by identifying system building, the type done in Ezumezu as the proper direction of African logic project. I will begin with the apologists.

4.2 The Apologists

The first school of thought in African logic is the apologists. Their goal is to defend the idea of African logic at any cost including using Afrocentricist propaganda and making African logic culture-bound. A form of logical radicalism that was apologetic in essence was heralded by Leopold Senghor who differentiated Western and African reasoning—the one being rational and the other being chiefly emotive (1964: 23–24). He has called this attempt "emotional" or "Affective" in which reason is suffused in positive human emotions. In a way, Senghor's articulation of black emotionality is not essentially devoid of reason as commentators have presented him. It is rather an emotional, call it humane reason—a sort of phenomenological presentation of the African person. In his logical vision, he enunciated a pattern that was to restore the middle value which the classical law of excluded-middle excluded. It was in all apparent promises to be an advancement of the idea of three-valued thought model which the likes of the Polish logician Jan Lukasiewicz had worked on earlier. This was to be his greatest legacy to humanity had he properly delineated and universalised it. He failed! Indeed, Senghor's unsuccessful attempt (failure to delineate and characterise the intermediate value, to formulate a proper system for his model and to universalise it) appears to raise the questions: should there not be more to reasoning than some strait-jacketed inferential appeal to stringent laws? Should we rather not be more committed to the categories of our thought? Is it absolutely necessary that we be structured to the laws guiding our thought processes at every turn and in every context and time? Our answer in this work supports some level of freedom and liberation of the human thought. This was for all intents and purposes, Senghor's unfinished and unrealised vision.

4.2 The Apologists

Perhaps he was mistaken as Ada Agada (2015: 18) enthused for not universalising his model. Certainly, this cannot be unconnected with the maze of nationalist solidarity that gripped African freedom fighters in different countries at the time. This must have robbed him of the vision of universal humanity as he articulated his thoughts on black emotionality and white rationality almost presupposing a duality.

Notwithstanding this apparent apologetic shortcoming, Senghor's forerunning description of a certain thought model which could be regarded as African is academically enterprising as it is notorious. This bifurcation is notorious for ascribing a supposedly culture-bound system to the Africans thus leading the continent away from humanity's common rational heritage. The daunting problem this poses could be formulated into the question: If Africans follow a different pattern in conducting their reasoning, would they be described as rational in what sense? If they are possibly rational at all, they would be, only by some otherworldly standard of rationality. In other words, Africans would be irrational by the standard of humanity's common laws of thought which Senghor supposedly decried as anathema for the African the moment he declared separate courses of reasoning for the African and for the rest of humankind.

Some have identified this slip as a telling weakness in Senghor's thoughts since it tends to present logic as socially acquired norm. With the emotion thesis, Senghor seems to imply that valid reasoning is dependent on regional circumstances. As Lansana Keita translates Senghor:

> In fact, I have often thought that the indo-European and Negro-African were situated at the extremes of objectivity and subjectivity, of discursive reason and intuitive reason, of thinking in concepts and thinking in images, of reflective thought and emotional thought. (1991: 153)[1]

For his critics, this is a critical shortcoming of Senghor's proposal for understanding the African humanity sorely stressed by the colonial ideology. He has been accused, particularly, of unwittingly approving the Eurocentric thesis that the European mode of thinking is diametrically opposed to that of the African, and superior to it. If the African is essentially emotional, then Senghor seems to affirm the Eurocentric assumption that African thought cannot distinguish between the rational, the irrational or the pre-rational (Keita 1991: 134). For Senghor, according to Tomaz Jacques (2011: 6), the African's relation to the world is of an essentially sensuous, emotional nature in which the mode of cognition does not objectify. It is rather intuitive, participatory, magical and holistic. Senghor further asserts that this cognitive affective relation also defines the African person's relation to others, family, society, politics and the divine. It is on these two scores, that Senghor has been criticised for (i) drawing a very sharp line between Western and African thought patterns, and (ii) subjecting the African pattern to an inferior treatment.

But it is possible that Senghor might have been misread and misunderstood by his critics. Yes, he identified a structural difference between Western and African

---

[1] See also Leopold Senghor. (1962 and 1977)

thoughts but he never simply meant one to be inferior to the other. Also, Senghor did not actually reject or sideline reason in his emotionality thesis, he so often uses the term emotional thought, intuitive reason, etc., so what he subscribed to was a type of reason that is moderated by humane emotion. I am of the view that had Senghor understood the wider logical implications of his thesis, he would have chosen different set of terms to explain his position and that careful formulation could have served as a basis for asserting that African thought was unique only in an inclusive sense of logic relativity and not, as he has been read, in an exclusive sense logic relativism that excludes any connection to a universal mode of reasoning.

But Senghor was not the only apologist for a unique African mode of reasoning. There are some others who attempted to synthesise the implications of the formulation. They are Peter Winch and Godwin Sogolo. When Senghor's myopism reinforced Levy-Bruhl's despicable position, it was Winch and much later Sogolo who found a way using apologetic strategies. Winch (1958 and 1964) presents strong arguments meant to defend the thesis that traditional thought possesses its own logic which is also valid within such contexts.[2] This was certainly a response to Levy-Bruhl. Winch argues that different modes of thought evidently require different rational procedures or criteria for their justification. As he puts it:

> Criteria of logic are not a direct gift of God, but arise out of, and are only intelligible in the context of, ways of living or modes of social life. It follows that one cannot apply criteria of logic to modes of social life as such. For instance, science is one such mode and religion is another; and each has criteria of intelligibility peculiar to itself. So within science or religion actions can be logical or illogical: in science, for example, it would be illogical to refuse to be bound by the results of a properly carried out experiment; in religion it would be illogical to suppose that one could pit one's own strength against God's; and so on. But we cannot sensibly say that either the practice of science itself or that of religion is either illogical or logical; both are non-logical. (1958: 100–101)

What Winch attempts to establish is that modes of thought that differ as much as science and religion differ cannot be bound by the same logical paradigm. In other words, by non-logical he means to say that there is no one universal algorithm that can axiomatise both. If there is, then the "logical" and "illogical" distinction between the civilised and the primitive societies will make sense.

Winch goes on to employ this in analysing the traditional thoughts of the Africans. His major argument is simply that criteria derived from one form of life cannot be used in judging a different form of life. In Sogolo's assessment, the African traditional form of life, like the European, has a designate universe of discourse or background logic, its own conception of reality and of course, its criteria of rationality. Its assumptions, like those of the Western form of life, are valid within their own very contexts (1993: 73). Winch's position therefore is that it smacks of racist indiscretion to judge one thought system from the logical lens of another. It is apparent that Winch advocates one of the extreme species of logic relativity. This is so when we realise that it can easily be inferred from Winch's position that the

---

[2] See also E. E. Evans-Pritchard (1965), M. Fortes and G. Dieterlen (1972) and C. B. Okolo (1993) who variously corroborate the position held by Winch.

traditional laws of thought, for example, do not have a place in the thought pattern of traditional societies. Scholars like Ijiomah, Etuk as well as Senghor before them have all fallen into a similar conceptual ditch.[3] But we know this to be incorrect. The likes of Hunnings, Uduma and Nze, etc., have all made it clear that the traditional laws of thought apply to a great extent in African languages.[4]

It is, therefore, a severe apologetic shortcoming when some actors tend to suggest that African logic is culturally exclusive. A sort of boundary sensitive logic exclusive to African thought system in much the same way African culture is. Unforgiving polemicists like Uduma Oji who approve the idea of logic in Africa but not African logic, have capitalised on this oversight in seeking to destroy the idea of African logic as a system (2009: 288, 2015: 100). Ademola K. Fayemi (2010) also groups the likes of Makinde, Oruka and Omoregbe among those who approve of the idea of logic in Africa but disapprove of African logic—where logic in Africa simply means the wholesale applicability of Western logic as a universe of discourse. According to Uduma, for instance, Etuk and especially Ijiomah are guilty of a terrible syllogism—If logic is a part of philosophy and philosophy is culture-bound, it follows necessarily that logic is culture-bound. This, for Uduma is an unwitting defence of cultural logic which is erroneous. I agree that African logic need not and ought not to be culture exclusive, but this criticism must not be extended to the idea of a universalisable system of an African logic as Uduma seeks to do.

Godwin Sogolo saw through the extreme relativism of Winch's arguments in the sense that they make any form of cross-cultural reasoning framework impossible. In Sogolo's assessment, conceding a unique thought framework to Africans and primitive societies only achieves Pyrrhic victory, the cost of which is extreme logic relativism. Sogolo then conceives a version of Winch's argument in which the extreme form of relativism is replaced by a mild one. This thesis simply suggests that two societies with different forms of life could, to a reasonable extent, interact even though their life-worlds require somewhat different universes of discourse to validate their assumptions. This does not eliminate the fact that they share certain elements in common which compel cross-cultural universe of discourse. This is because as Sogolo observes, they are both similarly marked by the same basic features of the human species:

> The difference lies in the ways the two societies conceive of reality and explain objects and events. This is so because they live different forms of life. And it is for this reason alone that an intelligible analysis of African thought demands the application of its own universe of discourse, its own logic and its own criteria of rationality. (1993: 74)

This difference in life forms, according to Sogolo, suggests a certain space of relative universe of discourse which cannot possibly be replaced by a common universe of discourse that cuts through different cultures. Yet, such relative systems do not in any way replace the necessity of a common universal criterion. It is on the basis of his recognition of the relative and universal character of logic that Sogolo

---

[3] See Ijiomah (2006), Etuk (2002) and Senghor (1962).
[4] See Hunnings (1975), Nze (1998) and Uduma (2009).

recommends just like Momoh (2000) that the African thinker should "fashion out these unique working tools (call it a system of African logic that is nonetheless universalisable) with which to unearth the complexities of the social form that confronts him" (Sogolo 1993: 74).

African logic also owes a lot to the audacious works of Meinrad Hebga and Gordon Hunnings who equally entertained and defended the idea of an alternative logic system that could come from Africa while the idea was not yet fashionable.

For them, it is easy to see with the survey of Western scholarship that the main problem it has with African thought system is the erroneous mindset that regards African system of thought as a collection of mystical and pre-logical traditions lacking in logical rigor. This might be so because the principles of Western logic i.e. the traditional laws of thought as some like Robin Horton claim and again, quite in error, are not present in African languages.

Akin Makinde criticised and rejected Horton's view accusing him of basing his conclusion on wrong premises. The first being that Horton misconceived philosophy as empirical science[5] and second being that he was wrong in supposing that philosophy was nothing but logic and epistemology. Makinde clarifies that philosophy predates logic and that people can reason logically without having being trained in the field. He goes on to show that logic and language are inseparable such that if Horton admitted there were languages in Africa, then he could not deny the presence of logic in those languages because, [W]here you have language there is logic, and where there is logic, there is language" (Makinde: 42).

The inferior treatment of the African system of thought was also rejected by Joseph Omoregbe (1985) who said that Africans of old may not have put their reasoning in the form of Aristotle's syllogism or Russell's logical form but they sure had their reasoning structure. The substance of Hunnings' advocacy is that the laws of thought are present in African languages and this enhances the possibility of an alternative logic system. Hebga on his part powerfully projected similar argument when he echoes the following golden words:

> The dogma of one standard and of one all-embracing prototype for civilisation and culture is losing its backers right along. If the fact of having arrived at the atom, of having probed nature in its depth and furthermost reaches gives legitimate pride to the discoveries and consecrates the civilisations which have produced them, all this still leaves an important place to the other cultures, embryonic though they may be called, a place which they occupy humbly, but at the same time to the advantage of all.... *A fortiori*, it is necessary to admit the existence of opposed logics, structures of thoughts, methods of research, contradictory in their methods or their conclusions. (1958: 222)

Hebga bemoans a prevalent system where the classical two-valued logic of Western thought is taken as the only prototype for civilisation. There could be other forms of logic as there are other cultures and thought systems. It is left for us to give them

---

[5] Kwasi Wiredu (1984) was the first to give detail criticism of Horton's similar position by drawing attention to the fact that Horton's comparison of African thought and Western science was greatly mistaken.

4.2 The Apologists

chance to be developed. He particularly points at philosophy's definition of logical truth as the agreement of thought with its object as strait-jacketed. For him:

> In this bivalence there is no place except for the true and the false. It excludes all intermediary value such as the "not altogether true" and "not altogether false." This basis of this bivalence seems to be the ambiguity of the intermediate value or, rather, the demands of the principle of contradiction which excludes one thing from being true and false at the same time under the same aspect. (1958: 223)

Hebga therefore offers the first clear suggestion on the actual structure of African logic as trivalent with the intermediate value capable of being judged both true and false under the same aspect; in a complementary mode. Hebga does not deny the applicability of logic in African thought system. His point is that the two-valued logic holds in African thought like in every other system but that it has operational limitations in much the same way African three-valued logic would have had some limitations when applied on a bivalent thought structure. He goes on to admonish: "But you must not attribute the exact application of this principle of contradiction as the monopoly of any particular system. Although it is metaphysical…, it does not keep two diametrically opposed systems from being true at the same time, their fundamental presuppositions being different" (Hebga 1958: 223). This is true, especially as the two standard values of African logic like in the system of Ezumezu are treated as sub-contraries rather than contradictories. Thus, if one holds, the other might still hold, so the possibility of "both/and" and "both/not" are in the variant of the three-valued logic I develop for African tradition.

Like Alexander Goldenwiser (1922), Harry Barnes (1965), as well as J. M. Bochenski (1965), Hebga holds the idea of relativity of logic at a promising end. As he puts it "At the same time, we must admit a certain logical relativism. This is recognized by common sense. How often is it said, such an idea is true—from your point of view" (1958: 224). This is the sort of idea Bertrand Russell sought to bring to prominence when writing on Chinese morals:

> The Duke of She addressed Confucius, saying: "We have an upright man in our country. His father stole a sheep and the son bore witness against him." In our country, Confucius replied, uprightness is something different from this. A father hides the guilt of his son, and son hides the guilty of his father. It is in such conduct that true uprightness is to be found. (Etuk 2002: 98)

Indeed, these types of nuances in the thought systems of different peoples of the world constitute the idea of relativity[6] in logic. Hebga, in the above, is pointing to the lacuna in Western logic which needs to be filled. He may not have filled this lacuna by way of alternative system building but his arguments are significant in laying the foundation for projects such as the Ezumezu system of logic.

---

[6] I contrast logic relativity with logic relativism. While the former describes a scenario where a system is culture-inspired in terms of the formulation of some of its principles, the latter describes a scenario where a system is not only culture-inspired but most importantly culture-bound in application of its principles. I accept the former and reject the latter as a mode of a system of African logic.

I come to the visionary quartet: Joseph Omoregbe, Chukwudum B. Okolo, C. S. Momoh, and Udo Etuk. I describe these men as visionary with regards to the project on African logic for the insights contained in their comments. Joseph Omoregbe is of the view that Africans of old may have reasoned in ways that did not correspond to the legal parameters in Western logic but it would be short-sighted to dismiss such alternative modes of inference as illogical because they were different. He argued forcefully that the idea of an alternative system is not outlandish.

Okolo (1993: 13–14) is one of the bold advocates of African logic. In his design of African philosophy curriculum, he lists African logic as one of the branches of study, the first. In his words: "[A]ll branches of philosophy indeed employ thinking. Whether the type of thinking is correct or not depends on whether it is in accord with the laws of logic." He goes on to say that "[T]his points to logic as perhaps the most important and fundamental branch of philosophy. Every philosophical system therefore must have logic." Okolo clarifies that the idea of African logic does not imply that Africans have a different kind of mental process from the rest of humanity as Makinde (2007) ridicules. The idea of African logic maintains difference with say, the Western logic in degree and not in kind. Ultimately, all logics have the same goal which is to clarify but different approaches which point to different worlds or cultures that inspire them. But since logic is the fundamental tool that drives each philosophical tradition, every system must have its own logic as this is what shapes its methods and distinguishes it from other traditions.

Udo Etuk (2002), an unsteady believer in African logic project also joins this league and in his paper "On the Possibility African logic" argues for the possibility of such logic that could be called African capable of axiomatising different experiences in the African life-world where the Western logic has demonstrated limitation. He calls his approach "Affective logic" in solidarity with the approach which Senghor pioneered.

Mention must also be made of C. S. Momoh, a general in the great debate on African philosophy and one that could be described as a thunderous voice on the debate on African logic. In his deeply argumentative paper earlier mentioned he affirms that the logic question is imperative and is one that must also be answered in the positive. He challenges Robin Horton who in his paper "African Traditional Thought and the Emerging African Philosophy Department: A Comment on the Current Debate" implies the non-existence of African logic. Momoh quotes Horton as saying that:

> Traditional cultures, though eminently logical, have never felt the need to develop logic. In the first place, it simply is not in the place of cultures to be logical. It is the individuals in a culture and not the culture itself that can be said to be logical. If there is any institution in a culture where things seem to hang together logically it should have some individuals in that culture at a certain point in space and time that made and arranged things that way. It is the individuals in a culture who feel the need to develop logic either in thought, action and indeed, or in relation to institutional arrangements. Secondly, since African traditional cultures were not, at any rate, literate it is difficult to see how they could have developed logic, even if the need was felt. (Momoh 2000: 179–180)

4.2 The Apologists

Momoh rejects some of these deductions made by Horton and insists that "…in every usage of natural language we talk of a person as being logical if he is reasonable, sensible and intelligent; if he can unemotionally and critically evaluate evidence or a situation; if he can avoid contradiction, inconsistency and incoherence, or if he can hold a point of view, argue for and from it, summon counter-examples and answer objections" (2000: 180). Momoh insists that there are individuals in every culture who are logical in this sense including in African culture. From the foregoing Momoh seems to conclude in opposition to Horton that Africa necessarily has a logic even though it may not have been systematised. He calls on Africans who are logicians to pick up this task.

Evidently from the foregoing, the contributions of Senghor, Hebga, Hunnings, Omoregbe, Momoh and Udo Etuk, in the African logic project can be described as geared towards philosophy of logic (*logica utens*) rather than system of logic (*logica docens*). Perhaps, Momoh knew this quite well hence his call for younger African logicians to take up the task of constructing the system of African logic. One of my goals in this work is not merely to repeat such but to gesture towards the existence of such projects already. The point is that these men had the vision and even though they did not construct the system, they laid an invaluable foundation for system building in African logic. In a later section, I will address the attempts by Helen Verran, Innocent Asouzu, Chris Ijiomah and the present author which are in part, a response to this call!

Finally, I come to the remotest part of the apologist cave. The occupants of this section of the cave can be called cultural logicians or ethnologicians. They are scholars who have in various ways attempted to demonstrate the presence of logic in different African cultures, though it does not mean that they actively developed these unique cultural logics far removed from the universal parameters of logic. Some of them include Bernadette Eboh's "The Structure of Igbo Logic (1983)," I. B. Francis' research on Efik logic, (1992), O. I. Francis' research on Ibibio logic (1997), C. B. Nze "Uncovering Logic in Igbo Language and Thought (1998)," Victor Ocaya' understanding of Acholi logic (2004), Ogugua's doctoral dissertation on symbolism in Igbo thought (2003), Enyimba's essay on the nature of logic in African thought (2011), Fayemi's "Logic in Yoruba Proverbs (2010)," Jones and Badey on Ibani and Ogoni logics (2012), Ogugua and Oduah on "Logic in Igbo-African Understanding (2013)," Ogugua and Ogugua's "Is there an Igbo-African Logic (2015)," Edwin Etieyibo's "Logic in Urhobo Proverbs" (2016), to name just a few. One common decimal among these is that they all seek to demonstrate the existence of logic in cultural thoughts. It is as if their goal was to counteract the Levy-Bruhlian thesis that the primitives are pre-logical, and Horton's argument that the principles of logic cannot be formulated in African languages. Clearly, Enyimba, Ocaya, Fayemi, Jones and Badey echo this emotion as the motivation for their researches.

The project of the ethnologicians is no doubt encouraging and academically interesting but I have serious doubt as to its usefulness. The challenge with this type of project is that at the surface emotional level, it tends to promote the feeling of cultural solidarity and identity but deep down, it appears backward looking. Cultural logic/ethnologic neither constitutes system of formal reasoning nor a solid and progressive discourse in philosophy of logic. It is more like a consolatory exercise. Do we really need to prove that principles of logic exist in African languages/culture? Do we really need to respond in this way to the cultural prejudices of Levy-Bruhl, Robin Horton, and the likes? The simple answer is that there really is no apparent benefit in doing so. Cultural exhibitionism is profoundly counterproductive, and sometimes often plays right into the very hand of those it is meant to answer. Rational people do not need to prove that they are rational unless and except in cases where they are not sure. What to my mind deserves our collective research attention is the construction of viable and universalisable logic systems/thought models (*logica docens*), as well as some rigorous intellectual exercises in the field of philosophy of logic (*logica utens*). This is the driving force behind the project of the system of Ezumezu thought model which is the focus of this book.

4.3 The Polemicists

Now I turn to the polemicists to discuss a few of them as space will permit. Members of this school of thought seek to reject or even destroy the idea of African logic at any cost. They are European iconoclasts or some African Évoléus who have taken to blind Eurocentricism. They argue that reason can have one absolute manifestation world over and on this basis dismiss the idea of African logic as anathema.

Robin Horton (1977) was one notable polemicist who made a monstrous claim that African languages do not contain principles of logic and as a result, it would be mistaken to talk of African philosophy. Horton not only indicts the African intellect by that assumption. He also denies the idea of African logic. He was riding on the inglorious crest of the misinformed French Anthropologist Lucien Levy-Bruhl who conceived quite in error that primitives are pre-logical meaning that they are not capable of logical reasoning of any form. These were the pervading opinions that were soon to be dismantled. Akin Makinde, Momoh and Maurice Makumba clearly decimated Horton's arguments.[7]

Between Horton and Levy-Bruhl who denied any form of rationality to Africans, and those African philosophers who have strenuously defended the idea and the possibility of African logic, comes a more subtle aggression from those who thought that the advocates of African logic were abusing their privilege. Akin Makinde, Kwasi Wiredu and Uduma Oji Uduma are the most vocal among the polemicists against the idea of an African logic.[8] These polemicists are opposed to the idea of a

---

[7] See: Makinde, M. A. (1977); Momoh (2000) and Makumba (2007).
[8] See Makinde (2010); Wiredu (1991); Uduma (1998, 2009, 2015).

culture-bound logic system because, for them, logic is a universal discipline like mathematics and cannot be relativised.[9] Such a project, they contend, is not only wrong but essentially inimical to the identity which the African shares with the rest of humanity. This point has seriously been made by Hountondji.[10]

Uduma's arguments, for example, began as a reaction to all those who suggest the possibility of African logic such as C. S. Momoh, C. B. Okolo, U. Etuk, C. O. Ijiomah etc.[11] Two most important characteristics of logic, according to Uduma, is that it is universal and topic-neutral. The idea of African logic contravenes these requirements, and therefore becomes, for him, unacceptable. In "Can there be an African Logic?" he raises critical questions on the possibility of constructing such a logic in the first place as well as the immense challenges that would face such project.

Makinde's contention is not different from Uduma's. Like Uduma, he declares that logic is universal and cannot possibly be relative without referring to an irrational mode of thought. He says that the principles of logic are universal and apply everywhere including in African thought system.[12] He demonstrated however that any suggestion of a regional logic system like African logic is mistaken because as he put it "…logic, like mathematics cannot be relativised." (2010: 42). He goes on to argue that since we cannot talk about American or African mathematics, we cannot also talk about such things as American or African logic, otherwise it would not be true that the principles of logic are assumed in all cultures. But this is a bad analogy because it is not based on facts as I have already shown in great detail in Chap. 3 above.

The same goes for Wiredu who, while commenting on Ocaya's work on logic in Acholi language dismisses the idea of African logic as "precipitous" and "blanket speculation" (1991: 101). For him, the African philosopher can rest content with showing the Westerner that the principles of logic can be found in African languages which was what Ocaya did. Here, he suggests that it is nonsensical to indicate that an African logic can exist. Wiredu wrote several essays on logic none of which was in the area of African logic tradition. Logic for him can only have one-standard. By this supposition, Wiredu is obviously a victim of what Hebga calls 'the dogma of one all-embracing standard' of logic. Even though Wiredu (1991: 93) challenges African scholars not to leave the advancement of the human understanding of such things as logic to other peoples forever, he obviously intended the African to join the Westerners in the discussions on their logic tradition. No wonder he spent a lifetime publishing several papers on Western logic most of which are in intellectual limbo

---

[9] See Makinde (2010: 42) and Uduma (2009)

[10] Hountondji (1996).

[11] See Momoh (2000), Okolo (1993) and Ijiomah (2014)

[12] I have had the privilege of joining this debate. I (2011) began by reacting to Uduma (2009). In reaction, Uduma (2015) sought again to undermine my arguments which I responded to, see Chimakonam (2015a). Whichever way one looks at the argument, it does look as though it is going to continue for some time to come.

with little notice or recognition by Western logicians. It is easy to see the line of his thought. Logic is like mathematics and it is simply outlandish to contemplate regional logics just as one cannot contemplate regional mathematics. But this analogy is out of place. Logic is not mathematics. While logic deals with signs and symbols with largely qualitative meanings—the type that refer to realities in their ontological states and their relationships thereof, mathematics deals essentially with numbers with quantitative meanings. It is therefore not the case that logic traditions are impossible.

From the foregoing, I wish to discountenance apologias and polemicism as veritable strategies for developing the field of African logic. While the former tries to establish it by all means, the latter tries to discourage it by all means that are not rigorous. This is based on the fact that both forms of intellectual campaign are directed by ethnic and tribal sentiments rather than objective scholarly and philosophical rigour. In their place, I recommend the strategy of conversational thinking for actors in the debate on African logic. This is a mechanism of the conversational philosophy, a new school of thought in African philosophy committed to critical engagements aimed at formulating and debating transgenerational problematics.[13] By its method, this school encourages the critical engagements between one called *nwa-nju* or the contestant and the other called *nwa-nsa* or the protestant.[14] This engagement is a dispassionate one aimed at deconstruction, reconstruction, theoretic purification and sophistication, discovering lacunas, filling them up, opening new vistas, unveiling new concepts and sustaining the culture of conversation.[15]

4.4 The System Builders

After the polemicists come the system building school of thought who are primarily interested in constructing specific systems of logic that could be called African. Their goal was and still is, as it were, to pick up the challenge thrown by Momoh in formulating basic syntactic rules and symbolism of a system of an African logic. Here, I will discuss the attempts of Helen Verran, Innocent Asouzu, Chris Ijiomah and the present author.

Helen Verran (2001), an Australian who lived among the Yoruba-speaking people of Western Nigeria for some 7 years, attempted a project on African logic in her book. This book contains an audacious attempt at presenting a certain African logic around a supposedly relativist Yoruba numeric system. The book concerns a demonstration that logic and number systems are relative rather than absolute; or in a way, that the Yoruba has a numeric system different from the Western system. When seen as an alternative system rather than as an inferior one, this will gesture towards a somewhat different set of principles of numbering which is an affirmation of a dif-

---

[13] See Chimakonam (2018).

[14] See Chimakonam (2015b).

[15] See Chimakonam, J.O. (2015c).

4.4 The System Builders

ferent logic system. Verran's discussion of this key point spreads across the four parts of the book. In part one, she prepares the ground by raising and attempting to answer the rather odd question: Could African numbers be different from the numbers of science? She explains her study of the Yoruba numeric system using series of experiments in abstract/qualitative numbering and concrete/quantitative numbering in which school children are put to tests involving qualitative and quantitative comprehension of number. Then she observes that while the Yoruba school children score well in quantitative exercises, they perform very poorly in qualitative exercises. This she suggests confirms previous researches which hold that Africans are somewhat incapable of abstract reasoning and that the Yoruba cannot be an exception.

But this is where Verran's work differs from the conclusions of others. Verran refuses to interpret this as a mark of mental inferiority. In part two, she finds another way. By comparing the Yoruba and the Western number systems and analysing the social lives of numbers, she observes that the quantitative nature of Yoruba number system is a question of approach and style rather than inferiority of individuals in the Yoruba culture. She singles out the ways number names function grammatically in English and Yoruba sentences and on the basis of this confirms her hypothesis of the relativity of number system. In part three, she uses further experiments to critique the universalist notion of generalising and reports that the Yoruba quantifying numeric model is as logical and abstract as the Western quantifying system. In other words, she suggests that the quantitative comprehension of number is abstract in some ways. In the final part, she argues that the principles of Yoruba number system may differ from those of Western numeric system but the two represent different approaches of arriving at the same result. She claims that they are both logically consistent suggesting the relativity of logics. And that an African logic must hold the underlying principles which characterise numbering in Yoruba culture and by extension, Africa.

On the whole, the highpoint of Verran's work is on the boldness of its arguments with examples, cases and experiments that support her claim about the existence of logical thinking in African culture. However, despite the significance of this attempt, for the task of constructing a system of African logic, it also has outstanding weak points.

To begin with, Verran's concession that the inability of the Yoruba and by extension Africans to frame the abstract notion of number should not be interpreted as a mark of mental inferiority to the West is not only incorrect but sounds more like a charitable remark and should be dismissed. If it is not a mark of inferiority what then is it? Suggesting that there are abstract spaces in the horizon of quantitative comprehension of number waters down the discourse and Verran knows that. What I think should be pointed out is that Verran misinterpreted the outcome of her experiments. That a people (Yoruba and Africans) are in the habit of quantitative conception of number does not imply that they are incapable of abstract conception of number. Those school children who failed in her strange experiments failed because they have not been taught the abstract conception of number. After all, Verran's assistants were all Yoruba and Africans and they could frame the abstract notion of number as her experiments show. It does appear therefore that Verran was lacking an important skill: she appears not to be versed in the Yoruba intellectual culture despite having spent some time in Yorubaland.

From the above, one can see that Verran does not have full grasp of Yoruba ontology. Embedded in the Yoruba ontology is the convention which tends to prioritise the concrete conception of number over the abstract. This is the contrast between empiricism and rationalism. British Empiricists are not incapable of following the reasoning of Continental Rationalists; they are simply saying that their model is better. Again, there is a way Verran comes to this point but her conclusion which suggests that the Yoruba just like other Africans are incapable of framing the abstract notions is incorrect.

Technically, one could also observe that her presentation which treats an African logic as a mechanism for description rather than a mechanism for reasoning is also limited. In other words, her case for an African logic is actually a description of the attitude or character of "being logical". This attitude is different from "logic" itself as a system. To do logic or to be logical is an attitude which any individual could demonstrate, but logic is far from being a mere human attitude. Logic is both an art and a science of reasoning on diverse topics with a set of linguistic rules. Verran fails to articulate the set of rules that undergird her so-called African logic. Similarly, Verran deploys so much energy in discussing the understanding with which the Yoruba people employ number and tries to show in many ways; for instance, (a) that such procedures are logical; and (b) that it implies the existence of Yoruba (African) logic. But there is a fundamental lacuna in the structure of this argument. If the various applications of number are said to be logical, as Verran deploys them, in what specific senses are they logical? In other words, which laws of thought and rules of logic do they obey? From Verran's presentation one could see the laws of Aristotelian logic at play. The nagging questions therefore are: how then can the laws of Aristotelian thought be the fulcrum of African thought system? And how can the rules of Aristotelian logic guide the logical inferences of an African logic?

Besides this, Verran's submission is that because the Yoruba arrive at the same correct result similar to those obtained in following Western logical procedure, their own procedures are logical. This spurious argument only demonstrates that the Yoruba are logical in light of Western logic! Verran, therefore, succeeds in establishing one point which also accounts for the disestablishment of her main point. In other words, that the Yoruba numeric system is logical in light of Western logic (rather than an African logic) readily disintegrates her argument that there exists an African logic. This is because if there exists an African logic then that the Yoruba number system is logical, ought to be so primarily in light of the laws of an African logic. Verran fails to establish this. Lastly, Verran makes no tangible attempt at discussing the substance of an African logic she projects in terms of its structures and the principles that hold them. Merely showing that Yoruba number system is logical in light of Western logic has said nothing about the system of an African logic.

The next system builder is Innocent Asouzu (2013) of the Calabar School of Philosophy. He made his name in the circle of African philosophy through his ontological theory of ibuanyidanda or complementary reflection. It was however in a recent book that he enunciated the logic of this theory clearly. This system of logic though specifically articulated to account for the ibuanyidanda theory is nonetheless capable of wider applications in many a discourse. Asouzu notes that:

> ...the rules guiding ibuanyidanda logical reasoning seeks to serve as a guarantor for the validity of all forms of logic of discourse by ensuring that they comply with the demands of the transcendent complementary circle. One of its major concerns is exploring credible ways of addressing an arbitrary imposition of any of our logical faculties on the way we relate to the world. This is mostly the case with the mode of operation of our disjunctive faculties. (2013: 91)

Asouzu argues that the transcendent complementary circle or the transcendent *ibuanyidanda* circle provides the context for the determination of the *ibuanyidandaness* of any action or judgement. Principles such as the truth and authenticity criterion, noetic propaedeutic, the *ibuanyidanda* imperative and other *ibuanyidanda* principles provide the legal framework in which reasoning proceeds without encountering problems such as *ihe mkpuchi anya* (phenomenon of concealment) which distorts judgements and actions. Asouzu is of the view that logical judgements proceeds from our innermost human consciousness which is open to influence by our emotions (*ihe mkpuchi anya*). This consciousness could be motivated towards a conjunctive or disjunctive reasoning pattern. When we reason through our conjunctive faculty, we tend to be accommodating whereas when we reason disjunctively, we tend to be divisive.

Ibuanyidanda therefore favours a conjunctive mode of reasoning in which realities are presented as missing links. This makes the complementary logic a "both/and" rather than "both/not" system. According to Asouzu, whereas our conjunctive faculty impels us to reach out to the world in the mode of "not only this but that thing" or in the mode of "this as well as that thing," our disjunctive faculty restricts us to "either this or that thing" (2013: 90). Asouzu (2013: 93–97) goes on to explain his logic thus, although these two faculties are part of the ambivalences of our being, complementary logic compels us to overcome the pressure of our disjunctive faculty which impedes harmonious reasoning in order to always reason conjunctively. Complementary logic, for Asouzu, is however not a regional logic or what he calls "the logic of geographical categorization." He is in this way against the idea of an African logic as a relative system. Conjunctive reasoning behind complementary logic, for him, provides human consciousness with the means to steer a more liberal, mediating and more accommodating course; one that makes room for the coexistence of opposites.

It is easy to see the deep insight in Asouzu's articulation of complementary logic. His idea of conjunctive reasoning is without doubt necessary in the formulation of the intermediate value that explains the "truth-value glut" or the "both/and" which has come to be a central aspect of the idea of a relative or an alternative African system. However, complementary logic still falls short of a complete system of logic. By its formulation, it can at best pass for a philosophical logic serving as a tool for explaining realities from the *ibuanyidanda* perspective. Some problems arise in the author's explanations. The author had rejected all forms of relative (geographical) systems of logic but forgot that in rejecting what he calls the disjunctive mode of reasoning, he was advocating a relative system in which the law of excluded middle was not effective. By advocating a system that reconciles opposites (logical contradictories), the author crossed the bounds of two-valued logic; decimated the laws of contradiction and excluded middle and reached out for an unnamed inclusive alternative.

Complementary logic becomes a relativised even if not a geographical system. He suggests it is pluri-valued which means it is an alternative, and all alternative logics are in some ways relative. But the question is: relative in what sense? Is it culture-inspired in formulation or geographical in application? He states it is not exclusivist and absolutist, and this implies it is inclusivist and relative. Hence, Asouzu's complementary logic falls short of a complete system on the one hand and rejects relative systems of any form on the other. And even if we conceive of it as a relative system, we find it incomplete enough to ground theories in African philosophy. Nevertheless, Asouzu's complementary logic definitely provides useful insights from which to proceed in African logic project.

Also, the Nigerian logician from the Calabar School of Philosophy, Chris Ijiomah (2006 and 2014), one of the contemporary advocates of an African logic, also makes a strong case for the relativity of logic systems. He argues not only for the existence of many logic systems besides the two-valued logic but more resolutely for the existence of an African logic system. He has recently published a treatise where he attempts developing a theory of an African logic called "Harmonious Monism." Obviously, the intellectual significance of such a step cannot be gainsaid. However, whilst we celebrate any attempt to create such a theory, what Ijiomah has done does not attain the kind of progress we hope to be making in the search for the parameters conducive to an African system of logic. The theory of harmonious monism, to say the very least, lacks the essential logical nutrients any such system requires in order to overcome basic legal and structural challenges.

In sum, Ijiomah explains in his book that logic is relative to cultures just as philosophies are. He argues that African philosophy springs from African cultures and raises questions pertaining to the African place. To understand these questions raised in the African place he goes on, one needs a specific type of logic—the African logic—which is formulated from the African thought system. It is only this logic for Ijiomah, that can interpret and explain the African lifeworld. Ijiomah therefore sets out to formulate a prototype of this logic and calls it "Harmonious Monism". Harmonious Monism for him is to be not only a philosophical logic for the explanation of realities in African ontology but a system of logic as well. The procedure of this logic will be to obtain the third value from two contrary values. In essence, harmonious monism is a three-valued logic. In a nine chapter work, Ijiomah devoted the first three chapters to giving the background of his project and establishing that logic is relative to cultures. From Chaps. 4, 5, 6, and 7, Ijiomah discusses the connection between logic and culture/ontology. He shows the difference between Western and African ontologies and suggested that these different ontologies cannot birth the same logic. In Chap. 8, he explains harmonious monism as a philosophical logic—a tool— for explaining realities in African world. In Chap. 9, he produced many samples of the application of harmonious monism in explaining realities in African lifeworld.

Despite these giant strides in unveiling Harmonious monism as a philosophical logic, there is no passage where Ijiomah attempted to formulate rules and principles of Harmonious monism as a system of logic neither did he formulate the laws that undergird the unique thought system on which he rests his system. This is the greatest weakness of Ijiomah's book in that it made claims at the beginning which it did not fulfil.

Consider the following question: Is harmonious monism a philosophical logic, a system of formal logic or a philosophy of logic? First, in the title of the work, the author gives the presumption that it was going to be a theory in philosophical logic but by the second page of his preface, we are presented with assumptions that presuppose it is an attempt at developing a system of logic. In his words:

> The objective of this work is therefore to construct that alternative logic otherwise shortened to answer the logic of Harmonious Monism which can take care of the prevalent configuration of realities in Africa….the logic plays a harmonious role as to bring out a holistic explanatory attempt to African experience. (2014: vii–viii)

And yet the substance of his discourse in the book presents his theory more like a philosophy of logic. Logic, when viewed as a theory of inference dealing with laws of thought, is a system that appeals to these laws in the determination of assumptions from certain observations to a certain conclusion. This is called formal logic. When these laws of logic are applied differently, for example, in induction and deduction, it gives birth to another aspect of logic called methodology or theory of methods. Furthermore, when philosophical questions are raised pertaining to the application of these laws in any scheme at all, it leads to philosophy of logic; in other words, as Roy Cook (2009: 221) explains, it becomes "the philosophical study of formal systems", their problems, applicability, efficacy and weaknesses.

Ijiomah in the Chaps. 3, 6 and in other passages in his book claimed his theory is a study of some formal systems (this, I think, is where harmonious monism appropriately belongs). There is a little difference between philosophy of logic and philosophical logic according to Cook. The latter differs from the former in that it does not study formal systems but rather uses them as "tools for solving basic philosophical problems" involving clusters of reality of the type Ijiomah dealt with in his book. The important thing, according to Bochenski (1965), is to always maintain a strict separation among these aspects of logic in any discourse for clarity and avoidance of confusions. Ijiomah unfortunately committed this grave mistake in articulating his theory in the book mentioned by not clearly separating these ideas.

In the final analysis, Ijiomah fails to construct a proper system he had promised at the beginning of the work if we understand by a system of logic, the formal theory equipped with laws specifying ways of their applications in revising assumptions out of which a certain conclusion could be drawn from certain observations. It is perfectly possible to have different systems of logic dealing with the same set of laws. The difference between them would be in the degrees of tightening and relaxation of those laws. Though the term "alternative," as Ijiomah employs it, could designate any proposal for a system of logic, the problem with his proposal is that it is presented as a radical alternative system where the classical laws may not apply and which may be equipped with its own laws that may be exclusive to it. But whichever the case, the author concluded the book without accomplishing his proposal to construct a system of formal logic even if constructed with different laws of thought. It was not even stated that the proposed system was going to be rested on the traditional principles of thought or any new set of principles whatsoever; the author simply went ahead discussing harmonious monism as a tool for explaining realities in African world-view.

It is imperative to clarify that when a body of knowledge is called "African," as in the case of "African logic," we may not mean an existing system approved by all African cultures. In affixing "African" to an enterprise, the intention may be (a) to produce a cultural or philosophical model by sifting elements that are common in many African world-views, and/or (b) to adopt and project others which may not be common but which are nonetheless in agreement with the basic notions and structures in African ontology. We do this bearing in mind that this is one of the ways knowledge can be improved upon and modified to acquire a universal appeal. Thus, it would not be out of place to argue that Western logic, science and numeric system etc., all rose through this same means. It was Maurice Ritcher (1973) who stated that science is a cultural process or group of interrelated processes through which we acquire our modern and dynamic knowledge of the natural world. Sandra Harding (1997) also confirms that modern science is an offspring of ethno-science. By this she means local knowledge system constantly modified and improved.

I come now to my contribution. The Ezumezu system is three-valued consisting of *ezu, izu* and *ezumezu*. The latter is the third and middle value from which the system derives its name Ezumezu spelt with capital 'E'. Symbolically, the three values are represented with letters 'T', 'F' and 'C'. Ezumezu is trivalent as opposed to the bivalent structure of the two-valued logic. The difference between them is that Ezumezu represents an extension of two-valued logic where the laws of identity, contradiction and excluded-middle were relaxed to formulate the supplementary laws of njikoka, nmekoka and onona-etiti respectively.

My proposal here is an intellectual climate in which scholars on the frontier of African logic will eschew apologias and reckless polemicism and engage in rigorous conversations aimed at developing a robust system of logic which will merit the prefix "African." Such a system when developed is expected to ground methodology in various areas of African Studies beginning with philosophy. Ezumezu represents such a system. All that is now required are critical insights from, for instance, conversational philosophy which encourages critical engagement between two contenders—between the *nwa-nju* and the *nwa-nsa*—in a creative attempts at continually opening new intellectual vistas for thought as well as expanding the culture of conversation. In latter chapters, I will lay out the structure of Ezumezu as philosophy of logic, methodology and formal system.

4.5 Conclusion

In conclusion, no one could truly claim that African philosophy has arrived in the absence of a logic system to ground its methodology. This is because such a system of logic will lie at the base of the intricate web of African lifeworld. I will present the Ezumezu logic as an exciting possibility in this regard. Its promises provide the context for outlining the methodological dynamism of African philosophy and Studies. In this chapter, I have surveyed various contributions to the discussion on African logic under schools of thought, from the apologists, the polemicists to the system builders and highlighted the need for continuing conversations among African logicians geared towards outlining a system of logic that can serve the crucial purpose of grounding African philosophy and studies.

References

Agada, Ada. 2015. In *Existence and consolation: Reinventing ontology, gnosis and values in African philosophy*, ed. Jonathan Chimakonam. Minnesota: Paragon House.

Asouzu, Innocent. 2013. *Ibuanyidanda (complementary reflection) and some basic philosophical problems in Africa today: Sense experience, "ihe mkpuchi anya" and the supermaxim*. Zurich: Lit Verlag GmbH and Co. Kg Wien.

Barnes, Harry. 1965. *An intellectual and cultural history of the western world*. Vol 1. 3rd rev. edn. New York: Dover Publications.

Bochenski, M. Jozef. 1965. *The methods of contemporary thought*. Dordrecht/Holland: Reidel Publishing.

Chimakonam, O. Jonathan. 2018. The 'demise' of philosophical universalism and the rise of conversational thinking in contemporary African philosophy. In *Method, substance, and the future of African philosophy*, ed. Edwin Etieyibo, 135–159. Cham: Palgrave Macmillan.

———. 2015a. The criteria question in African philosophy: Escape from the horns of jingoism and Afrocentrism. In *Atuolu omalu: Some unanswered questions in contemporary African philosophy*, ed. Jonathan O. Chimakonam, 101–123. Lanham: University Press of America.

———. 2015b. Transforming the African philosophical place through conversations: An inquiry into the Global Expansion of Thought (GET). *South African Journal of Philosophy* 34 (4): 462–479.

———. 2015c. Conversational philosophy as a new school of thought in African philosophy: A conversation with Bruce Janz on the concept of 'philosophical space'. *Confluence: Journal of World Philosophies* 3: 9–40.

Cook, Roy. 2009. *A dictionary of philosophical logic*. Edinburgh: Edinburgh University Press.

Eboh, N. Bernadette. 1983. *The structure of Igbo logic as shown in dispute settlement in Igbo land with special reference to Nzerem town*. Rome: Gregorian University.

Enyimba, Maduka. 2011. The nature of logic in African philosophy. *Integrative Humanism Journal* 1: 1 153–1 167.

Etieyibo, Edwin. 2016. African philosophy and proverbs: The case of logic in Urhobo proverbs. *Philosophia Africana* 18: 1 12–1 39.

Etuk, Udo. 2002. The possibility of African logic. In *The third way in African philosophy*, ed. Olusegun Oladipo, 98–116. Ibadan: Hope Publications.

Evans-Pritchard, E. Edward. 1965. *Theories of primitive religion*. Oxford: Oxford University Press.

Fayemi, K. Ademola. 2010. Logic in Yoruba proverbs. *Itupale: Online Journal of African Studies* 2: 1–14.
Fortes, M., and G. Dieterlen, eds. 1972. *African systems of thought*. New York: Oxford University Press.
Francis, B. I. (1992). *Logic among the Efiks*. Unpublished B.A. Thesis, Department of Philosophy, University of Calabar, Nigeria.
Francis, O. I. (1997). The Ibibio logic. Unpublished B.A. Thesis, Department of Philosophy, University of Calabar, Nigeria.
Goldenweiser, Alexander. 1922. *Early civilisation: An introduction to anthropology*. New York: Knopf.
Harding, Sandra. 1997. Is modern science an ethnoscience? Rethinking epistemological assumptions. In *Postcolonial African philosophy: A critical reader*, ed. Emmanuel C. Eze, 45–70. Cambridge, MA: Blackwell Publishers.
Hebga, Meinrad. 1958. Logic in Africa. *Philosophy Today* 11 (4): 221–229.
Horton, Robin. 1977. Traditional, thought and the emerging African philosophy department: A comment on the current debate. *Second Order: An African Journal of Philosophy* 3 (1): 64–80.
Hountondji, Paulin. 1996. *African philosophy: Myth and reality*. 2nd Rev. ed. Bloomington: University Press.
Hunnings, Gordon. 1975. Logic, language and culture. *Second Order: An African Journal of Philosophy* 4 (1): 3–13.
Ijiomah, Chris. 2006. An excavation of a logic in African world-view. *African Journal of Religion, Culture and Society* 1 (1): 29–35.
———. 2014. *Harmonious monism: A philosophical logic of explanation for ontological issues in supernaturalism in African thought*. Calabar: Jochrisam Publishers.
Jacques, Tomaz. 2011. Philosophy in black: African philosophy as a negritude. *Sartre Studies International* 17 (1): 1–19.
Jones, M. Jaja, and Badey Paul. 2012. Logic in African philosophy: Examples from two Niger Delta societies. *International Journal of Academic Research in Business and Social Sciences* 2 (4): 95–102.
Keita, L. 1991. Contemporary African philosophy: The search for a method. In *African philosophy: The essential readings*, ed. Tsenay Serequeberhan, 132–155. New York: Paragon House.
Makinde, M. Akin. 1977. Formal logic and the paradox of excluded middle. *International Logic Review* 15: 40–52.
———. 2010. *African philosophy: The Demise of a controversy*. Rev ed. Ile Ife: Obafemi Awolowo University Press.
Momoh, S. Campbell. 2000. Nature, issues and substance of African philosophy. In *The substance of African philosophy*, ed. Campbell S. Momoh, 1–22. Auchi: African Philosophy Projects Publication.
Nze, B. Chukwuemeka. 1998. Uncovering logic in Igbo language and thought. *WAJOPS* 1: 131–142.
Ocaya, Victor. 2004. Logic in the Acholi language. In *A companion to African philosophy*, ed. Kwasi Wiredu, 285–295. Cambridge, MA: Blackwell Publishing.
Ogugua, I. P. (2003). The epistemological conditions of African understanding (a study of the functions of symbolism in Igbo systems of thought). Unpublished Ph.D. Thesis, Department of Philosophy, University of Nigeria, Nsukka.
Ogugua, I. Paul, and I.C. Oduah. 2013. Logic in Igbo-African understanding. *African Research Review: An International Multidisciplinary Journal* 7 (2): 193–205. https://doi.org/10.4314/afrrev.7i2.13.
Ogugua, I. Paul, and I.C. Ogugua. 2015. Is there an Igbo-African logic. *Open Journal of Philosophy* 5: 243–251. https://doi.org/10.4236/ojpp.2015.54031.
Okolo, B. Chukwudum. 1993. *What is African philosophy? A short introduction*. Enugu: Cecta.

References

Omoregbe, Joseph. 1985. African philosophy: Yesterday and today. In *Philosophy in Africa: Trends and perspectives*, ed. Peter Bodunrin, 1–14. Ile Ife: University of Ife Press.

Ritchter, Maurice. 1973. *Science as a cultural process*. London: Fredericia Muller.

Senghor, S. Leopold. 1962. On negrohood: Psychology of the African negro. *Diogenes* 10 (37): 1–15.

———. 1964. *Liberte 3*. Paris: Editions du Seuil.

Sogolo, S. Godwin. 1993. *Foundations of African philosophy: A definitive analysis of conceptual issues in African thought*. Ibadan: University of Ibadan Press.

Uduma, O. Uduma. 1998. Logic as an element of culture. In *Metaphysics, phenomenology and African philosophy*, ed. Jim Unah, 374–393. Ibadan: Hope Publications.

———. 2009. Can there be an African logic? In *From footmarks to landmarks on African philosophy*, ed. Andrew F. Uduigwomen, 2nd ed., 289–311. Lagos: Obaroh & Ogbinaka Publishers.

———. 2015. The logic question in African philosophy: Between the horns of irredentism and jingoism. In *Atuolu omalu: Some unanswered questions in contemporary African philosophy*, ed. Jonathan O. Chimakonam, 83–100. Lanham: University Press of America.

Verran, Helen. 2001. *Science and an African logic*. Chicago: University of Chicago Press.

Winch, Peter. 1958. *The idea of a social science and its relation to philosophy*. 2nd ed. London: Routledge.

———. 1964. Understanding a primitive society. *American Philosophical Quarterly* 1: 4 307–4 324.

Wiredu, Kwasi. 1991. On defining African philosophy. In *African philosophy: The essential readings*, ed. Tsenay Serequeberhan, 87–110. New York: Paragon House.

Wiredu, J.E. Kwasi. 1984. How not to compare African thought with Western thought. In *African philosophy: An introduction*, ed. Richard Wright, 3rd ed., 149–162. Lanham: University Press of America.

Chapter 5
African Logic and the Question of Method: Towards Villagisation of Knowledge

Abstract Do we need new methods for African philosophy? Or, are the methods of Western philosophy adequate for African philosophy? These questions are not some of the easiest to answer in African philosophy. In charting the course of future direction in African philosophy, one must be confronted with these questions. On the one hand, if one agrees that we sure need new methods for African philosophy, a serious but perhaps not far reaching implication could be drawn: does it mean that all we have been doing using methods developed in Western philosophy is not African philosophy? On the other hand, if one says that Western-developed methods are more than adequate for African philosophy, a further implication could be drawn: does it mean that African philosophy is not truly African as yet?

In this chapter, I seek to, in practical terms, undertake the task of methodological reconstruction in African philosophy through the framework of Ezumezu. To accomplish this task, I seek to mount a defence for postmodern thinking and then project Ezumezu from this methodological purview. To do all this, I will first demolish the pretensions of European philosophy weaved into the modern mindview which erroneously projects the European methodological particular as a synonym for the universal.

5.1 Introduction

Do we need new methods for African philosophy? Or, are the methods of Western philosophy adequate for African philosophy? These questions are not some of the easiest to answer in African philosophy. In charting the course of future direction in African philosophy, one must be confronted with these questions. On the one hand, if one agrees that we sure need new methods for African philosophy, a serious but perhaps not far reaching implication could be drawn: does it mean that all we have been doing using methods developed in Western philosophy is not African philosophy? On the other hand, if one said that Western-developed methods are more than adequate for African philosophy, a further implication could be drawn: does it mean that African philosophy is not truly African as yet? It is beyond the scope of this work to indulge in this dilemma. I have stated it to bring to life the enormity of what

Lucius Outlaw (2003) calls the deconstructive and the reconstructive challenges facing African philosophy in our time. These challenges among others, point to methodological re-direction. On this score, I pitch my tent with those who hold that we need new methods for African philosophy. The burden of justification shall be mine here.

A clever logician by name Udo Etuk (2002: 107) in a rather shrewd paper observes that, "[T]he problem for us therefore, has to start with challenging the view that the methods of discovery and the methods of doing things which we have inherited from the West are the only legitimate ways of discovery and of doing [things]." Etuk was in the above making it clear that there are many ways of doing things and there is no one way to doing things. From the foregoing, one thing appears certain, African philosophy in this age needs a methodological re-direction to free its discourse from the spell of Plato and Aristotle. The question is how do we proceed? Tsenay Serequeberhan suggests that the main task of the African philosopher in this troubled time should be to lead a recovery that "requires a rethinking of much that we inherited—consciously and subliminally—from the colonial past" (1991: 23). This rethinking technically involves what he calls the "unmasking of the Eurocentric residues in modern Africa..." (1991: 22). Evidently, Serequeberhan's advocacy for the dethronement of logocentricism aligns with Outlaw's identification of deconstructive and reconstructive challenges confronting African philosophers in the postcolonial (2003: 169–174). Basically, Outlaw sees the starting point of African philosophy as necessarily deconstructive (2003: 174). African philosophers must therefore undertake the task of deconstructing European-instituted logocentric methodology to free the African from intellectual prison of European hegemony. For Outlaw, a reconstructive effort should properly commence after this deconstructive exercise. In his words:

> The reconstructive aspects of this challenge are to be found in the self-definition, the specification, and reappropriation of an African authenticity and legitimacy, in the disproving—the displacing—of the inventive discourse, and, most importantly, in the efforts to reclaim control over African historicity and the interpretation of African history in general, and African philosophical history in particular... (2003: 176)

Some of the cardinal points made by Outlaw in the above include; supplying African authenticity and legitimacy as well as reclaiming African historicity. Method, it appears stands at the helm of these endeavours. Now, granted that many a scholar of African philosophy has creditably undertaken the deconstructive challenge, much of all there is in the reconstructive challenge in the past has amounted to prescriptions and lip service. In this chapter, I seek to, in practical terms, undertake the task of methodological reconstruction in African philosophy through the framework of Ezumezu. To accomplish this task, I seek to mount a defence for postmodern thinking and then project Ezumezu from this methodological purview. To do all this, I will first demolish the pretensions of European philosophy weaved into the modern mindview which according to Serequeberhan (1991: 4–5) erroneously projects the European methodological particular as a synonym for the universal.

5.2 The Issues of Scope and Methodology

We cannot define African philosophy satisfactorily. We simply cannot, even if we want it so desperately. This is because to attempt this task, we must first supply answers to the following two questions: when is a discourse philosophy? And when is a philosophy African? C. B. Okolo (1993) and Kwasi Wiredu (1991) have both highlighted the difficulty involved in this task. Thus the best we can hope for is a clear demarcation of its scope. Such that we may be able to say: this is what constitutes African philosophy; this is what we shall take as African philosophy and this is what we shall not take. The reason for this is not farfetched. The genetics of African philosophy is encumbered on all sides by possible controversies. Thus every attempt to define the discipline would immediately bring one or two of those controversies alive. For example, a definition of African philosophy may commit us to geography i.e. a philosophy done in a particular place namely, Africa, which excludes other places. A commitment to place therefore, would make geography the ultimate criterion for African philosophy. Again, another definition may commit us to race, i.e. a philosophy done by a certain race of people which excludes non members. Such a commitment also, would make race the criterion for African philosophy. On the whole, any definition that does not commit us to the two above would almost certainly commit us to the emphasis on the African theme. The subject matter would therefore become the ultimate criterion for African philosophy which literally excludes other discourses that are not African. None of these approaches is acceptable in defining any intellectual tradition that is called philosophy. Bruce Janz has amply defended this position as well as noting that any such attempt would be vitiated by problems (2009). He goes on to recommend a culture that focuses on questions as the best way to think of African philosophy. But this is not the issue. The issue is whether it was worthwhile to define African philosophy from the staccato house of philosophy in general.

Apparently, we both agree that it is not but Janz fails to address a proper alternative. Urging us to think more of the questions which African philosophy has to ask simply avoids the main issue. I submit that in the absence of a satisfactory definition for African philosophy, we should rest content with the delineation and clear description of its scope. Somewhere down the passage Janz came close to this view when he offered a second alternative as a description of its movements and subdivisions (2009). But the scope of the disciple is not exhausted in its movements and subdivisions. In failing to provide a proper definition of African philosophy, we must be able to give a clear and comprehensive presentation of its scope at least, which offers the reader or any newcomer a clear picture of the discipline. Thus for me, the scope of African philosophy is broad and limited to those forms of life that are discussed through the African background mode of thought. This is exactly what definitions are meant to do anyway and as such where we cannot define, we must find an alternative that does the job. It was this failure to define and then the failure to clearly mark the scope of the discipline that led to the confused wrangling among members of disparate schools of thought in African philosophy.

Perhaps it should be stated that plotting the scope of African philosophy is necessarily a methodological question and the latter, is a proper concern of logic. I should also point out that the difficulty that manifests in defining African philosophy is present in Western, Oriental, Polynesian and indeed all other philosophical traditions. We can define philosophy but we simply cannot define Western, Oriental, Polynesian and African philosophies. The best logical thing we can do is to delineate them and this delineation is a methodological question. So, different philosophical traditions would be methodological nuances in philosophy. Thus we cannot define them but we can describe them from their different methodological purviews. The problem of discrimination in the house of philosophy is as a result of one philosophy tradition (Western) elevating itself as an absolute instance, i.e. that its particular is synonymous with universal manifestation of reason. This is however a mere pretension because all philosophical traditions are particular, the only philosophy that is universal is philosophy itself. And this thing called philosophy without the burden of any predicate is what we can define. If we make any attempt to define Western, Oriental, Polynesian and African philosophies, then these definitions will have different *definiendum* from that of the definition of philosophy itself. And if this is the case, then what would make such traditions philosophy? We must understand that different philosophical traditions are sub-sets of philosophy and always and at all times treat them as such.

It is like different children from the same mother. From one end, you could say there is a unity and from the other you could see the plurality. Philosophy can be defined from the perspective of its unity but described from its pluralist dimension. Plurality in philosophy is inevitably anarchistic not in the sense of lawlessness but in that of diversity. Plurality in question is a plurality of methods. Paul Feyerabend (1975) broaches something akin to methodological anarchism or epistemological anarchism. In these methodological nuances consists the postmodern mindview in philosophy. This work which is in African philosophy, aims to approach from the postmodern angle by projecting Ezumezu logical model as purveying the African philosophical methodology. Before I move on, let me first dwell on the pretensions of European philosophy.

5.3 The Pretensions of European Philosophy

I will like to stretch the point I mentioned about delineating the scope of African philosophy even though arriving at a clear scope and focus is not enough. One also needs to identify and highlight the principle that guides discourses within the scope he delineates. To do this, one necessarily has to ask: what is that basic principle which different platial philosophies have in common? The answer that beckons is 'reason' or what can be called philosophical reason. It is reason that makes a

5.3 The Pretensions of European Philosophy

discourse philosophy. Its manifestation in different philosophical places is a prognostic to the shared universality of different philosophical traditions. All true philosophical traditions whether Western, Asian, Arabic, Native American, Latin American, Polynesian or African should be universalisable. None is absolute. And because no philosophical tradition is absolute, all traditions are alternatives[1] to one another. The African philosophical tradition is an alternative to say Western philosophy and vice versa. None can be regarded as first among equals because it is the same reason that manifests in all these places. The self-image of Western philosophy that portrays it not only as a universal model but even as an absolute instance is a mere pretension. Janz writes that "… the Western pretension is that the development of universal reason and the reflection on particular issues within the West are identical" (2009: 66). It is in effort to demolish this pretension which is taking root in African philosophy that Outlaw (2003) and Jay van Hook (2002) recommend methodological reconstruction for African philosophy. However, in undertaking this task, we must not at the same time, lose sight of the basic philosophical index—reason—that makes a discourse philosophy.

But if a discourse is philosophy because of reason, how does a philosophy become African? Obviously we cannot talk about the colour of reason.[2] We cannot also say that a philosophy is African because it is produced in Africa or by Africans as some have argued.[3] This leads to phony myopism as I tried to gesture in connection with geography and race earlier. Validly, we can argue that a philosophy is African, or Western or Asian because of its background logic. This is the cultural inspiration of a place that defines the working mode of thought of the people. It is primarily ontological but can be transformed into the logical. The ontological appurtenances of Western cultural mindview were what Aristotle systematised into a thought model and is now called the Aristotelian logic. This Aristotelian logical system became the backbone of Western philosophy. Thus one way of describing philosophical traditions would be to say that they are those philosophies in which reason guides discourse through the Western or Asian or African mode of thought. In essence, what different philosophical traditions bring to the table is simply different ways of looking at the same reality.

Thus when philosophers in the global north, according to Serequeberhan (1991: 4) 'other' the rest of cultures by violently universalising their own singular particularity and seeking to annihilate the history of the rest of humanity, philosophers in the global south owe them the duty to point out the consequences of their action.

---

[1] The actual expression when one tradition is mentioned in reference to another should really be 'alternative with' and not 'alternative to.' This is the sense in which I employ the term 'alternative' in this book.

[2] Emmanuel Eze (1995) as well as Tsenay Serequeberhan (1991) both presented Kant as relating rationality to colour. In fact, Serequeberhan quoted Kant to have said "this fellow was quite black from head to foot, a clear proof that what he said was stupid" (1991: 6).

[3] Paulin Hountondji (1996) makes this argument. A position I have elsewhere criticised as "Hountondji's Dilemma" (Chimakonam 2015, xiii).

One of such obvious consequences is that the West will isolate and endanger itself in this attempt to 'other' the rest of humanity. Western philosophy's othering of the rest of philosophical traditions places it at a dangerous position of 'uniqueness,' and to be unique in this sense is to be culture-bound. This can be called 'involuntary re-othering'—a self-inflicted othering. If the West is so unique then, it shares nothing in common with the rest of humanity. By this measure, the Westerners discount themselves from the family of humans, unbeknownst to them. Technological advancement is not a proof of humanity after all, aliens have been speculated to have sophisticated technology yet, they are not humans, something that should make them really jealous of our kind I suppose.

In this maze of confusion where members of different schools in African philosophy opposed to each other's mode of thought engage in endless wrangling; in this charade of uncertainty where hardly any school has been able to give an objective justification for the study of African philosophy; and in this cacophony of arguments in which no one has been able to paint a clear picture of the discipline, we must learn to ask: what is the scope of African philosophy? In articulating this scope, care must be taken not to draw restrictive lines or what Boaventura Santos calls abyssal lines[4] that polarise humanity. For example, we admit the importance of focus on African issues but must not make it a restriction because what affects people in the far end of the globe affects the African as well. So our scope encompasses the rigorous study of any issue whatsoever by anybody, from anywhere and in any place. This scope of African philosophy is broad and limited to those forms of life that are discussed through the Africa-inspired background logic. In other words, insofar as there is an Africa-inspired logical background orientation guiding the methodology of one's philosophising, such a philosophy is African irrespective of the topics, issues, who does it and where it is done.

A good number of scholars have discussed the influence of the predicate 'African' on philosophy (Okolo 1990, 1993). While some have questioned the application of the predicate to a discipline such as philosophy (Wright 1984), many others have argued in favour on the basis of shared commonality (Abraham 1962; Jahn 1961; Metz and Gaie 2010). A few others have also argued in favour on the basis of system building (Verran 2001; Metz 2014). So I will not rehash these ideas and arguments here. What I will however do is attempt to articulate Ezumezu as a veritable logical system/background for African philosophy. Thus from the premise that reason characterises philosophy and that a philosophy is African by the reach of its scope delineated by a logical system systematised from the African ontological vision, I will proceed in this work, to present a formulation and an interpretation of that logic and how it might serve as a veritable framework for African philosophy and studies. Where such a system of logic yields a methodology that could be described as African, and where we admit that there should be different methodologies for different philosophical traditions, there would be no qualms in declaring such a condition postmodernist.

---

[4] See B. S. Santos. (2016a).

5.4 African Philosophy and the Question of Method

In a way, almost all the questions of postmodernism can be reduced to one ultimate question: that of method. Philosophy on its part can be compressed to three questions namely, what is ultimately real? What is ultimately true? And what is the ultimate value? Thus it would appear that the postmodern disagreement with the modern is that of most credible methodology for the philosophical inquiry. Modernism, it can be argued, favours a unified system built on the framework of Plato and Aristotle; postmodernism wants this system brought down in favour of a more liberal philosophical community even if that leads to a form of anarchism. Feyerabend (1975) on his part thinks that a liberal approach to inquiry is better for knowledge and progress in the sciences than the hegemonic modern condition. But where does African philosophy come into all this? It should be observed that the unified modern research framework whether in the sciences or in philosophy is a Western particular elevated to an absolute instance. Sandra Harding (1997) makes important allusion to the fact that the so-called modern science emerged from the Western ethno-science. That the Western advance in knowledge which has come to be treated in modernism not just as *a* model but as *the* model for all humanity is an indication of an unchallenged hegemony and not an accurate depiction of human intellectual history. This is what Janz calls the Western pretension as earlier noted—the erroneous supposition that the Western particular is synonymous with the universal. The postmodern agitation therefore is an onslaught against this falsehood.

In knowledge acquisition, method is strategic. It is method that describes the authenticity of the process, the accuracy of the outcome and the nativity of the accomplishment or failure. The intellectual history of the world is drawn up not only to document events but to historicise the progress of peoples. It is in this connection that Georg Hegel (1975) states that Africa has no dignified place in human history because it has made no contributions to world civilisations. So, a lot is at stake here, identity, dignity and the likes. Postmodernism is an outcry against the systemic domination and silencing of cultures. African philosophy through postmodernism seeks to reclaim its voice. To do this, there is a need to orchestrate a shift from the basic Western philosophical methodology. As methodology is a by-product of logic, the Western modern methodology stems from Plato's and Aristotle's framework logicised by Aristotle in his *Organon*. This Platonic and Aristotelian framework lies at the foundation of philosophy which grew architectonically and blossomed in the modern time, in the works of Rene Descartes and Immanuel Kant. Modernism is simply a continuation of that tradition.

African philosophers must seek to dislodge this framework in African philosophy. In African philosophy today, there are ghosts of Plato and Aristotle hovering around. These ghosts were imported into the African place in the twentieth century mainly by those who were later to be known as members of the universalist school but who gave themselves the flamboyant name: professional philosophers (Oruka 1975; Bodunrin 1984) thereby announcing their influence from Plato and Aristotle. By calling themselves professional philosophers, they had drawn a line between themselves and those they ridiculed as unprofessional or which is worse, ethnophilosophers. This is essentialist—the foremost trademark of Plato and Aristotle. Plato's framework had recognised the superior world of idea and the inferior world of matter and Aristotle's framework recognised the superior essence and the inferior accident. This framework has become the Greco-European model of thought segregating and discriminating against other cultures. Playing stooges in the hands of their Western tutors, the so-called members of the professional school who had been educated or in the words of Amos Wilson (1993) miseducated by the European iconoclasts, imported and affirmed the hegemony of Western philosophical methodology. Apparently too lazy to do the needful, (which was to construct the African philosophical methodology), or having been in the words of Wilson (1993) educated away from creativity, they took advantage of the lack of rigour in traditional philosophy and transformed their philosophical enterprise into a mere philosophy of commentary. At one end eulogising Western thought and at the other, deploring African traditional thought. Indeed, the legacy of the professional school despite their very important intervention to quell the tide of ethnophilosophising, is a brazen lack of creativity.

The arrival of this set of African philosophers in the 1940s representing the colonial European mission derailed the development of original thinking in African philosophy and held it back for decades. African philosophy began to find proper direction (in the creation of original ideas) theoretically in the early 1990s. With the publication of works like "African Philosophy: Deconstructive and Reconstructive Challenges" by Outlaw and "African Philosophy: the Point in Question" by Serequeberhan, and many others which raised creative questions, the future direction of the discipline was activated. In this vein, the Nigeria philosopher Ada Agada (2015) in addressing the future direction question in African philosophy states that "it demands great innovation, diversity and originality." His view is that the future direction of African philosophy should be the one that promotes "independent and innovative thinking that seeks original answers to fundamental questions of philosophy." Practically, the development of Uwa ontology by Pantaleon Iroegbu (1995) and the Complementary ontology by Innocent Asouzu (2004) to name just two examples provided concrete impetus to the new direction. In the period between 1940s to the late 1980s, the professional school held African philosophy to ransom variously castigating traditional thought. Hountondji, a prominent member of this school made this endeavour his life's work. Granted that their campaign for rigour was timely, it nonetheless was not supposed to be the ultimate focus. That the African traditional thought was not rigorous, so what?, that was not the task facing African philosophers. The task before them was the construction of a philosophical paradigm or methodology which foundation would not be the Platonic and the Aristotelian framework. Had they focused on constructing this methodological paradigm, the need to show that the traditional philosophers were in error would not have arisen.

Karl Popper (2003) would talk about the spell of Plato in the history of philosophy. It was the professional philosophers who brought home this spell and attempted casting it upon emerging philosophers who had the misfortune of being their students. In a fairly recent work, Agada (2015) appears to de-emphasise the question of methodology but intelligently argues that enough methods have been articulated in African philosophy that are now adequate to guide the discipline to future development of original ideas. My disagreement is with some others who suggest that the methods of Western philosophy are adequate for African philosophy and as such the methodological question in African philosophy does not arise. Some of these people include the egg-heads of the universalist school like Paulin Hountondji and Peter Bodunrin and others like Marcien Towa. Recent developments show that there may be emerging scholars who are sympathetic to their cause. How else can one know that the spell of Plato cast by the professional philosophers is still very much efficacious in the mainstream African philosophy today? All those who share the methodological sentiment of the universalists are obviously under the influence of this spell when they trivialise an issue as crucial as methodology. What then would make their discourses African philosophy and not Africans' exercise in Western philosophy? This is what makes Outlaw's and Serequeberhan's contributions strategic in marking the African philosophy's postmodern resurgence.

5.5 The Need for Villagisation of Knowledge

The need for villagisation of knowledge stems from the facts that, (1) there is no knowledge perspective that is absolute and comprehensive and as a result suffices for all places and times. (2) True justice demands the accommodation of all cultural perspectives. (3) We cannot have social, economic and political justices without epistemic justice. (4) The villagisation of knowledge entails the accommodation of different cultural epistemic visions and the recognition of their epistemic canons.

I see villagisation of knowledge as the last frontier in the battle to dethrone Plato's and Aristotle's hegemony. It is what will bring the end of a "cognitive empire,"[5] to adopt Boaventura du Sousa Santos' metaphor, set up more than 2000 years ago in Athens. With this powerful metaphor, Santos shows how theoretical, methodological, and pedagogical frameworks could be utilised in dethroning the epistemic hegemony of Eurocentric thought. For him, the Eurocentric cognitive empire not only exports the Western epistemic vision but imposes it on the rest of humanity as the one, all-embracing standard. It universalised the Western perspective of reality and through conquest, colonialism, neo-colonialism and imperialism, sought to decimate the particular epistemic visions of other cultures in what Santos termed epistemicide. Epistemicide as he put it, is,

> …the murder of knowledge. Unequal exchanges among cultures have always implied the death of the knowledge of the subordinated culture, hence the death of the social groups that possessed it. In the most extreme cases, such as that of European expansion, epistemicide was one of the conditions of genocide. The loss of epistemological confidence that currently afflicts modern science has facilitated the identification of the scope and gravity of the epistemicides perpetrated by hegemonic Eurocentric modernity. (2016a: 135)

---

[5] See Boaventura du Sousa Santos (2018).

In the above, Santos tries to show that some of the implications of epistemicide could be far-reaching. For example, he indicates that genocides and indeed all crimes against humanity have basis in epistemicide. When the epistemic and cultural paraphernalia of a marginalised group are discounted, members of the dominant group begin to see them as less humans or see themselves as more humans. The inferiorisation of the subordinated thus begins to set in. This was the case in Nazi Germany against the Jews where about six million Jews were murdered and in King Leopold's Belgium against native Congolese where about 20 million Congolese were murdered. The justification for these terrible crimes appears to have their motivation is a successfully conducted epistemicide of the subordinated culture. This is probably why Santos (2016a: 229) explained that "[T]he destruction of knowledge is not an epistemological artifact without consequences. It involves the destruction of the social practices and the disqualification of the social agents that operate according to such knowledges." Once this destruction is accomplished, anything from racism, to xenophobia attacks and even to the scale of genocide becomes possible.

For more than 2000 years, since the golden age of Greek philosophy, Western philosophers have abandoned the world and took flight to the top of mount Olympus where they built a city of gods for themselves, talking to themselves alone and legislating stuffs which the average human finds either unrealistic or anti-realistic hence, holding knowledge captive. In their isolated city, they dream of one universal ideal exported from their cultural particular for all of humanity setting aside the facts that as much as this ideal might be appealing, it neglects the fact that individual identities have stronger appeal and that the diversity that comes with differentiation is a lot more beautiful. Santos even argues that this diversity should be valorised.[6] The gods of this city, call them philosophizens not only despise this diversity but wryly look down at the world and regard its cultures as somewhat unenlightened. But despite this pride of place which philosophizens on top of mount Olympus think they occupy, something has happened in these intervening centuries. The philosophizens have become increasingly isolated in their own *romcom* edgy world, arguing and then much later babbling amongst themselves. No one seems to care anymore about the next big idea from Western philosophers. A romantic comedy has become a tragedy. Indeed, who has Western philosophy helped nowadays?

There was a time, and that time was not so distant in the past, when Western philosophy positioned itself as the standard by which other philosophical traditions must measure themselves. That time is no more. Beginning with the later part of the twentieth century, other philosophical traditions started to waft great energy and by the turn of the millennium years, a new consciousness was found among other philosophical traditions to unhook themselves from the hold of Western philosophy and move on. Now, they think more of finding new conversations with sister traditions from the south as per Chinese and Indian or African, African and Chinese or Indian, etc., than in continuing the endless courting of an aging bride.

---

[6] See B. S. Santos. (2016a).

This new consciousness was stimulated by the feeling that the self-styled gods on top of mount Olympus who needed to be persuaded to come down, if ever they needed to be persuaded at all, have been persuaded enough. They would be left alone from now on. Philosophical reason is therefore leaving the West and making its way into the various cultures in the south. Hedged up on the mountain top, within the bulwarks erected by Plato and Aristotle, there is no more room for the next big idea to emerge. It is all a regurgitation now. Research funds have dried up for the Western philosopher and are increasing for philosophers in the south. There are new and exciting conversations going on in the south while the Western philosopher is out in the cold obsessed with logos. Philosophical reason is thriving in the south where it is unveiling new concepts, ideas and opening new vistas for thought whereas the voice of reason echoes now, only in the distant mirage of past glories, from Plato to Aristotle and from Descartes to Kant.

In the midst of this tragedy of knowledge, the need for villagisation of knowledge has never been as timely as it is now. By villagisation of knowledge I do not mean building new epistemic structures, no, these structures are already there in many cultures; by villagisation of knowledge I mean the recognition of these structures and accommodation of their canons. This recognition is about contexualistion of reason, the endorsement of the particular and the authentication of its principles. This recognition is sought from outside, it is sought from within the geography of epistemologies of the south and it is a recognition that reality is an arena of unities rather than what is popularly misconstrued by the mountain-top philosophers as a growing pillar of unity whose foundation rests on the ideas of Plato and Aristotle. This is an important component of the postmodern posturing in epistemology and it is on this ground that I advocate the disbanding of the philosophical city in which *philosophizens* maintain exclusion from those they othered (on the basis of superior-inferior dichotomy) and the reconstitution of, this time, not a philosophical village (the Greco-European thought as an absolute instance) but philosophical villages where philosophers of varied persuasions in their different villages emerge as *ichie*[7] and hold conversations with philosophy and non-philosophy, and philosophers as well as non-philosophers alike. This is also in keeping with the duty of philosophy as a second order discipline to adjudicate and pass judgements on the results of other disciplines.

The need for villagisation of knowledge is in agreement with Santos' campaign and promotion of what he calls epistemologies of the south.[8] These are those epistemic perspectives from other cultures which the global north looks at as not focused on any knowledge that is relevant, "...because they are concerned with things, ways of knowing, that very often do not count as knowledge. They are viewed as superstitions, opinions, subjectivities, common sense. They are not rigorous, they are not monumental and therefore they are discounted" (Santos 2016b: 20). Santos goes on to indicate that the basic idea on which epistemologies of the south rests is that of

---

[7] Igbo word for chief(s) skilled in ways of conversational engagement, adjudication and value prescription.
[8] See B S Santos. (2016a, b, 2018).

abyssal line. This is an imaginary divisive and discriminatory line created by thinkers in the global north to polarise the world between them and the rest or this side and the other side. Thus as Santos put it, for some five centuries, "[A]ll our theories have been based and developed on the experiences from this side of the line. Our universalisms have been based on the realities of this side of the line; the other side of the line has remained invisible" (2016b: 20). They have remained invisible not because they cannot be seen, but because the actors on the European side have refused to see them. So we can see that Santos uses the concept of epistemologies of the south to draw attention to a carefully orchestrated scheme by global north global south to isolate, exclude and discriminate against knowledge perspectives from the global south. This amounts to a systemic silencing of the voices from the south. But as I have explained earlier, epistemologies of the south have now reached a new consciousness since the millennial that informs new waves of conversations amongst them which might lead to the eventual isolation of the epistemology of the north.

It is my view that this isolation and possible re-othering of the global north can be averted if thinkers in the global north breaks down Plato's and Aristotle's bulwarks of essentialism and reaches out to re-engage with their counterparts in the global south. It should be averted because, whilst it might degrade epistemology from the global north and make thinkers on that side of the line dissidents to the new dominant order in the global south, re-othering sustains Santos' abyssal line. The victory by those on the global south would then be trivial and pyrrhic since they would become the new devils they fought in the twentieth century.

5.6 Conclusion

A host of African philosophers, including those that are self-styled are yet to have a firm grasp of issues bordering on scope, methodology and content of African philosophy. Unfortunately, the field of African philosophy became a hunting ground for all kinds of people from the 1970s. Some of these phony characters were actors from outside the African philosophy culture area and those from within who failed tremendously to make a mark in the tradition of their primary training. The staggering, sick son of nobody called African philosophy provided ground for these uninvited mercenaries to invade the African intellectual space. These African philosophy mercenaries did not stop at making some really bad claims, some of them have courageously gone on to legislate for Africans—and I am here referring to some really bad legislations—how to do African philosophy, its history and what have you.[9]

---

[9] See Placide Tempels (1959) on the structure of being in Bantu philosophy; Anke Graness (2016) on where to begin in writing the history of African philosophy. There are exceptions of course; some non-Africans have produced remarkable works in African philosophy and studies. Our displeasure is about those who, guided and perhaps, funded by Eurocentric institutions seek to control minds and misrepresent African intellectual history to appear residual to the West.

Writing about the cultures and history of the so-called primitive peoples has always been a cheap path to fame for many Westerners in the past. Who would have known Placide Tempels or Claude Sumner or Robin Horton, and the list could really be very long if you choose to go into the areas of African history, cultures and archaeology, if not for the works they published about Africa. Agonisingly, most of these works by these mercenaries can fairly range between complete nonsense or falsehood or misrepresentation to really very shaky and questionable presentations, indeed, not one of these works is not embroiled in fatiguing controversies.

My concern in this chapter has been to address some issues about scope and method that might throw sands into the eyes of a new reader of African philosophy and logic in order to make a case for what I call villagisation of knowledge. No one can properly follow the trend in African studies without first being clear on the scope of discourse and its methods. This was why Odera Oruka warned and insisted that being versed in Africa's intellectual history and cultures was a prerequisite to doing African philosophy, something some African philosophy mercenaries ignore these days. In the same vein, understanding the structure of African logic is the prerequisite for doing African studies as a whole. In the next three chapters, I will unfold Ezumezu, a prototype African logic, as philosophy of logic, as methodology and as formal system respectively.

References

Abraham, William. 1962. *The mind of Africa*. Chicago: University of Chicago.
Agada, Ada. 2015. The future question in African philosophy. In *Atuolu omalu: Some unanswered questions in contemporary African philosophy*, ed. Jonathan Chimakonam, 241–267. Lanham: University Press of America.
Asouzu, I. Innocent. 2004. *The method and principles of complementary reflection in and beyond African philosophy*. Calabar: University of Calabar Press.
Bodunrin, Peter. 1984. The question of African philosophy. In *African philosophy: An introduction.*, 3rd edn., ed. Richard Wright, 1–23. Lanham: University Press of America.
Chimakonam, O. Jonathan. 2015. Preface. In *Atuolu omalu: Some unanswered questions in contemporary African philosophy*, ed. Jonathan O. Chimakonam, xi–xv. Lanham: University Press of America.
Etuk, Udo. 2002. The possibility of African logic. In *The third way in African philosophy*, ed. Olusegun Oladipo, 98-116. Ibadan: Hope Publications.
Eze, Emmanuel Chukwudi. 1995. The color of reason: The idea of 'race' in Kant's anthropology. In *Anthropology and the German enlightenment: Perspectives on humanity*, ed. Katherine M. Faull. Lewisburg: Bucknell University Press.
Feyerabend, Paul. 1975. Against Method: Outline of an Anarchist Theory of Knowledge. London: Verso Books.
Graness, Anke. 2016. Writing the history of philosophy in Africa: Where to begin. *Journal of African Cultural Studies* 28 (2): 132–146. https://doi.org/10.1080/13696815.2015.1053799.
Harding, Sandra. 1997. Is modern science an ethnoscience? Rethinking epistemological assumptions. In *Postcolonial African philosophy: A critical reader*, ed. Emmanuel C. Eze, 45–70. Cambridge, MA: Blackwell Publishers.
Hegel, W. F. Georg. 1975. *Lectures on the Philosophy of World History*. Trans. H. B. Nisbet. Cambridge: Cambridge University Press.

Hountondji, Paulin. 1996. *African philosophy: myth and reality*. 2nd rev. edn. Bloomington: University Press.

Iroegbu, Pantaleon. 1995. *Metaphysics: The kpim of philosophy*. Owerri: International Universities Press.

Jahn, Janheinz. 1961. *Muntu: An outline of neo-African culture*. New York: Grove Press.

Janz, Bruce. 2009. *Philosophy in an African place*. Lanham: Lexington Books.

Metz, Thaddeus. 2014. Just the beginning for ubuntu: Reply to Matolino and Kwindingwi. *South African Journal of Philosophy* 33: 1 65–1 72.

Metz, Thaddeus, and J.B.R. Gaie. 2010. The African ethic of ubuntu/botho: Implications for research on morality. *Journal of Moral Education* 39: 3 273–3 290.

Okolo, Chukwudum. 1990. *Problems of African philosophy*. Enugu: Cecta Nigeria Press.

Okolo, B. Chukwudum. 1993. *What is African philosophy? A short introduction*. Enugu: Cecta.

Oruka, Odera. 1975. The fundamental principles in the question of African philosophy. *Second Order* 4 (1): 44–65.

Outlaw, Lucius. 1987/2003. African philosophy: Deconstructive and reconstructive challenges. In *The African philosophy reader*, ed. P.H. Coetzee and A.P.J. Roux, 2nd ed., 162–191. London: Routledge.

Popper, Karl. 2003. *The open society and its enemies, vol 1: The spell of Plato*. London: Routledge.

Santos, Boaventura de Sousa. 2016a. *Epistemologies of the south: Justice against epistemicide*. New York: Routledge.

———. 2016b. Epistemologies of the south and the future. *European South* 1: 17–29.

———. 2018. *The end of the cognitive empire: The coming of age of epistemologies of the south*. Durham: Duke University Press.

Serequeberhan, Tsenay. 1991. African philosophy: The point in question. In *African philosophy: The essential reading*, ed. Tsenay Serequeberhan, 3–28. New York: Paragon House.

Tempels, Placid. 1959. *Bantu philosophy*. Paris: Presence Africaine.

Van Hook, Jay M. 2002. The universalist thesis revisited: What direction for African philosophy in the new millennium? In *Thought and practice in African philosophy*, ed. G. Presbey, D. Smith, P. Abuya, and O. Nyarwath, 87–93. Nairobi: Konrad Adenauer Stiftung.

Verran, Helen. 2001. *Science and an African logic*. Chicago: University of Chicago Press.

Wilson, Amos. 1993. *The falsification of Afrikan consciousness: Eurocentric history, psychiatry and the politics of white supremacy*. New York: Afrikan World InfoSystems.

Wiredu, Kwasi. 1991. On defining African philosophy. In African philosophy: The essential readings, ed. Tsenay Serequeberhan, 87–110. New York: Paragon House.

Wright, Richard. 1984. Investigating African philosophy. In *African philosophy: An introduction*, ed. Richard Wright, 3rd ed., 41–55. Lanham: University Press of America.

Part II
Unveiling Ezumezu as a System of African Logic

Chapter 6
Ezumezu as Philosophy of Logic

Abstract In this chapter, I aim to discuss the philosophy of African logic from the perspective of Ezumezu (an African) logic. In the first section, I will present some principles of African logic and show how they justify system of African logic. The interesting thing to note here is that these principles, in addition to being articulated from the African background ontology and world-view, will be universalised. I contend that this is where African philosophical assessment of African logic ought to begin because most critics of the idea of African logic agitate that an African system of logic, if it is ever possible will necessarily lack the tincture of universal applicability. I will narrow my inquiry down to the appraisal of African logic with an example of Ezumezu system. I will discuss some emergent issues in the scope and nature of African logic. This point is especially critical because it purveys a demonstration of a prototype system of an African logic. I will conclude by throwing further light on the merits, nature and promises of an African logic tradition.

6.1 Introduction

In this chapter, I aim to discuss the philosophy of African logic from the perspective of Ezumezu (an African) logic. In the first section, I will present some principles of African logic and show how they justify system of African logic. The interesting thing to note here is that these principles, in addition to being articulated from the African background ontology and world-view, will be universalised. I believe that this is where African philosophical assessment of African logic ought to begin because most critics of the idea of African logic agitate that an African system of logic, if it is ever possible will necessarily lack the tincture of universal applicability. But the principles I shall present will prove otherwise. Afterwards, I will narrow my inquiry down to the appraisal of African logic with an example of Ezumezu system. I will discuss some emergent issues in the scope and nature of African logic. This point is especially critical because it purveys a demonstration of a prototype system of an African logic. I will conclude by throwing further light on the merits, nature and promises of an African logic tradition.

Here, I want to show that logic is central to how African philosophers interpret the world and relate to reality within it as against the position of those who think otherwise. And I want to unveil that prototype African logic. Concerning the latter, I will do a presentation of philosophy of African logic from the perspective of Ezumezu system.

Possibly, one challenge which a scholar trained in Western philosophy and logic will encounter in reading this book will be a struggle to make logical sense of my discussions within the Western logical schema. This is because, such a scholar will be constrained by the paradigm of Western philosophy and logic he is familiar with. But the truth is that if my presentation here can be realised straight-forwardly within the paradigm of Western philosophy and logic, then it would not really qualify as a discourse in African philosophy of logic. To be worth its name therefore, my discussions here have to generate a few controversies and perhaps stagger anyone encountering the African thought system for the first time when such a person assesses it with the tool of Western logic. I describe the Aristotelian tradition of logic as Western without meaning to say that it does not apply in other places including Africa. Let me begin with some elementary conceptualisations.

The synonym for the word logic in Igbo (an African language) is *nghọ* which means dynamic or flexible reasoning. *ịtụ nghọ* therefore becomes an expression for "to do a dynamic or flexible reasoning" or simply to do logic. Thus Ezumezu logic is that type of logic that is dynamic or flexible which is why it is an alternative system. It is called African because it is developed in Africa and is largely inspired by African ontology and world-view. It might be instructive to note that African ontology is that ontology which holds that reality could be viewed or interpreted from three perspectives namely; the physical, the non-physical and the combination of the two. Returning to my focus, being dynamic makes reference to the laws guiding thought, to the character of the third value described as *ezumezu* where the two polar values (truth and falsity) complement, as well as to the character of context-dependence which refers to the idea of evaluating each proposition within specific contexts; and the often noticed shifts in modes which has to do with the evaluation of propositions either in the mode of complementary unity (the intermediate third value called ezumezu) or that of specific contexts (the polar values called truth and falsity respectively). We may for this obvious difference state that while Ezumezu logic is dynamic, Western logic is strict in their applications of the laws of thought and in their modes of reasoning.

Ezumezu is an Igbo word meaning 'the collective, the aggregate or the totality of all that is most viable, most potent and most powerful'. Nwafor Orizu explains it as the "aggregate of all…" (Orizu 1994: 14). This is however a mystical word in Igbo eschatology. My conceptualisation of the word to explain the third and intermediate value in the system of African logic was to demonstrate the power of the complementary point of the two standard values. I felt that this point needed some emphasis hence; I derived the name of the logical system from the same concept, only this time written with uppercase letter 'E'. Ezumezu then becomes a prototype African logic.

However, the talk about African logic must not be construed as an intellectual pastime or given skewed political interpretation. It must be addressed squarely as a research paradigm and the interests and insights it raises must be taken seriously. My goal in this chapter is to attempt an understanding of the philosophy of African logic from the perspective of Ezumezu system. To do this, we must first describe the structure of a logic system and then try to fit in Ezumezu into the structure created. J. M. Bochenski (1965: 8–10) has done a simple but wonderful classification of logic. He builds a tree at the root of which is formal logic consisting of the application of the laws of logic in reasoning; and then methodology, which is the study of methods or different applications of the same laws of logic. A method then, for him, would be "the manner of proceeding in any particular field; that is, of organising activity and of coordinating its objectives". Then at the top is philosophy of logic which is a kind of metaphilosophical inquiry about scope and nature of logic, i.e. the nature of its laws and the issues that arise from their applications. The question is: does African logic reflect this structure? Can this be demonstrated with Ezumezu which is a prototype African logic?

To the first question, we take the answer yes for granted because the second question somewhat insures it. So, it is the task of showing that Ezumezu reflects this structure that I must undertake however briefly. Ezumezu as I shall show later relaxes the traditional laws of thought in order to accommodate three other supplementary laws namely njikoka, nmekoka and onona-etiti. The application of these laws in analysing propositions and argument structures captures the formal landscape of African logic which will be the focus of Chap. 8. Also, it is the different applications of these supplementary laws that yield the two inferential methods in Ezumezu system namely, arumaristics and ohakaristics, the study of which is methodology. Discussions on these methods will be done in the next chapter. The philosophy of African logic from the foregoing would consist of the philosophical appraisal of African logic, its laws and the applications of those laws. I will offer a conception of African logic, explaining and clarifying its main assumptions before I narrow my inquiry down to the African philosophy explication and appraisal of Ezumezu logic. This will be my concern in this chapter.

6.2 Towards a Conception of African Logic

To give a conception of African logic, I will like to begin with the basics such as thought system. Thought system is the metaphysical characterisation of that worldview which describes the reasoning trend in a given culture. As the structure of thought system vary from culture to culture, so do the structure of logic borne out of them. The Western logic was systematised out of the native thought system of the West by Aristotle, following that illustrious example; African logic is an attempt to do the same for the African people. The question what is African logic therefore would definitely attract a slightly different answer from the question what is Western or Indian or Chinese logic? Although, under the same umbrella, they all qualify, as Dale Jacquette (2006) defined generically, the systematic study of the principles of correct reasoning. The difference marker among the relative systems of logic would then lie on what constitutes the gauge for correctness from one system to the other and this depends above all else on the contextual applications or relaxation of the rules of reasoning.

African logic therefore is a tradition in logic which is a function partly of principles of reasoning adapted to the African background ontology and world-view. Further, it is that tradition in logic in which the distinction between correct and incorrect reasoning is sanctioned by rules that were adapted from the African thought system. This tradition has a number of characters that make it a tradition of logic in its own right. For example, we talk of contextual analysis and interdependence of variables and values, the idea of relevance and the various laws and principles including the supplementary laws of thought. All these put together constitute the principles which determine correct reasoning in an African logical system. However, as this logic could also hold in many a different culture, it is the African cultural determination of its systematisation that distinguishes it from other traditions of logic.

The history of thought in Africa is witnessing a debate between two schools in the last few decades: the one called the universalists and the other called the relativists. While the former deny the possibility of African logic, the latter affirm this possibility. Some of the actors in this debate include Leopold Senghor, Meinrad Hebga, Lucien Levy-Bruhl, Robin Horton, Kwasi Wiredu, C. S. Momoh, Gordon Hunning, Joseph Omoregbe, Udo Etuk, Chris Ijiomah, Uduma Oji, Helen Verran, J. O. Chimakonam, Ademola K. Fayemi, Edwin Etieyibo, to mention just a few. A detailed account of each person's contribution has been given in Chap. 4.

Here, I shall narrow my focus on Ezumezu logic as a prototype of African logic. Ezumezu logic thus would be that system whose principles of correct reasoning are derived from the African thought system. It obeys the laws of Nmekọka, Njikọka and Ọnọna-etiti all of the time in addition to those of traditional thought such as contradiction, identity and excluded-middle which it obeys some of the times. Ezumezu logic also gives credence to inferences of relevance and beyond the formal consequence relation emphasises the place of subject matter of an argument. In other words, Ezumezu as a prototype of African logic studies values, meanings and understanding of logical language. Nothing is treated without content. It is both an art and science which studies the logical relationship among realities expressed in terms of propositions and symbols. Ezumezu therefore is a logical framework that can be used to explain and analyse experiences in African world-view. I will provide further clarifications of this conception in Chap. 10 below.

6.3 Some Notations and Principles of Ezumezu System

System building and the type called *logica docens* requires the articulation of certain conventions and the formulation of syntactical rules to guide reasoning in a formal sense. Any theory is a system of rules guiding the structure and structuring of phenomena within a specialised field. A theory of logic therefore, would be a system of the systems of rules guiding interpretation of phenomena in different fields. In this connection, I have attempted to formulate some of the basic principles that shall undergird my system of Ezumezu logic (Chimakonam 2012, 2013, 2014a, b) and I shall formulate a few additional ones in this chapter. In this section, I will show how I relaxed the traditional laws of thought and was thus able to formulate additional three laws to supplement them. As a result, instead of three, Ezumezu operates on six laws of thought. In loosening the laws of excluded middle and contradiction on the one hand and identity on the other as we shall see later, I mitigated the characters of absolute difference and absolute identity thereby shaded determinism from bivalence and transformed the latter into trivalence. Like in every progressive system, these principles shall not be sacrosanct. But unlike the Western system, these principles shall not be too strict. One would like to hear the terms "dynamic", "fluid", "flexible" whenever anyone wishes to describe the system, its effect or any new development in it. These are the very attributes of the word *nghọ*, an Igbo-African word we adopted for logic. Some of the defining structures of Ezumezu logic are as follows:

6.3.1 Trivalence

To formulate a genuine African logic, it was necessary that I first obtain the accurate mappings of African system of thought. I traced the various stages of development of metaphysics in what I call the theory of ontological quadrant (Chimakonam 2012). This theory holds that the structure of metaphysics developed across four stages of human thinking leading to the emergence of logic. The first stage is worldview where metaphysics is dormant and inactive comprising of superstitions and religious concerns. The second stage is the cosmology/ontology where metaphysics becomes active offering critical explanations to phenomena. Questions like what is being? Is being physical, non-physical or both? began to demand answers. The second question specifically sets the stage for the emergence of two and three pronged valuations. The third stage which is the emergence of thought system represents the purest development of metaphysics. At this stage, common beliefs as we have in the world-view stage are separated from basic beliefs. The latter are such beliefs with rational explanations. It is here that the diversities in cultures manifest with regards to how a given people look at reality. On the one hand, people who reason that being is either physical or non-physical automatically reveal their indigenous thought system to be two-valued or bivalent. On the other hand, people who reason that being can be either physical or non-physical or both reveal their thought system to be three-valued or trivalent, and so on.

The type of logic mechanised in any tradition eventually is a confirmation of the structure of thought system that inheres in that culture. So, the fourth stage is where metaphysics births logic. This is why I regard thought system as a transitional stage.

Fig. 6.1 Diagram of trivalent thought structure. (Source: Chimakonam 2015a)

Fig. 6.2 Diagram of integrative sub-contrary valuations. (Sourrce: Chimakonam 2015a)

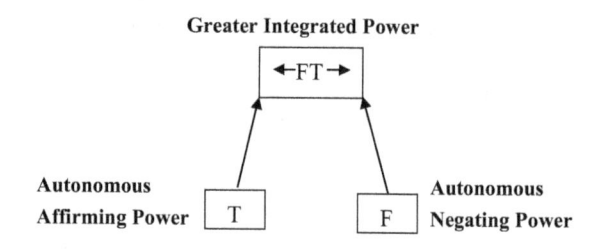

It is by this study that we were able to map African thought system as three-valued, hence trivalent.[1] See Fig. 6.1.

The diagram of trivalence shown above consists of three values namely; truth (ezu), falsity (izu) and ezumezu with small letter 'e' (complemented). A system of logic is trivalent if it has three-values. This is opposed to bivalence in which a system of logic boasts of two-values namely; truth and falsity. The difference between the two structures is further demonstrated by the diagrams in the rest of the principles below.

6.3.2 Sub-contrary Valuations

That two standard values in the diagram above can complement each other without in the words of Bochenski (1965: 79) "contradiction in the simplest way" demonstrates the viability of the third value in Ezumezu logic. This led me into thinking that the two standard values in logic must in African thought be treated as sub-contraries and not contradictories. As Hebga (1958: 223) carefully explains; in African thought the principle of contradiction "does not keep two diametrically opposed systems from being true at the same time, their fundamental presuppositions being different". These presuppositions point at the sub-contrary valuations of the two standard values. In the square of opposition, when two variables are said to be sub-contraries, it means if one holds, the other might still hold hence two seemingly opposed variables can both hold. See Fig. 6.2.

The diagram above demonstrates the thought structure in African ontology where the intermediate is possible.

---

[1] See Animalu, O.E. Alexander and Jonathan O. Chimakonam. (2012) for a detailed discussion of this structure.

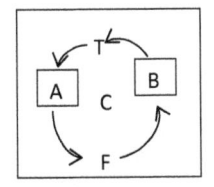

Fig. 6.3 The complementary mode, where A and B represent logical sub-contraries, T and F represent truth and falsity and C represents the Complemented value. (Source: Chimakonam 2015a)

6.3.3 The Modes

Granted that the two standard values in African thought system are sub-contraries thus capable of complementing each other in the third value called ezumezu; it does not annihilate the inherent two values of Western logic. It only means that inferences switch from one platform to the other. So we break the modes into two to account for this namely: (i) the contextual and (ii) the complementary modes of thought. Standing on their own, the two sub-contrary values, called ezu and izu or true and false are treated as peripheries to the centre. Where cmi^1 is an acronym for Complementary Mode of Interpretation, cmi^2 would be an acronym for Contextual Mode of Interpretation; the difference lies in the superscripted indicators ^{1} and ^{2} respectively. At such a platform, each of the two standard values is in a contextual mode interpreting variables on contextual basis. But joined together through the conjunctive motion in the intermediary third value, the product called ezumezu is said to be in a complementary mode treating variables no longer at a contextual but at a complementary level until complementation breaks down and variables return to the contextual modes through disjunctive motion. See Fig. 6.3.

One other thing that these modes teach us is the dynamism of African logic. Specific contexts represent autonomous identities or the peripheries of reality in an African logical schema while inferences that go beyond the specific contexts point to the centre of reality.

6.3.4 Context Principle

Whatever that is stated, is a statement about something and that which is stated to be meaningful, must be stated within a context. Variables shed their meanings and acquire new ones from context to context. There are two sub-contrary contexts which have in-between them an intermediary context. This third intermediary context is a mode at which the sub-contrary contexts complement. Because African logic is three-valued which admits of the intermediary third option i.e. truth-value glut, to assert that a variable strictly holds or that it strictly does not hold (Western logic undertone of African logic) it would be imperative to reduce each given inference to a context. This entails working with live variables or at least asserting them as though they were out there, objective and verifiable. It is only at such a context that one can assert that an object is or is not…when objects are employed in terms

Fig. 6.4 Sub-contraries move to contextual modes. (Source: Chimakonam 2015a)

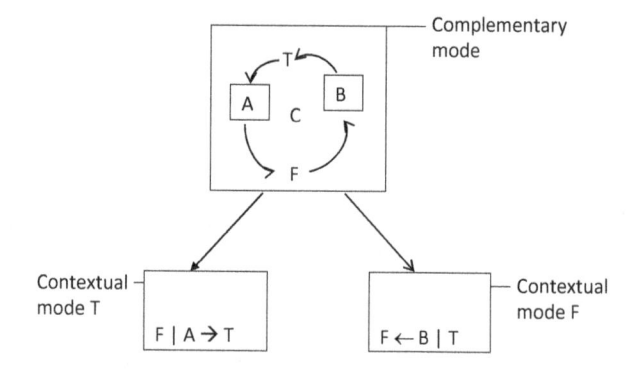

of their opposed assemblages, the inference switches to complementary mode. At such a mode, one cannot assert that objects "are or are not" but "both and" or "both not." See Fig. 6.4.

Context principle therefore helps in determining the relevance of subject matter to the inference and mode in African logic.

6.3.5 The Three Supplementary Laws of Thought

From the foregoing discussions, one would readily agree that the three old laws of thought do not hold absolutely in the mapped out thought system. There are bound to be some limitations in the application of identity, contradiction and excluded-middle. Things are not always as they seem; there is no strict polarity between one thing and its opposite; and there is always the intermediary position. To augment them, I promulgated additional three laws namely Njikoka, Nmekoka and Onona-etiti which may be referred to as the three supplementary laws of thought.

Njikoka states: (T) A $\updownarrow$ (T) A $|$ → (T) (A ∧ B) which reads A is true iff A is true wedge-implies A and B is true.

Nmekoka states: (T| ⊃ F) = C which reads, C is or equals a complement of T and F. Here, I introduce the new notation '|⊃' to stand for the idea of 'complementation.' This means C is the third value called ezumezu or nwa-izugbe consisting of ezu and izu. C is a complete or whole variable that consists of the complementing variables T and F. The variables ezu and izu when in the contextual mode are either true or false but C cannot be so evaluated, it is simply complemented meaning at the very minimum that the values of the ezu and izu are both present.

Onona-etiti states: (T) A ∧ (T) ~ A or (T) A ∧ (F) A which reads A is both true and false (both and). This law accounts for the intermediary values (not altogether true and not altogether false) and includes what was excluded by the old law of excluded middle. Thus, Ezumezu logic boasts of six laws of thought in all.

6.3.6 The Wedged-Implication (Conditional)

The notation wedged-implication "|→" does not replace material implication "⊃" neither was it intended to accomplish this. It was invented to strengthen material implication. So, when the sign is employed, it carries the original meaning of material implication and more. Let me also add that when the intention is strictly "⊃" the additional meaning which "|→ "carries does not interfere or cause any form of disruption. Hence, since "⊃" cannot completely stand for "|→" without a loss of some meanings and "|→" can stand for "⊃" without import of unintended meanings, it becomes merely convenient to always employ "|→" in Ezumezu system. So the adoption of "|→" in Ezumezu logic does not mean the rejection of "⊃". This particular clarification is especially important to address the erroneous reading of my works by some who consequently accused me of banishing material implication and the inferential rules containing it from African logic.[2] My position is, if I must make it explicit, that material implication when not strengthened does not fully account for the inferences in African thought not that it does not do so at all.

The wedge-implication "|→" therefore introduces "context-analysis" in-between an antecedent and its consequent. Variables imply others directly at a complementary level but at a contextual level, it is imperative that they do so through relevant contexts. The context principle is used to determine the relevance of each subject-matter to the inference and mode.

On the whole, I have also discussed in my previous works the characteristics of African logic, added more rules to the inference and replacements rules, developed the syntactic and semantic languages of this logic, invented additional notations and symbols and in my recent publications, have begun taken it to quantificational level.[3]

6.4 On Principles of Consent

There are additional principles I wish to formulate or strengthen in this work. In studying different modern applications of reasoning, I observed that some people sometimes find a justification for their inference outside the inference itself ignoring what has come to be thought of as "necessary connection" factor among propositions in a syllogism. There is a sense to which this form of reasoning guards against autological orientation and or self-referential tendencies. The place of these principles is obviously significant to the semantic component of African logic. The following are to be called principles of consent in Ezumezu logic because of the vital roles they play in the system. They ease-up the weight of determinism and neutralise the deadlock imposed by the law of contradiction, so Ezumezu logical system necessarily *consents* to their application even though *abinitio* they may appear to

---

[2] See Uduma (2015: 99).
[3] See Chimakonam (2013).

have no connection with the system. They are also meta-theoretic which opens them up to more semantic evaluations than syntactic analysis. These principles of consent are as follows:

6.4.1 Permissibility Principle

This principle helps to indicate which context a logician's inference is tied to since context is vital in African logical inferences. The earliest formulation of this principle occurred in the papers of the present author. It is abbreviated as "perm" and can be stated as: a given variable p wedge-implies another q if, and only if it does so through a relevant context. This is employed with the aid of the wedged–arrow " | → " and the three universal contexts [M, A, N] or their corresponding particular ones [m, a, n].[4] So in essence, the permissibility principle also serves as a context indicator principle. This is why implication in Ezumezu logic is not merely material but wedged hence the wedged-arrow is called wedged-implication. The idea behind the concept of "Wedged" is to indicate that the implication process is not direct but mediatory.

6.4.2 Ohakarasi Principle

This principle was formerly tagged *dispositionality* principle in my previous writings. The word disposition meaning inclination was originally chosen to depict a general spirit but has been found a little cumbrous to that service. To that effect I fall back to the Igbo word "Ohakarasi" as a suitable replacement in this work. Ohakarasi literally means "the public says what counts" but figuratively means "authority lies with the generality" or at the centre from where the influence reaches down to its constituents or the peripheries. On the basis of this new conceptualisation, *Ohakarasi* is a meta-theoretic principle of Ezumezu logic which states 'that the truth of the centre accounts for the truths of its peripheries, all things being equal'. In other words the truth of the universal determines the truth of the particulars.

This principle can be contrasted with the principle of *Arumaruka* which states that "the truth of the peripheries account for the truth of the centre, all things being equal." This is also similar to the compositionality principle in Western logic which states "that the meaning of a complex expression, such as a compound statement, is a function solely of the meaning of its constituent parts" (Cook 2009: 54). These two seemingly opposing principles of *Ohakarasi* and Compositionality tell a story of two different thought systems namely; African, which is largely communitarian and Western, which is largely individualistic.

---

[4]The acronyms stand for the worlds of matter, anti-matter and non-matter in African cosmology but while 'MAN' represents the abstract universals of these worlds, 'man' represents the particulars/definite entities in these worlds. See J. O. Chimakonam. 2012, pp. 29–32.

A classical statement of both and *Arumaruka* is the one attributed to John Mbiti from East Africa in his *African Religions and Philosophy* which captures the very essence of the two principles in the African thought system. It says "I am because we are and since we are therefore I am" (1969: 108). In the Southern Africa, there is a train of thought called ubuntu whose statement "a person is a person through other persons" (Eze 2010: 11) also captures the frame of Ohakarasi principle. In Africa generally, it is more common to reason from collective to individual and less common to reason from individual to community because the community as some have argued is supreme and subsumes the individual even though it does not necessarily consume it (Menkiti 1984; Iroegbu 1995; Ikuenobe 2006; Molefe 2017).

One thing that must also be noted is the status of the object of reasoning. The variables of this reasoning process are not abstract accretions, notations or numbers; these are mere prognostics pointing towards the humanist factors. Variables are treated as beings in much the same way as population is treated ontologically as a question of people not mathematically as a question of number. Numbers and notations are therefore signs for concrete ontological beings. For this reason, concrete is more important than abstract, in much the same way as the group is more important than the individual in it or the centre more important than the peripheries. Thus while subsuming the individual; the group does not consume it. The reverse to individual-community dynamics appears to be the case in Western thought system characterised by the libertarian ethos. There, the group gains only when the individual gives up his power to it. In African communitarian set up, the reverse is the case; the group is in possession of power, the individual gains power and existence by associating with the group. In set theory, this can be demonstrated as follows:

If A be a set and b, c, d its elements then b, c, d iff A

Opposed to the libertarian ethos is the communitarian ethos which characterises the African thought system. The individual in African communitarian system, especially the radical version propagated by the menkitians can be likened to a bee, the colony is everything. If a bee wanders from its colony, it ceases to produce, it loses its name and it ceases to exist. Outside it, it is simply nothing. This is why in African thought system, the group is more important than the individual. African philosophers like Pantaleon Iroegbu, Udobata Onunwa, Ifeanyi Menkiti and Emmanuel Edeh emphasise this point in various ways. It is not a numeric classification, it is an ontological arrangement. Logically, therefore, this explains why the principle of Ohakarasi stipulates that the truth of the whole accounts for the truths of the parts, all things being equal.

6.4.3 Unification Principle

There have been so many speculations on the imperativeness of this principle in African thought. Udobata Onunwa, C. S. Momoh, K. C. Anyanwu and E. A. Ruch and some other writers in African philosophy have attempted to describe a context where opposed variables meet. Udo Etuk (1999) and Godfrey Ozumba (2010) gave it a humanistic interpretation; Innocent Asouzu (2004) gave it a metaphysical interpretation; the present author gave it a methodological interpretation; Chris Ijiomah (2014) also came close to describing it although with a cumbrous name "harmonious monism". In a different paper (2013) the present author describes it with the name unification context or context of nzụkọ. That no longer represents the author's full conviction hence, in this work, the present-author wishes to rename it "unification principle". Others who demonstrated this principle in logical discourse like Ijiomah above, came short of any theoretic and metatheroetic formulation of this principle as a useful tool in African logic. This is the task the present author wishes to undertake here.

I define the unification principle as a class functional relation say ị that holds between two functions ọ and ụ such that the proof of one becomes the proof of the other, or for all inputs e:

$$\dot{i}(e) \leftrightarrow \underset{.}{o}(\underset{.}{u}(e))$$

That is to say ọ and ụ are elements of the set of opposed variables ị within which, R ọ ụ is symmetrical. The ọ-ary $ọ^1$, $ọ^2$, ..., $ọ^n$ are elements of ị just as ụ-ary $ụ^1$, $ụ^2$, ..., $ụ^n$, while ị is a class function of mode cmi^1. This makes it possible for ọ and ụ functions though opposed at mode cmi^2 to be "possibly" symmetrical at mode cmi^1.

6.4.4 Thesis of Regimented Ontology

This thesis which derives from the Igbo maxim 'uwa ezu oke' literally means that 'nothing is complete or comprehensive.' As a principle of consent it states: "there is no grand norm in knowledge". This implies that there is no metanarrative or theory that accounts for the ontological structure of everything or that says or explains it all. In other words, the thesis opposes the existence of a discourse with absolutistic flavour. There is no absolute truth; there can be no absolute standards of inquiry. No comprehensive criterion of thought. All discourses are relative resulting from disparate cultures though may be universally applicable. Ontology is on the whole regimented! Being is micro. Being might be studied in relation to others but on its own, it is regimented, everything is therefore, relative. Being or reality might exist in a network or in a chain of many links or as elements in the whole from which the particulars can be understood but there is always a missing link (Asouzu 2007) or a necessary link' that missing link is an individual, a unit, a point and it is relative. Without the whole, we might not understand the particulars, but it is the particular when finally understood that enriches our knowledge of being as a whole. This thesis is thus opposed to any absolutistic conception of reality or knowledge. Logically, we can formulate this thesis as follows:

$$(Kw)_h (T_h \rightarrow_{MAN} \sim G_h) [\text{where Kw is a universal quantifier}]$$

In all metanarratives h, if h is a theory T_h then h is in no world a grand norm $\sim G_h$.

One of the things I have been able to demonstrate in the above is that African logic represents a tradition in logic. The principles I have formulated project Ezumezu as a prototype logic system from Africa. In contrast to the Western system which is bivalent, I have presented the African system as trivalent. And when placed side by side, these two systems betray a tension. This tension will be the focus of the next two sections.

6.5 The Philosophy of Ezumezu Logic

There are so far three systems that have been formulated in African logic tradition namely; Complementary Logic developed by Innocent Asouzu (2004, 2013); Harmonious Monism worked out by Chris Ijiomah (2006, 2014); and Ezumezu logic formulated by the present author. The earlier attempt by Helen Verran (2001) was replete with errors that one cannot truly say it was an African system. It was a caricature of African thought system from a Western logical lens. Interestingly, the three actors whose systems can be described as African are members of the Calabar School of Philosophy—a bourgeoning philosophical movement founded at the University of Calabar, Nigeria. It is not surprising that this is the case because the University of Calabar is now leading African philosophy research globally at least, since the first decade of the millennium years. My focus here, in analysing the African philosophy of logic will be on Ezumezu system. The other two systems are well beyond the scope of this book but a brief discussion on them has been done in Chap. 4 and will again be highlighted in Chap. 8.

There should be a strong connection between African philosophy and African logic and indeed, there is. As a matter of fact, we cannot truly undertake the project of reconstruction in African philosophy without beginning from the methodological premise. A worshipper for example would not claim to be Mohammedan if his order of worship was Christian, even if he worships inside a mosque. I conceive African philosophy elementarily as a deconstructive and reconstructive discourse that is conversational[5] from the background of African thought system or methodological purview aimed at formulating transgenerational problematics and finding solutions, opening new vistas, creating new concepts and sustaining the conversation (Chimakonam 2017a, b).

African philosophy generally focuses on the African experience of reality. How Africans structure reality says a lot about the logic of their world-view. The structure of this logic has been identified in literature as three-valued. But there are a number of issues that arise in the project of African logic. I will discuss a few of them as space will permit under two broad sub-headings below.

---

[5] Conversational philosophy is a new school of thought in African philosophy that sees the tool of conversational thinking as the most viable approach to doing African philosophy. See Chimakonam, J. O. (2015a, b, 2018); Chimakonam and Nweke, V. C. A. (2018), Nweke, V. C. A (2015).

6.5.1 The Issue of the Third Value, Scope of the Laws

The intermediate value in Ezumezu logic is of the nature of both/and in which two standard values truth and falsity converge but only tentatively. Many people have interpreted the third value differently according to the variant of three-valued logic they propagate. The Polish logician Jan Lukasiewicz (1920) offered both an epistemic and a realist reading of the third value which is somewhat cumbrous. He of course, denotes it as undetermined read as neither true nor false (truth-value gap). Stephen Kleene (1952) according to Jacquette (2000), was more consistent offering a strict epistemic reading of undetermined neither true nor false (truth-vale gap). The question that is generated then is: how does one justify the both/and structure in Ezumezu logic?

In Ezumezu logic where two standard values are treated as sub-contraries rather than contradictories as in Lukasiewicz and Kleene, the complementary mode where they converge becomes a truth glut. This is because the complementary mode (ezumezu) is a distinct value in itself where the other two standard values ezu and izu converge and complement. But this convergence does not lead to a synthesis where the two values lose their identities, it is a tentative mode which disintegrates by means of a conversational mechanism called creative struggle to re-instate each truth value in their different contextual modes. The interpretation of the third value is the "complement" or "complemented" and is read roughly as 'it is known that it could be both true and false.' It is strictly true or false when ezumezu is disintegrated into ezu and izu during a contextual inference. One might question the realist status of ezumezu which would be both true and false. Strict semantic evaluations in African thought are read contextually similar to situation semantics where statements of formal systems are interpreted as true or false relative to situations (Cook 2009). In contextual semantics, that which is true; is true only in a context, it could be false in another. This is a realist rather than an epistemic reading of the three-valued thought model. Under this reading, the Ezumezu truth table definition of the wedge-conditional " $|\rightarrow$ " would be T, C = T; C, F = C; and C, C = C where C replaces U in Lukasiewicz and Kleene and is used to denote complement or "complemented". Notice our notation " $|\rightarrow$ " invented to strengthen the conditional "⊃". See Fig. 6.5.

From the diagram above, one could see that the values T and F are insufficient in themselves in that one affirms but does not negate; while the other negates but does not affirm. It is in the complemented value C that they both achieve sufficiency

Fig. 6.5 Diagram of complementary thought. (Source: Chimakonam 2015a)

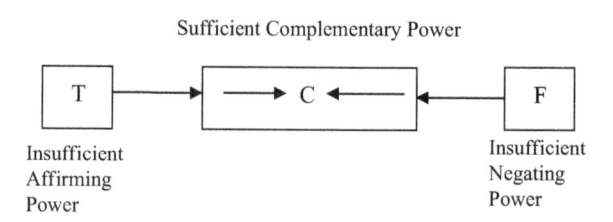

6.5 The Philosophy of Ezumezu Logic

according to the law of nmekoka. The affirming power of T becomes complemented by the negating power of F as shown above.

Another point I must mention in this connection is the scope of these so-called laws (or broadly, principles) of logic. Are the numbers of these principles specific? Well, I would not want to think about it in this numerically strict way even though we have the traditional laws of thought said to be three in number but the principles of thought are not really exhausted in those three laws of thought. Many are rules, principles and even axioms that guide human thought. The reason why I would not subscribe to a numerical strictness is because, in logic, there is no Sanhedrin. Almost anybody can add to the existing corpus so long as the new laws or rules or principles are properly formulated. But even though there is no Sanhedrin, logicians of different generations have acted as if the principles of logic were sanctioned by a fail-safe Sanhedrin. Some even speak as if they were/are members of this supreme legislative body. Take the example of Immanuel Kant (1991: 8) who in the preface to the second edition of his *Critique of Pure Reason* declares (quite in error) that formal logic thus far "has been unable to advance a step, and thus to all appearance has reached its completion". I had commented elsewhere that soon after this importunate declaration, the mathematically-minded logicians like George Boole, Charles Pierce, Giuseppe Peano, John Venn, Gottfried Leibniz, etc., began making exponential contributions to the subject of logic remarkable among which eventually was the complete formulation of a symbolic language by Gottlob Frege (1967) in his *Bergriffsschrift* of 1879. Now, Aristotelian logic is somewhat regarded as old-fashioned or an earlier version of the doctrine of modern logic sometimes, flamboyantly referred to as quantificational or symbolic or predicate logic. In a realistic sense, everyone is capable of thinking logically and illogically so, logic is for everyone. Trained logicians may however feel more obligated to study, monitor and report the accurate/inaccurate formulation of these principles but that is where it actually ends really. Anybody that has followed the historicity of logic long and well enough can formulate additional principles where he deems such necessary. But just as he is at liberty to formulate them, no logician is obligated to accept them the way they have been formulated. But all logicians are obligated to study them, criticise and report their accuracy or inaccuracy. A good example is the Frege-Russell exchanges on what has come to be known as 'Russell paradox' which Bertrand Russell discovered and on that basis faulted certain conclusions in the work of Gottlob Frege.[6] In this case, Russell found reasons not to accept Frege's logical formulation even though the other had the right to formulate them. Russell also had the right to criticise and establish the inaccuracy in Frege which he exercised.

In making these formulations, one perhaps, unstated rule of the thumb is to keep in mind, that such principles will be universally applicable. A set of logical principles that applies only in one culture area draws an incorrect line between humans with reference to their pattern of thought. It is admissible that humans may think and react differently to the same circumstance but the basic physical structure of thought in our world almost always remains the same. For example, when one

---

[6] See the exchange of letters between Russell and Frege in Jean van Heijenoort, ed., (1967).

throws up an object, it will surely fall down in any part of the world. Similarly, people all over the world look left and right before crossing a motor way. But then again, we must not gloss over the fact that some principles may apply in one culture more than they do in another culture. This is due to preferences in approach which different cultures adopt. Also, in discussing say the traditional laws of thought (by far the most basic of all the principles of logic), it may be possible to strengthen or weaken their basic formulations in order to map out approaches to thought favoured by different cultures. As soon as this is done, a new logic system is born.

But it is regarded almost as a scandal by some logicians that the basic formulations of the three laws of thought could be tampered with. Arguments of the likes of Uduma Oji Uduma (2015) and Fayemi (2010) against what they call African logic have been weaved to suggest this scandal. These scholars like many others we cannot discuss here treat the traditional laws of thought as the untouchables of philosophy. One wonders why this old-fashioned intellectual stubbornness, even when some scholars like Georg Hegel, Karl Marx and Friedrich Engels (Korner 1967) have raised credible objections to the inviolability of the traditional laws of thought. My intention here however, is not to 'target the bad guys' but to provide an African philosophy assessment of Ezumezu logic.

6.5.2 Between Logical Bivalence and Trivalence: Unveiling the Essential Tension

The emergence of the *Évoléus*[7] in the colonial Africa is not the only essential challenge confronting Ezumezu as a system of a three-valued system of logic. While logical determinism is a sterling problem for the system of Western logic which is two-valued (bivalent), the one most vicious obstacle on the path of any system of three-valued logic is what I shall call the 'glut paradox'. For the system of two-valued logic, it is the 'gap paradox'. I shall explain all these terms momentarily. The thesis of determinism can be formulated as saying 'every statement is either necessary or impossible' this connects with the thesis of bivalence which states that 'every statement is either true or false'. Determinism is said to constitute a serious problem for bivalence in that it presents the two values as predetermined. If something holds, it was because it was already determined to hold. It could not have been otherwise. Questions therefore naturally arise as to the value of attaching the values in the first place? Logic would be helpless and logicians themselves would be surplus to requirement among the world's intellectuals.

In a milieu governed by fate, what is the use of logic? In wrecking this havoc, determinism leads to the 'gap paradox' which can be captured in the following: (1). every statement is either true or false, (2). the future contingent statements are neither

---

[7] Or the *deracinés* are those Africans who in their quest to ape the ways of the colonialists have lost touch with their native African cultures, and are yet not Europeans. So they are stuck in-between in cultural limbo.

6.5 The Philosophy of Ezumezu Logic

true nor false, (3). Thus if statement 1 is true then it is false at the same time. All the attempts at a veritable African system beginning with three-valued logic are efforts aimed at resolving this paradox. A three-valued system aims at transcending the gap paradox by creating truth-value-glut in which statements could be true, false and possibly both. This throws up a quick promise of resolving the gap paradox but at a great cost. Exactly how could one explain the possibility of a statement being both true and false at the same time is what I now call the 'glut paradox'. For any system of three-valued thought model to break through this wall, a proper resolution of the glut paradox is imperative. The brilliant systems built by Lukasiewiscz as well as that of Kleene, etc., bowed before this paradox. It is unlikely that one can make any head way in constructing an African system without first toppling this paradox.

Ezumezu accomplishes this through what can be called the 'analogy of Nkita eke-uke'. Eke-uke is a popular market somewhere in eastern Nigeria notorious for a special kind of merchandise. The merchandise is a species of dog that is oddly too playful with strangers including thieves and annoyingly mischievous, stealing meat from the soup pot, eating chicken eggs and even the chicks, etc. When one's dog develops into this form of habit, it is immediately marked to be sold at eke-uke market. Nkita being the Igbo name for dog implies that any dog of this mold is quickly dismissed as Nkita eke-uke—bad breed. Traders come from far and wide to this day to sell and buy Nkita eke-uke. One other remarkable thing about these dogs and I should say about all dogs is that if it breaks away from its cage, it will return home no matter how far the market is from its original home.

Now, supposing that one has travelled tens of miles to sell her dog at eke-uke market and soon after she left the market, the dog, let us call it Nkita eke-uke broke away from the cage where the buyer had restrained it and escaped into the nearby bush. There is one possibility: (1). Nkita eke-uke will surely return to its original home alive. But supposing also that the bush stretching tens of miles is paraded by dog hunters who hunt and kill wild dogs, there is again a second possibility: (2). Nkita eke-uke will be hunted down and killed by these vicious hunters. In this context, these two possibilities are equally probable. In other words, there is 50/50 chance for either to hold. So 1 and 2 above can both be true but cannot both be false. Hence, in Ezumezu, we describe two seemingly opposed variables as logical subcontraries rather than contradictories as is the case in the two-valued and the Lukaseiwicz's three-valued systems.

The analogy of Nkita eke-uke above clearly resolves the glut paradox but throws up another problem I shall call the 'non-bivalence case'. This problem shows how so easily we are prepared to throw away the baby alongside the bathwater. The analogy of Nkita eke-uke establishes trivalence and undermines bivalence. Every statement could be true, false and both. We know however that besides the telling problem of determinism, bivalence is as real as the palm tree in Okonkwo's farm. We still look both ways to cross the road because it is either us or the car. Both certainly cannot cross at the same time without a contradiction.

The essence of trivalence mode of thought as far as African logic is concerned is not to replace bivalence but to extend it into trivalence forestalling the weaknesses of bivalence and molding an alternative thought model. To this end, the elimination of bivalence by the analogy of Nkita eke-uke which generates conspicuously the 'non-bivalence case' requires another resolution. For this, I propose again a second analogy to be called the 'analogy of onye-nso' or the analogy of the dog tracker. Let us capture it briefly. Supposing at the moment Nkita eke-uke ran into the bush, a by-standing bushman experienced in tracking wild dogs followed it such that he keeps pace with Nkita eke-uke in the bush at a relative distance. There are two conditions but only one possibility at a time which can be expressed in the following bivalence: either Nkita eke-uke reaches its original home or it gets hunted down and killed by the vicious dog hunters. The analogy of onye-nso clearly explains that the experienced bushman tracking Nkita eke-uke can only observe one of these at a time not both. Thus, by inserting the tracker, trivalence is reduced once again to bivalence. That this is possible in the first place shows that both are closely connected. Hence, what can be called the 'bivalence-trivalence continuum thesis' (meaning the possibility of bivalence transiting to trivalence and vice versa), in Ezumezu logic. It is in the unveiling and resolution of this tension that the foundation of Ezumezu three-valued thought model as a logic tradition in Africa is firmly rooted.

In this same way also, the Lukaseiwicz's three-valued logic[8] could be viewed as logic in Polish tradition. Similarly, Paraconsistent logic is a variant of many-valued logic first formulated by Argentinian logician F. G. Asenjo in 1966 (Priest 2002) but popularised by the Australian logician Graham Priest. The name was first coined in 1976, by the brilliant Peruvian philosopher Francisco Miró Quesada (Priest 2002). There have been many proponents in paraconsistent logic in the recent times including Alan Ross Anderson (USA), Diderik Batens (Belgium), Nuel Belnap (USA), Jean-Yves Béziau (France/Switzerland), Ross Brady (Australia), Bryson Brown (Canada) to name just a few. Even though, paraconsistent logic has become cosmopolitan in the recent years we might still term it logic in the Latin American and Australian traditions following the roots of its initial developments.

Also, the three or many-valued logic of the Indian, Jaina and Buddhist traditions formulated by the likes of Gautama, S. R. Saha, S.C. Vidyabhusana, T. Stcherbasky, T.K. Sarkar, B. K. Matilal, etc., (Mohanty et al. 2009) as well as the Chinese logic which could be three or many valued formulated by the Pre-Qin and Mohist thinkers but promoted and further developed by the likes of Tan, Hu, Chen, Graham, Harbsmeiser and in the recent time Chris Fraser (2003, 2011) of the University of Hong Kong. The logic tradition in Africa is therefore a variant of three-valued logic. Udo Etuk (2002) in keeping with Senghor suggested the name Affective logic,[9] Asouzu calls his own complementary logic, Ijiomah calls his project Harmonious

---

[8] See Łukasiewicz J., 1920, "O logice trójwartościowej" (in Polish). Ruch filozoficzny 5:170–171. English translation: "On three-valued logic", in L. Borkowski (ed.), (1970). Selected works by Jan Łukasiewicz, North–Holland, Amsterdam, pp. 87–88. In this initial work Lukasiewicz formulated and defined his theory as three-valued, although much later it has been generalized for all n-valued systems.

[9] It must be noted that Etuk was heavily influenced to this choice of concept by Leopold Sedar Senghor who had described African thought as some sort of emotive rationality.

Monism (2014),[10] and I call the system I am developing Ezumezu logic (2014b).[11] Before four of us, the likes of Meinrad Hebga, Leopold Senghor, C. S. Momoh and Gordon Hunnings have all worked on the vine yard of African logic on a proposal level. I took it upon myself to transcend the level of proposal which has characterised discourse on African logic and began formulating its principles.[12]

6.6 Conclusion

In the sections of this chapter, I have appraised African logic such that instead of philosophy of logic, one can describe the endeavour as African philosophy of African logic. I want to conclude by arguing that a well-formulated logic tradition is the ultimate foundation upon which a philosophy tradition nay African philosophy can be erected. It is the tool of logic positioned as a background framework that makes a discourse philosophy and as such it is the tool of African logic tradition serving in the capacity of background framework that makes a discourse African philosophy or that drives its methodology. But one may ask: what then makes a discourse logic and what makes a logic African? A discourse is logic if it provides principles that serve as yardsticks for intelligible communications and draws a line between correct and incorrect reasoning in accordance with those principles. Then, a logic is in a given tradition if it provides for a set of principles that either expands or contracts such yardsticks for intelligibility and correctness of reasoning. In the case of logic tradition in Africa, like in most other traditions, the principles that serve as yardsticks for reasoning are slightly expanded and relaxed as I have done in this chapter.

In the convention of logic, the two-valued logic is basic as it is difficult to formulate a single-valued logic where everything is viewed from one perspective.[13] But three-valued, many-valued, n-valued logics, etc., can, and have been formulated. These formulations represent logic in various traditions. So, it is safe to say that logic in the traditions provide for a set of principles that expand the criteria for intel-

---

[10] Ijiomah's derivative, harmonious monism is in tune with the intermediate value where the two standard values achieve a functional bonding.

[11] See J. O. Chimakonam. "Ezumezu: A Variant of Three-valued Logic" (2014b). Earlier than this I had used this concept in other unpublished works. The first articulation of this theory began in 2008 and was first given in a conference lecture "Outline of African Logic for the Development of Thought, Science and Technology in Africa" (2011a).

[12] Most of the principles which now underscore my theory of African logic can be found in my previous works ibid (2011a); "Project on African Logic, From Thought System to Algorithmic Model: Impact on Science, Technology and Human Development" (2011b); *Introducing African Science: Systematic and Philosophical Approach* (2012); Alexander Animalu and Jonathan O. Chimakonam (2012).

[13] The likes of Ron Hubbard in his Scientology 0–1 describes single-valued logic as neither A nor ~A; but for Brad Hicks it simply states that "everything is x". Some have also viewed single-valued logic as other-worldly. Like in Christianity, heaven is a place where there is absolute goodness.

ligibility and correct reasoning. The three, four, five, multi, n-values, etc., in logic therefore speak of the various expansions of the principles which serve as yardsticks for correct and incorrect reasoning from the base of two-valued logic.

References

Animalu, O.E. Alexander, and Jonathan O. Chimakonam. 2012. 4x4 magic square representation of complementary duality of African three-valued thought logic. *African Journal of Physics* 5: 141–168.

Asouzu, I. Innocent. 2004. *The method and principles of complementary reflection in and beyond African philosophy*. Calabar: University of Calabar Press.

———. 2007. *Ibuaru: The heavy burden of philosophy beyond African philosophy*. Zurich: Lit Verlag GmbH and Co. Kg Wien.

Asouzu, Innocent. 2013. *Ibuanyidanda (complementary reflection) and some basic philosophical problems in Africa today: Sense experience, "ihe mkpuchi anya" and the supermaxim*. Zurich: Lit Verlag GmbH and Co. Kg Wien.

Bochenski, M. Jozef. 1965. *The methods of contemporary thought*. Dordrecht-Holland: Reidel Publishing.

Chimakonam, O. Jonathan. 2011a. *Outline of African logic for the development of thought, science and technology in Africa*. Paper Presented at the Sixth annual international conference on research and innovation for sustainable development: Prospects and challenges in the third world. University of Port Harcourt, Nigeria, October 25–28, 2011.

———. 2011b. *Project on African logic, from thought system to algorithmic model: Impact on science, technology and human development*. Paper Presented at the second international conference and home coming. University of Nigeria, Nsukka, November 30–December 3, 2011.

———. 2012. *Introducing African science: Systematic and philosophical approach*. Bloomington: Authorhouse.

———. 2013. Quantification in African logic. *Filosofia Theoretica: Journal of African Philosophy, Culture and Religion* 2 (2): 409–422.

———. 2014a. Ezumezu (African) logic as an algorithm for scientific research in Africa. In *Philosophy, science and human development: International conference papers 2011*, ed. C.N. Ogbozo and C.I. Asogwa, 58–77. Enugu: Snaap Press.

———. 2014b. *Ezumezu: A variant of three-valued logic*. Paper presented at the Philosophical Society of the Southern Africa PSSA. Free State University, Bloemfontein, South Africa, January 20–22.

———. 2015a. The criteria question in African philosophy: Escape from the horns of jingoism and Afrocentrism. In *Atuolu omalu: Some unanswered questions in contemporary African philosophy*, ed. Jonathan O. Chimakonam, 101–123. Lanham: University Press of America.

———. 2015b. Transforming the African philosophical place through conversations: An inquiry into the Global Expansion of Thought (GET). *South African Journal of Philosophy* 34 (4): 462–479.

———. 2017a. Conversationalism as an emerging method of thinking in and beyond African philosophy. *Acta Academica* 47 (2): 11–33.

———. 2017b. What is conversational philosophy? A prescription of a new doctrine and method of philosophy, in and beyond African philosophy. *Phronimon* 18: 114–130.

———. 2018. The 'demise' of philosophical universalism and the rise of conversational thinking in contemporary African philosophy. In *Method, substance, and the future of African philosophy*, ed. Edwin Etieyibo, 135–159. Cham: Palgrave Macmillan.

Cook, Roy. 2009. *A dictionary of philosophical logic*. Edinburgh: Edinburgh University Press.

Etuk, Udo. 1999. *The new humanism*. Uyo: Afahide Publishing.

References

———. 2002. The possibility of African logic. In *The third way in African philosophy*, ed. Olusegun Oladipo, 98–116. Ibadan: Hope Publications.
Eze, O. Michael. 2010. *Intellectual history in contemporary South Africa*. New York: Palgrave and Macmillan.
Fayemi, K. Ademola. 2010. Logic in Yoruba proverbs. *Itupale: Online Journal of African Studies* 2: 1–14.
Fraser, Chris. 2003. Introduction: *Later mohist logic, ethics and science* after twenty-five years. In *Later Mohist logic, ethics and science*, ed. Graham, xvii–xxxiv. Hong Kong: Chinese University of Hong Kong Press.
———. 2011. Knowledge and error in early Chinese thought. *Dao: A Journal of Comparative Philosophy* 10: 127–148.
Frege, Gottlob. 1879/1967. Begriffsschrift, a formular language, modelled upon that of arithmetic, for pure thought. In *From Frege to Godel: A source book in mathematical logic*, (1879–1931), ed. Jean van Heijenoort, 1–82. Cambridge: Harvard University Press.
Hebga, Meinrad. 1958. Logic in Africa. *Philosophy Today* 11 (4): 221–229.
Ijiomah, Chris. 2006. An excavation of a logic in African world-view. *African Journal of Religion, Culture and Society* 1:1 29–35.
———. 2014. *Harmonious monism: A philosophical logic of explanation for ontological issues in supernaturalism in African thought*. Calabar: Jochrisam Publishers.
Ikuenobe, Polycarp. 2006. The idea of personhood in Chinua Achebe's things *fall apart*. *Philosophia Africana* 9 (2): 117–131.
Iroegbu, Pantaleon. 1995. *Metaphysics: The kpim of philosophy*. Owerri: International Universities Press.
Jacquette, Dale. 2000. An internal determinacy metatheorem for Lukasiewicz's Aussagenkalkuls. *Bulletin of the Section of Logic* 29 (3): 115–124.
———. (ed.). 2006. Introduction. In *A companion to philosophical logic*. Malden: Blackwell publishing.
Kant, Immanuel. 1934/1991. *Critique of Pure Reason*. Trans. J.M.D. Mieklejohn. London: Everyman's Library.
Kleene, Stephen Cole. 1952. *Introduction to metamathematics*. Amsterdam: North Holland.
Korner, Stephen. 1967. Laws of thought. In *Encyclopedia of philosophy*, ed. Paul Edwards, vol. iv. New York: Macmillan Publishing Company.
Łukasiewicz, Jan. 1920/1970. On three-valued logic. In *Selected works by Jan Łukasiewicz*, ed. Borkowski, L., 87–88. Amsterdam: North–Holland.
Mbiti, John. 1969. *African religions and philosophy*. London: Heinemann.
Menkiti, Ifeanyi. 1984. Person and community in African traditional thought. In *African philosophy: An introduction*, ed. Richard Wright, 3rd ed., 41–55. Lanham: University Press of America.
Mohanty, J.N., S.A. Saha, A. Chatterjee, T.K. Sarker, and S. Bhattacharyya. 2009. Indian logic. In *The development of modern logic*, ed. Leila Haaparanta, 903–961. Oxford: Oxford University Press.
Molefe, Motsamai. 2017. Critical comments on Afro-communitarianism: The community versus individual. *Filosofia Theoretica: Journal of African Philosophy, Culture and Religions* 6 (1): 1–22.
Nweke, C.A. Victor. 2015. David Oyedola and the imperative to disambiguate the term "African philosopher": A conversation from the standpoint of the Conversational School of Philosophy (CSP). *Filosofia Theoretica: Journal of African Philosophy, Culture and Religions* 4 (2): 94–99.
Orizu, Nwafor. 1994. *Liberty or chains, Africa must be: An autobiography*. Enugu: Horizontal Publishers.
Ozumba, O. Godfrey. 2010. *Philosophy and method of integrative humanism*. Calabar: Jochrisam Publishers.
Priest, Graham. 2002. Paraconsistent logic. In *Handbook of philosophical logic*, ed. D. Gabbay and F. Guenthner, vol. 6, 2nd ed., 287–393. Amsterdam: Kluwer Academic Publishers.

———. 2015. The logic question in African philosophy: Between the horns of irredentism and jingoism. In *Atuolu omalu: Some unanswered questions in contemporary African philosophy*, ed. Jonathan O. Chimakonam, 83–100. Lanham: University Press of America.

Van Heijenoort, Jean. 1967. *From frege to godel: A source book in mathematical logic,* (1879–1931), ed. Jean van Heijenoort. Cambridge: Harvard University Press.

Verran, Helen. 2001. *Science and an African logic*. Chicago: University of Chicago Press.

Chapter 7
Ezumezu as Methodology

Abstract My main aim in this chapter is to lead a charge against the Western methodological hegemony and lay down principles that will demonstrate the independence of African philosophy and intellectual tradition. To do this, I will first identify and discuss three pillars of thought in Ezumezu methodology namely, nwa-nju, nwa-nsa and nwa-izugbe. I will show how they play foundational roles in the construction of the system of Ezumezu logic. Second, I will unveil and discuss the two main methods or modes of inference or reasoning in Ezumezu logic namely, Arumaristic and Ohakaristic. I will further identify the concept of *nmeko* easily translated as our notion of relationship and use it as a twine to bind the three pillars as epistemic agents and employ the latter to bring about a functional release of the two methods. Finally, I will show with the examples of five leading theories in contemporary African philosophy namely, Afro-communitarianism, ubuntu, complementary reflection, consolation philosophy and conversational philosophy, the cenrality of nmeko to the methodology of African philosophy tradition.

7.1 Introduction

In philosophy, method is everything. It is the manifestation of reason, the shape of inherent logic and the guide to reasoning. It is the compass for thought. Plato and Aristotle, two of the biggest names that shaped the methodological leaning of Western philosophy and now threatening to do so for all other philosophical traditions in the universe, including the African philosophical tradition are difficult to challenge. This is because, the success story and reputation of Western philosophy, besides being intimidating are also earned and well-deserved. But behind this success story are two towering, giant shadows of Plato and Aristotle, the former wielding epistemological and metaphysical batons of essentialism and the latter wielding metaphysical and ultimately logical batons of essentialism. Together, these wardens of Hellenistic civilisation shepherded modern Western civilisation and are now casting their shadows to the far reaches of the world. Nowadays, to some, Western philosophy can fairly be described as *the* philosophy and this judgement would be almost infallible except that it is not. There are other philosophical traditions besides the Western model and they must rise to resist the spell of Plato and Aristotle.

I believe that confronting the intellectual and methodological hegemony of these Hellenic wardens is a task every epistemology of the south must seek to surmount before it can truly establish its standing as a distinct philosophical tradition. At the foundation of this Hellenic influence is methodology. Indeed, no tradition of philosophy today can be regarded as truly different from Western tradition if it subscribes to the dichotonomous, essentialist and divisive epistemic and metaphysical visions propelled by the logic of non-contradiction.

My main aim in this chapter is to lead a charge against this hegemony and lay down principles that will demonstrate the independence of African philosophy and intellectual tradition from the Hellenic wardens. To do this, I will first identify and discuss three pillars of thought in Ezumezu methodology namely, nwa-nju, nwa-nsa and nwa-izugbe. I will show how they play foundational roles in the construction of the system of Ezumezu logic. Second, I will unveil and discuss the two main methods or modes of inference or reasoning in Ezumezu logic namely, Arumaristic and Ohakaristic. I will further identify the concept of nmeko easily translated as our notion of relationship and use it as a twine to bring the three pillars into live epistemic agents and employ the latter to bring about a functional release of the two methods. Finally, I will show with the examples of five leading theories in contemporary African philosophy namely, Afro-communitarianism, ubuntu, complementary reflection, consolation philosophy and conversational philosophy, the centrality of nmeko to the methodology of African philosophy tradition.

7.2 Unfolding the Three Pillars of Thought in Ezumezu Methodology

I want to identify three main pillars of thought namely nwa-nsa, nwa-nju, and nwa-izugbe in African philosophy and studies, which together could form the triangle of thought in Ezumezu methodology. I conceive nwa-nsa as a peripheral variable or an agent that proposes and protests the criticisms of its proposals; nwa-nju as a peripheral variable or an agent that opposes or contests the proposals of nwa-nsa, and nwa-izugbe as a central variable that represents the complement or conversations of nwa-nsa and nwa-nju. In other words, nwa-izugbe is a product of a creative struggle between the peripheries. These three pillars are at the tips of the triangle and are connected together by a line of relationship that could be called nmeko characterised by contestations, protestations and conversations. This triangle is enclosed in an imaginary existential circle in which nwa-izugbe represents the centre and nwa-nsa and nwa-nju represent the peripheries. Nmeko connects nwa-nsa and nwa-nju otherwise called the peripheries at the base to nwa-izugbe which is at the top of the triangle. Whilst these three can stand as pillars of thought in Ezumezu methodology, it is nmeko that activates them by bringing them together. Nmeko is our notion of relationship but a relationship of a kind. It is a logical relationship that follows two patterns namely, arumaristics and ohakaristics.[1]

Arumaristics is when the peripheries move towards the centre for a logical relationship of inclusion in the complementary mode marshalled by the law of onona-etiti, and ohakaristics is when the centre moves towards the peripheries for the logical relationships of integration and complementation to occur between the peripheries from their contextual modes. In other words, nwa-nsa and nwa-nju are contexts which can come into a logical relationship marshalled by the laws of njikoka and nmekoka. In these modes, nwa-nsa and nwa-nju can engage in logical relationships in which their individual identities come together to strengthen the collective (njikoka) and in which their individual identities are strengthened in the collective (nmekoka).[2]

Nmeko thus brings the three pillars to live by orchestrating two forms of logical relationships amongst them. By the application of the three supplementary laws of thought, nmeko again, transforms the two types of logical relationships into full blown inferential methods in Ezumezu logic.

7.3 The Two Inferential Methods in Ezumezu Logic

Methodology roughly is the study of methods of logical reasoning, where the latter represents different applications of the same laws of thought. In this context, the laws implied are the three supplementary laws of thought which I had formulated in Chap. 6 above. The two methods I generate from the application of the supplementary laws are arumaruka and ohakarasi. These are the noun forms of the adjectives, arumaristics and ohakaristics inferences, in much the same way they talk about deduction and induction as noun forms of deductive and inductive inferences.

Method describes a specific way of applying the laws of logic in research and methodology gives an account of the methodic differences that exist in a field. I would like to think that it is the latter that defines what we normally regard as schools or trends of thought in a given field. It does seem to me therefore that the possibility of creating different methods in a field depends entirely on the elasticity of human imagination in meddling with the traditional laws of thought.

As methods, arumaruka and ohakarasi prescribe how we can reason correctly in Ezumezu logic. The inference from premises to conclusion in Ezumezu logic is either from the peripheries to the centre (arumaruka) or from the centre to the peripheries (ohakarasi). In both, the same laws are applied but differently as already explained in the preceding section concerning the nature of logical relationships.

---

[1] For a discussion of arumaristics and ohakaristics as argument structures in Ezumezu logic, see Chap. 8 below.

[2] See the statement of the three supplementary laws of thought in Chap. 6 above and see the discussion of the laws in Chap. 8 below.

On the one hand, arumaruka as a method of reasoning prescribes how the law of nmekoka brings two seemingly opposed variables into a logical relationship in which the identity of the separate variables can be strengthened in the collective. In this method, the law of onona-etiti comes in to justify this relationship as something in which the truth of the separate variables can account for the truth of the collective, all things being equal.

On the other hand, ohakarasi prescribes how the law of njikoka brings two seemingly opposed variables into a logical relationship in which the identity of the separate variables come together to strengthened the collective. In this method, the law of onona-etiti comes in to justify this relationship as something in which the truth of the collective can account for the truth of the individual variables, all things being equal.

To examine Ezumezu as methodology further, I observe that realities are expressed as variables in African philosophy and studies. But that two variables can complement does not mean that they can lose their identities and merge into one or synthesis as the dialecticians hold. This structure can be observed in various theories and methods in African philosophy.

For example, the method of conversational thinking in African philosophy, demonstrates the encounter or relationship of variables as arumaristic which means that they come together to forge a stronger identity and break up into individual contexts according to necessity. Thus the conversationalists hold that two seemingly opposed variables can be in a disjunctive motion determined by their ontological variance and can revert to a conjunctive motion determined by their ontological equality.[3] These motions represent the continuing reshuffling of sets of nwa-nsa and nwa-nju. A disjunctive motion is slowed down by what can be called 'concessional bridge'—defined as a mechanism for determining when complementation has become necessary and has begun to take place. It is this steep bridge that eventually transforms the disjunctive motion into a conjunctive motion. At the other end, a conjunctive motion begins to bring opposed variables into a relationship at what can be called 'complementary turn'—defined as a mechanism for determining when the point of complementation has been reached—and is transformed into another disjunctive motion by what can be called 'tension of incommensurables'—defined as a mechanism for determining when complementary relationship between nwa-nsa and nwa-nju or the peripheries has reached benoke point and collapsed. Benoke point is a point beyond which complementing variables cannot come any close.

In practical terms, let us imagine that agent X (code-named *nwa-nsa*) develops a theory A that claims to have systematised ubuntu as an ethical framework fit for modern application with a load of new concepts to drive the theory; agent Y (code-named *nwa-nju*) may decide to take agent X to task on the viability and veracity of his theory. He raises questions that will stagger the theory and as a result compels agent Y to continue to fortify his theory, revise it or even abandon it. This process is known as creative struggle or nmeko—a relationship of contestation, protestation

---

[3] Ontological variance refers to existential properties that make two entities different while ontological equality refers to existential properties that make two entities similar.

and conversation. Now this is where one might raise the curious question; is this all about the method of conversational thinking? The answer is No! The turning point occurs at this juncture in that the conversationalists i.e. *nwa-nsa* and *nwa-nju* are not expected to end this struggle, ever! On the one hand, every answer will give birth to new questions and with it new concepts. On the other hand, every question is expected to open new vistas for thought and elevate the discourse to a higher level. Thus the ultimate goal of the conversational method is the sustenance of the conversation and not the final resolution of questions. What this implies is that while methods such as dialogue and polylogue, following from Hegelian type of dialectics, are open to the unity of opposed variables in a synthesis, conversational thinking which rides on the crest of arumaristics regards synthesis as anathema.

Nwa-izugbe is not a synthesis but a phase in the ever unfolding outcomes of creative struggle. It is a product of conjunctive motion which turns into a disjunctive motion at the moment when the peripheral variables reach the benoke point. This is a point in conversational thinking where two complementing variables cannot continue doing so. It is a breaking point motivated by what is called tension of incommensurables—the charging up of those ontological factors that make two variables different.[4] Once the benoke point is reached, the peripheral variables at nwa-izugbe which is the complementary mode disintegrate into a disjunctive motion and relapse into their various contextual modes. The process is without end because of the importance of context in Ezumezu logical evaluation. I will further explore the radical dimension of the methods of thought in Ezumezu by analysing the CdV principle which is the offshoot of the logical thesis.[5]

7.4 Further Justification of the Ezumezu Methodology: The Context-dependence of Value (CdV)

The 'principle of Context-Dependence of Value' (CdV) which states that 'credible value judgements are the ones based on contexts' is formulated to justify the claim of the 'logical thesis' that 'what we call truth may not always be dependent on the collection of facts which a proposition asserts but rather, on the context in which that proposition is asserted.' In Ezumezu methodology, epistemic agents and contexts can be thought of in geometrical terms as points, each capable of independent self-manifestation, meaning that it can be analysed in ways not subject to its interaction with other entities and, complementary self-manifestation, meaning that it can be analysed in ways subject to its interaction with other entities. Think of independent self-manifestation as points without lines connecting them and think of complementary self-manifestation as points connected together by a line or lines. As any distance between two points for example is a line, think of this line as nmeko—our

---

[4] See Chap. 8 for detailed discussion of conversational curve and its appurtenances.

[5] For the discussions on the logical and ontological theses of Ezumezu, see Chap. 8 below.

notion of logical relationship between epistemic agents and contexts represented by such points. CdV then affirms the individual identities of epistemic agents and contexts which are captured in various African philosophy theories and upholds their viability such that we may now be able to, following the complementary mode of the Ezumezu methods, talk about facts relative to contexts and their interrelation rather than stop at the framework of propositions that carry such facts in a non-complementary mode.

Ezumezu as methodological consideration begins from the premise that realities which are sorted in terms of nwa-nsa and nwa-nju, though independent exist in a network of interrelation in which the ideas of difference and equality are inherent[6], and not as isolated units. In this complementary framework, nwa-izugbe, which represents the convergence of nwa-nsa and nwa-nju promotes equal inter-party engagement in a special way, i.e. by levelling the ground and ensuring a totally horizontal relationship. It focuses on the process that leads to the production of new concepts and thoughts rather than on a final outcome and it upholds the critical rigour of philosophy by discouraging terminal answers; and relocates truth value from the facts expressed in propositions to the context of propositions themselves thereby making the notion of truth function in African logic dynamic.

From the preceding, CdV seems to affirm relativity and opposes the universality of truth. The question is; what is my motivation for urging us to switch from an universal analysis of truth captured in theories like correspondence to a relativised option? My motivation is due to the apparent fluctuations inherent in history. What is asserted true at one point in history turns out to become false at some other later historical time when circumstances change or when other facts become available. Take the example of the geocentric and the heliocentric models of the universe as one case. Consider also the case of colonialism thought to be just at some historical time, now, it is considered to be an unjust ideology that decimated, robbed and even underdeveloped a continent like Africa as Walter Rodney and Amos Wilson state.[7] Cases like these abound in our epistemic edifice. Are we supposed to pretend that they have no credibility? No, we should not! This was what motivated the Einstenian physics in modern science.

As much as the idea of truth relativity alarmed the scientific world in Einstein's time, in practice, experiments showed that it is a fact of life. Whether in the sciences or in the humanities, many cases abound in which contexts determined the values of facts. Yet, this does not in any way, vitiate the credibility of objective universal truth. We also know from common sense that objective truth makes a lot of logical sense. Where then does this apparent paradox lead us? One way to look at it would be to think about a middle course, something that removes the straitjacket that appears to characterise both universal and relative truths. The straitjacket is not only a problem

---

[6] This is known as the ontological thesis discussed in detail in Chap. 8.
[7] See Walter Rodney. *How Europe Under-developed Africa*. (2009). This work describes in horrific details the evils of colonialism on Africa; Wilson, Amos. The Falsification of Afrikan Consciousness: Eurocentric History, Psychiatry and the Politics of White Supremacy. (1993). This book exposes the dangers of colonialism, neo-colonialism and cultural imperialism.

for universal truth; it is also a problem for relativism. For example, relativism says that every truth is relative except the truth of its own assertion. That would make the truth of relativism universal at least, and this straitjacket contradicts its basic assertion. So, the problem is, if we remove this straitjacket from universalism, it would lose its meaning; and if we remove it from relativism, it would lose its foundation and collapse. This is a problem in foundationalism as well as in theory of justification broadly conceived. I here admit quite humbly that the methodology of Ezumezu and the handmaid of the logical thesis, i.e. the CdV, may not escape from this problem and I do not have an immediate solution either. But the encouraging thing is that I do not think that the presentment of this problem constitutes adequate grounds to deter me from constructing a pro-relativism methodology as I do in this work. My reasons are as follows: (1) History teaches us that contexts play vital roles in determining the values of facts. (2) Philosophy in our time seems destined to cross borders and if intercultural philosophy is to make any sense at all, we must be charitable to defend a certain strand of epistemic relativism. This definitely would come at a cost but I will prefer to invite other thinkers to dwell on what happens as a consequence rather than shy away from making what I think is a reasonable epistemic commitment.

However, I do believe that my inclination to relativism can profit from a reasonable moderation. Thus I am motivated to anchor my idea of CdV on Kwasi Wiredu's position concerning John Dewey's warranted assertibility embedded in the idea of notions of truth[8]. Wiredu however quarrels with Dewey for failing to highlight the importance of 'point of view' as contrasted from 'notions of truth'. In this regard, Wiredu appears to claim that besides universal truth, there may be another point of view which is a rationally warranted judgement. What this suggests is that the truth or falsity of propositions can be analysed relative to the contexts in which they are stated and such may be judged to be rationally warranted. So, for example, while CdV taken alone, implies that person X's assertion in the eighteenth century that colonialism was justified is true relative to the context in which person X asserts it, this alternative point of view, based on the reading of Wiredu, would imply that although we take seriously the context in which the proposition is asserted, we nevertheless can judge person X's assertion to be false in light of what we now know, i.e., that there are overwhelming context-independent reasons for thinking that colonialism was unjustifiable–notwithstanding the particular context in which its truth was previously asserted. The advantage of this alternative approach is that it is not committed to some objective, mind-independent truth which I have described as a straitjacket but nevertheless it supports the goal of intercultural philosophising which aims at affirming the epistemic credibility of different cultures or philosophical traditions as rationally warrantable judgements. On the basis of the accommodation of another point of view capable of being rationally warranted, progress in philosophy may be imagined as approximating as much as possible these types of judgements through intercultural engagements. This is the main focus of my argument for the relative evaluation of the truth of propositions.

---

[8] See Kwasi Wiredu. *Philosophy and an African Culture*. (1980: 157–158). See foot note 11 also.

One of the direct implications of the principle of CdV is that facts would not be the primary ingredients for determining the values of propositions, contexts would be. And of course, this may upset the notion of truth peddled in the old theories of truth in which there is a primary focus on the relationship between facts and propositions that assert them. I would like to think of this seeming anomaly as a scenario in which context upsets fact. Call it 'factual anomaly' if you will, but it points to a revelation that facts may not always be what they seem to be. Metaphorically, we can say with hesitation that facts *prostitute* themselves from context to context.

Another implication is that in intercultural philosophy, different philosophical traditions represent viable contexts as opposed to the dogma of one universal tradition. So, truth manifests from context to context from which they are able to exercise a form of intercommunication or solidarity. To engage across borders, different philosophical traditions require a tool that is not only accessible to all, but usable as well. It is for this need that I formulate conversational thinking[9] as a method grounded in Ezumezu logic that is not border-biased to guide African philosophy specifically and intercultural inquiries generally.

On the whole, what the CdV really indicates to philosophers from the perspective of the logical thesis is: 'never ask for the value of a proposition except in a specific context'.[10] When extended, this also applies to the truths of philosophy. Here, I take philosophy to be a tradition by tradition activity rather than a towering architectonic structure that imposes one cultural mindview on the rest of other cultures. On their own, when not placed in any contexts, most propositions are value-neutral. For example, consider the proposition: 'you need to drink water to stay alive'. When considered from the Boolean algebraic equation, this proposition will have the value 1. But this may be a little hasty if we take into consideration, as I think we should, such a serious concern as the context of that proposition. For one who is in the middle of the Sahara desert on a hot afternoon, the value of the proposition will be 1; but for one who is drowning in the River Niger, even if on a hot afternoon, that proposition cannot be true, its Boolean value will be 0. A drowning man may not need to drink water to stay alive. What he needs to stay alive is air, water will simply kill him. The preceding water analogy is one of several examples in which context upsets fact. The importance of context in Ezumezu methodology is further highlighted by our notion of nmeko which will occupy my attention in the next section.

---

[9] See Jonathan O. Chimakonam. 2015a, b, 2017a, b, etc.

[10] In his book, *The foundations of Arithmentic: A logico-mathematical enquiry into the concept of number,* Gottlob Frege was the first to state this criterion when discussing the subject of meaning he admonishes: "never to ask for the meaning of a word in isolation, but only in the context of a proposition" (1960: xxii).

7.5 The Centrality of the Concept of Nmeko for Theorisations in African Philosophy and Studies

Nmeko, an Igbo word that roughly translates to relationship is central to theorisations in African philosophy and studies. It has its taproot in African logic where it marshals different types of logical relationships as earlier discussed. The idea of relationship is something that occupies a prominent place in the works of other African thinkers for example, Chris Ijiomah defines African logic as the science of relationships among realities (2014: 118–126). He provides a highlight of some African philosophers like Kwame Gyekye, Pantaleon Iroegbu, Olusegun Oladipo, Emmanuel Edeh, etc., who have made the concept of relationship central in their discourses. Also, Thaddeus Metz[11] has in the last decade been exploring various ways in which the concept of relationship plays pivotal roles in African philosophy and studies. Themes such as human rights, dignity and the broad areas of Afro-communitarianism and ubuntu ethics have featured in his analysis. He is nowadays noted for his coinage, "capacity for relationship or communion" on which his theory of relational ethics is based. With this concept of relationship tapped from African world-view, Metz is able to go beyond the bar set by Immanuel Kant's Categorical Imperative to formulate a plausible ethical theory inspired by sub-Saharan world-views.

However, with the exception of Ijiomah, no other African thinker to the best of my knowledge has been able to connect the concept of relationship to African logic. Here, I will also go beyond Ijiomah who merely gave this concept presence in African logic to properly locate it as the livewire of the system of African logic and by extension, theories in African philosophy and studies.

I will begin with a claim that states that no properly formulated system or methodology in African philosophy and studies will be worth its name and function accordingly without nmeko occupying a central role. To show why this is the case, I will articulate what can be called three axioms of Nmeko presently. These axioms, among others show how nmeko is a central hub in any system that is called African.

1. The Axiom of Truth

No variable, no matter how viable is without a context.

2. The Axiom of Solidarity

Every variable needs to interact with other viable variable(s) to maximise its potentials.

3. The Axiom of Re-generation

When viable variables interact, new variables are produced.

In the above, axiom 1 explains that every variable or proposition or fact has a context no matter how universal it is. Axiom 2 follows from axiom 1 to state the fact

---

[11] See Thaddeus Metz. (2011, 2013, 2015, 2016, 2017), Metz and J. B. Gaie (2010).

that each variable or reality stands a better chance of fulfilling its inherent abilities when it combines with other realities. And finally, axiom 3 establishes the fact that new ideas are created from the creative encounter between old ones. Thus, because of the self-evident nature of these axioms, nmeko becomes a necessity that makes systems in African philosophy and studies viable.

It can even be argued that the primary concern of various theories in African philosophy and studies is to study different ways nmeko connects realities. Other concerns come after this primary concern. For example, if we take nmeko to roughly translate to 'relationship' then the well-known theory of Afro-communitarianism primarily seeks to study the factors in the relationship between the community and the individual in order to determine which is more powerful and influential. In ubuntu, the primary aim would be to study the two types of relationships which moral agents can enter into in a human society namely, mutual interdependence and mutual non-dependence in order to prioritise the former over the latter. For complementary reflection, the primary goal would be to study the actors in a relationship so as to establish that individually they are not self-sufficient and show the necessity for mutual complementarity. In consolation philosophy, the primary aim would be to study how yearning motivates actors to enter into a relationship and why such relationships inevitably transform actors into melancholy beings. Finally, in conversational philosophy, the primary aim would be to study the types, objectives and implications of relationships of creative struggle for actors that enter into them, and how and why such relationships might be sustained.

So, one can see with the few examples above that the notion of nmeko or relationship plays a central role in theorisations in African philosophy. What is true of African philosophy is also true of the sundry areas of African studies. But it is in African logic that this notion finds its root because it is logical relationship that determines metaphysical, ethical and epistemological relationships. The methodology of African logic depends on this notion as has been shown earlier in this chapter.

7.6 Ezumezu and Methodological Anarchy

Because Ezumezu is a liberal theory and libertarianism allows for many cocks to crow, it is possible to think of Ezumezu in light of methodological anarchism. In this way, Ezumezu as methodology could contribute to epistemic disagreements in the postmodern condition. I believe that there is an intuitive element that ensures orderliness in these disagreements, conversational thinking being a rule-guided system. To begin with, conversational thinking which is a method grounded in Ezumezu logic, is anarchistic in that it is not geared towards agreements rather; it is geared towards disagreements, large scale disagreements! Extrapolating this idea shall be my concern in this final section. I will begin with elementary conceptual clarifications.

7.6 Ezumezu and Methodological Anarchy

Here, I conceive anarchy not in terms of lawlessness or disorderliness. I suppose this is a common literal conception of the word. Instead of the noun form of the word, I will employ its adjectival form 'anarchistic' and conceive it technically for our purpose here, as disagreements—large scale disagreements. I equate anarchistic with conversational; and disagreement with 'arumaristic engagement' (the creative process in conversational engagements). Conversational thinking does not broach finality, it constantly seeks the continuation of conversations thus disagreements are courted. Disagreement here employed technically does not refer to quarrels or the fabled old wives chatter, but to an outcome of a systematic and methodic process. This process is conversational thinking characterised by attitudes of protestations from nwa-nsa that proposes new ideas and contestations from nwa-nju that opposes the new ideas.

Thus the word anarchistic would mean for our purpose here, something that tends to disagreements or tending towards large scale disagreements. So, when I say anarchistic, I mean disagreements, and when I say disagreements, I mean arumaristic engagement as a creative conversational process. I now apply this technical term so conceived to another concept 'orderliness' to obtain the twin concept 'anarchistic orderliness'[12] where the latter is synonymous with 'conversational orderliness'. It is the second concept 'orderliness' that mitigates the parent word 'anarchy' and downgrades its meaning from lawlessness to disagreements. In other words, anarchy arises when we realise that, multiple methods can exist, which do not obey the same set of laws, the same way. This lack of uniformity (protestation and contestation) could be described as anarchistic but only insofar as it refers to disagreements where to converse technically means to disagree. That many methods do not uphold the same laws of thought in the same way does not in any way suggest lawlessness. Even though it suggests anarchy, the interpretation is that of disagreement, perhaps large scale disagreements but never truly a form of lawlessness.

This large scale disagreement, it is fair to admit, might portend a form of disorderliness but only insofar as such multiple methods do not agree and disagree consistently. If they do, what then would be the reason for the multiplication of entities? And how can they yield conclusions that could also be contradictory in themselves? Put differently, orderliness, the type I talk about, is possible in this seeming methodological chaos insofar as 'rival methods consistently agree in the areas of their disagreements and consistently disagree in the areas of their agreements'. This will yield an X-model of methodological anarchism which is ordered as against the P-model (where P stands for parallel) which lacks this order.

I want to argue here that admitting the necessity of many methods of thought as Hebga suggests heralds postmodern thinking. Admitting again as Hebga states that these many and different methods might be contradictory in their conclusions

---

[12] I first stumbled on the idea that informed this concept in V. C. Uchendu (1965: 46) who reported that the British viewed the pre-colonial Igbo system of government which did not have powerful central figures as 'ordered anarchy'. Here I employ it to characterise a philosophical scenario in which there is a presentment of order in the absence of (presence of different relative laws) an absolute law.

suggests a form of what has been discussed as postmodern romance with anarchy or lawlessness. But I want to theorise here following the principles of arumaristic complementarity and arumaristic concession—that these methods despite being different and opposed, still portend a form of conversational orderliness. It does not really follow that disagreement portends anarchy of the lawless type. At a commonsense level, it does appear quite convincing that when there is no agreement, law breaks down. This is however not correct if we look at it from another perspective. Disagreement is not necessarily with reference to a common legal parameter; contextually, and in the sense I convey here, disagreement results from conflicting or rival legal parameters. In this scenario, different methods/conversing philosophers disagree (without strictness) in the areas in which they each affirm. This absence of strictness means that these affirmations may or may not be different; but they agree (consistently) in the areas in which they each deny differently. This means that what one denies is necessarily different from what the other denies. Thus the disagreement is not in their disagreeing (as different methods) but in what they may affirm differently; and likewise, their agreement is not in what they deny jointly, but in what they necessarily deny differently. Ezumezu logical order therefore is not founded on geometrical parallel but on geometrical intersection—something I have designated above as the X-model of thought. (See Fig. 7.1 below)

In the above, method 1 and method 2 represent random samples from many possible methods. The existence of these numerous methods sounds the horn of postmodernism. Anti-postmodernists conclude that the cacophony would lack harmony and thus become anarchistic in a literal sense—a hypothesis I do not accept. By the X-model of thought I developed above, I seek to demonstrate that though anarchical in the sense of the existence of many a different (disagreeing) method; the postmodern mindview/methodology could nonetheless be perfectly ordered, such that one could describe the process as ordered anarchy or in the flamboyant concept I have adopted as "anarchistic orderliness".

In the above diagram, A and B are contraries, C and D are sub-contraries, A and C are contradictories just as B and D are contradictories, following the basic definition of the traditional square of opposition. The trick is this; 'A' being a contrary agrees consistently with 'B' another contrary in the areas (C and D) in which they

Method 1   **Method 2**

Agreement   Agreement
   A   B

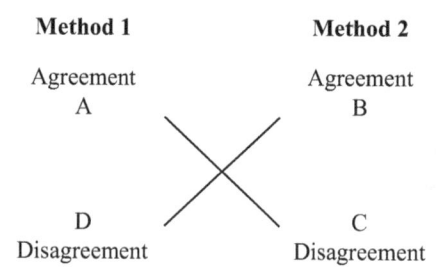

   D   C
Disagreement   Disagreement

Fig 7.1 Diagram of X-Model of thought. (Source: Chimakonam, O. Jonathan. 2018. Ezumezu as a methodological reconstruction in African philosophy. In *Ka-Osi-SQ-Onye: African Philosophy in the Postmodern Era*, ed. Jonathan. O. Chimakonam and Edwin Etieyibo, 125–148. Delaware: Vernon Press)

7.6 Ezumezu and Methodological Anarchy

deny differently. So their contrariety manifests in C and D whereby they both cannot hold—one must hold a different position from the other. Thus, their agreement is not in what they deny jointly, but in what they deny differently. In the same way, 'C' being a sub-contrary disagrees consistently with 'D' another sub-contrary in the areas (A and B) in which they each affirm which may or may not be different. So their sub-contrariety manifests in A and B whereby both might hold. In sum, A and B agree in differently denying C and D; and C and D may or may not disagree in differently affirming A and B.

The contrary and sub-contrary relations in our X-model diagram would become clearer when we consider the contradictory relations between A and C and B and D respectively. In each pair, where one agrees, the other disagrees. Thus on the whole, even though there are many disagreements including on what they disagree on, there is order. This postmodern order is founded not on any empirical law, but on an intuitive law. This intuitive law may be articulated as *egbe-bere, ugo-bere* or the EBUB law for short!

Subjectivity can only be prosecuted at the court of intuition. Subjectivities can only be assessed, questioned and reconciled in intuition. There are no known objective parameters for interpreting subjectivity. So, it appears we cannot imagine a postmodern methodological order since there is no empirical law we can appeal to for this task. Inasmuch as I agree with this, I have reservations concerning the popular assessment of the postmodern condition so far. It is not truly lawless. Yes, there might not be a grand norm to which all postmodern methodologies subscribe as we have in the modern methodology (which is 'rationally warranted, universal, demonstrable protocol'), this only suggests large scale disagreement not out-right anarchy. Even though, it suggests the absence of a grand norm, it does not still prove it. Even though the idea of postmodernism entails the impossibility of a grand norm, it clearly does so with it as a system. But every system whether modern or postmodern requires legitimation and this can only be constructed outside of such a system. Where it is possible to found the legitimation of a modern system on an empirical law, such appears impossible for a postmodern system which internal dynamics negate this. But there is no law that insists that structural legitimation must be founded on empirical laws. It is in this connection that I move here to found the legitimation of postmodernism on an intuitive law namely, EBUB. This law simply states that 'reality is a web in which every variable depends on others as a result of its lack of self-sufficiency'.

EBUB which is an acronym for 'Egbe-bere, ugo-bere' is worded from the Igbo-African language and refers to the authentication of otherness. This authentication occurs at the intuitive level through what can be called 'critical re-othering'. Critical re-othering can be contrasted with 'othering'. Othering for me is that polarising and bifurcating disposition inherent in systems which compels us to draw a discriminating line between what has been flogged as the dichotomy of "self and other," in which the superior-inferior mindset is promoted. The works of Plato and Aristotle laid this foundation in the history of Western thought and have been sustained in the modern time in the works of Descartes and Kant. Deconstructionists have in the contemporary time attacked this mindview. Jacques Derrida to be specific made it a lifetime project. I do not however intend to bug my readers by surveying the leading Western postmodern ideas of Ludwig Wittgenstein, Hans-Georg Gadamer, Richard Rorty, Donald Davidson, Willard Orman Quine, Gilles Deleuze, Michel Foucault, Emmanuel Levinas and Jacques Derrida to name a few. I would want to avoid all that and focus on unravelling my proposal here.

Unlike othering which draws a rigid 'vertical' line across existence, critical re-othering urges us to see the self as a form of otherness and the other as a form of self. This ultimately eliminates the rigid 'vertical' line but re-introduces another type of line—a grid line—that runs through the gamut of existence connecting all into a massive web. In this interconnection and interconnectedness, existence becomes replete with *othernesses* and not a single self would remain manifest. This exercise is a re-othering because it attempts to eliminate the vertical line and connect all existence with a grid line. It is critical because it confronts the self wherever it can be found and exposes its flaws and pretences which will transform it into an otherness subservient to yet another self. The possibility of reducing any self whatsoever, no matter where it manifests into a subservient otherness imposes a burden of humility on all 'selfs' and makes possible the idea of critical re-othering of existence. Articulating the basic principles of critical re-othering would be a concern of another work.

7.7 Conclusion

I have unveiled Ezumezu in this chapter as methodology where I discussed the pillars of thought, the two inferential methods, the concept of nmeko and the Context-dependence of Value. I also drew out the postmodern implication of Ezumezu methodology among other things. It is, therefore, my conclusion that the postmodern mindview/methodology is not without legitimation. EBUB, which is an intuitive law, provides this legitimation. Such that, even in a postmodern condition replete with disagreements, there can be orderliness orchestrated by the intuitive awareness of the insufficiency of every existence; which necessitates mutual interdependence that in turn authenticates the manifestation of every existent.

I have raised a justification for methodological deconstruction of the framework of Plato and Aristotle. I followed this up with an attempt at a methodological reconstruction of the African philosophical place. I planted the beacon of this enterprise on my doctrine of Ezumezu logical model. Finally, I drew the postmodern connection of these efforts from the African philosophy perspective. In this, I equated the methodological resurgence in African philosophy with basic postmodern assumptions. I gestured to the theoretic offshoot of this methodological shift and came up with what I call conversational orderliness, where conversational is taken as a synonym for anarchistic; and where anarchistic refers to multiplicity rather than lawlessness.

Finally, the major fruit of anarchistic orderliness is the EBUB law from which the theses of othering and critical re-othering are forged. I explained that EBUB ensures the authentication of otherness and that this authentication occurs at the intuitive level through what can be called 'critical re-othering'. I contrasted critical re-othering with 'othering'. While the former urges us to see the self as a form of otherness and the other as a form of self which transforms existence into forms of *othernesses,* othering is that polarising disposition inherent in systems which compels us to draw a discriminating line between the "self and other" in which the superior-inferior mindview is promoted. I clarified that this mindview was promoted in the works of Plato and Aristotle in the history of Western thought and have been sustained in the modern time in the works of Descartes and Kant. This amounts to, among others, a serious methodological influence. Something Karl Popper castigates as the spell of Plato, and I dare add, of Aristotle as well. To neutralise this spell through methodological reconstruction in African philosophy was the foremost task undertaken in this work.

References

Chimakonam, O. Jonathan. 2015a. Transforming the African philosophical place through conversations: An inquiry into the Global Expansion of Thought (GET). *South African Journal of Philosophy* 34 (4): 462–479.
———. 2015b. Conversational philosophy as a new school of thought in African philosophy: A conversation with Bruce Janz on the concept of "philosophical space". *Confluence: Journal of World Philosophies* 3: 9–40.
Chimakonam, Jonathan O. 2017a. African philosophy and global epistemic injustice. *Journal of Global Ethics* 13 (2): 120–137.
Chimakonam, O. Jonathan. 2017b. Conversationalism as an emerging method of thinking in and beyond African philosophy. *Acta Academica* 47 (2): 11–33.
Frege, Gottlob. 1960. *The foundations of Arithmentic: A logico-mathematical enquiry into the concept of number.* 2nd Rev. ed. Trans. J. L. Austin. New York: Harper Torchbooks, Gottlob Frege
Ijiomah, Chris. 2014. *Harmonious monism: A philosophical logic of explanation for ontological issues in supernaturalism in African thought.* Calabar: Jochrisam Publishers.
Metz, Thaddeus. 2011. Ubuntu as a moral theory and human rights in South Africa. *African Human Rights Law Journal* 11: 532–559.
———. 2013. The Western ethic of care or an Afro-communitarian ethic? Specifying the right relational morality. *Journal of Global Ethics* 9 (1): 77–92. https://doi.org/10.1080/17449626.2012.756421.
———. 2015. An African egalitarianism: Bringing community to bear on equality. In *The equal society: Essays on equality in theory and practice*, ed. George Hull, 185–208. Lanham: Lexington Books.
———. 2016. An African theory of social justice: Relationship as the ground of rights, resources and recognition. In *Distributive justice debates in political and social thoughts: Perspectives on finding a fair share*, ed. Camilla Boisen and Mathew Murray, 171–190. London: Routledge.
———. 2017. Replacing development: An Afro-communal approach to global justice. *Philosophical Papers* 46 (1): 111–137.
Metz, Thaddeus, and J.B.R. Gaie. 2010. The African ethic of ubuntu/botho: Implications for research on morality. *Journal of Moral Education* 39 (3): 273–290.
Rodney, Walter. 2009. *How Europe under-developed Africa.* Lagos: Panaf.
Uchendu, C. Victor. 1965. *The Igbo of southeast Nigeria.* New York: Holt, Rinehart and Winston.
Wilson, Amos. 1993. *The falsification of Afrikan consciousness: Eurocentric history, psychiatry and the politics of white supremacy.* New York: Afrikan World InfoSystems.
Wiredu, Kwasi. 1980. *Philosophy and an African culture.* Cambridge: Cambridge University Press.

Chapter 8
Ezumezu as a Formal System

Abstract A system of logic is a formal theory equipped with laws and elementary syntactic and semantic definitions specifying ways of applying those laws in reasoning and revising assumptions out of which certain conclusions could be drawn from certain premises. Here, I shall discuss the universe of discourse to a variant of three-valued logic called Ezumezu and show that the traditional laws of thought are inadequate hence, I will discuss the three new supplementary laws of thought which were introduced in chapter six. Having already formulated some of its syntactic and semantic rules in the previous chapters, I will show that in logic, Ezumezu system is comparable to systems developed by the likes of Lukasiewicz, Graham Priest, Stephen Read and other alternative logics. I will discuss two important theses namely, ontological and logical theses that will enable us to further understand the three pillars of Ezumezu logic namely, nwa-nsa, nwa-nju and nwa-izugbe already discussed in the preceding chapter. Finally, I will demonstrate the formal structure of Ezumezu logic using its two argument types called arumaristic and ohakaristic to show how conclusions could be drawn from premises.

8.1 Introduction

A system of logic is a formal theory equipped with laws and elementary syntactic and semantic definitions specifying ways of applying those laws in reasoning and revising assumptions out of which certain conclusions could be drawn from certain premises. It is perfectly possible to have different systems of formal logic dealing with the same set of laws of thought. The difference between them would be in the degrees of tightening and relaxing of those laws. In formulating Ezumezu, I am going to loosen the three traditional laws of thought in order to formulate three additional laws to supplement them. This is something which other workers in alternative logic like the Calabar School of Philosophy duo of Innocent Asouzu and Chris Ijiomah did not take into consideration and so ended up proposing systems in which some or all of the traditional laws of thought are comatose. I will return to this in a later section.

In Western logic governed exclusively by the traditional laws of thought, deductive and inductive reasonings are the main formal procedures for drawing conclusions from sets of premises. In Ezumezu logic, the supplementary laws of thought will govern the two alternative formal procedures called arumaristics and ohakaristics for drawing conclusions from a set of premises.

The system of Ezumezu logic will dilute the deterministic property in contradiction and extend bivalence into trivalence as I have explained in the preceding chapters. Two opposed variables only seem to be contradictory in some modes of inference, in other modes, they may not strictly be so. This is because, the A and O or the E and I propositions in the square of opposition are sub-contraries in Ezumezu system and two sub-contrary positions could both hold depicting the character of truth-value glut as against truth-value gap of Lukasiewicz's three-valued system.

The Polish logician Jan Lukasiewicz was said to have rejected the bivalent system of Aristotelian tradition on the basis of its commitment to determinism (Betti 2001; Kachi 1996). This is not an outlandish claim given Lukasiewicz's arguments in the 1918 and 1922 works (1970a, b, c: 110–128). The thesis of determinism can be formulated as saying "every statement is either necessary or impossible". We can easily see the connection between this and the thesis of bivalence which states that "every statement is either true or false". Bivalence seems a bit innocuous until you interpret it in light of determinism. To bring out the seriousness of logical determinism inherent in the two-valued system, Lukasiewicz had to appeal to the problem of future contingents. The future contingent statements are those propositions of future events which given the limitations imposed by the present cannot immediately be evaluated in light of the bivalence principle. This ultimately brought out the constraints of two-valued system.

The Lukasiewicz's three-valued system apparently aimed at accommodating the future contingents by admitting the intermediate value. His reading of this third value is neither true nor false otherwise called the undetermined. But did this escape determinism? I say no and that constitutes the main reason why I am abandoning ship with Lukasiewicz's three-valued system to construct an alternative system I call Ezumezu. Given the contingent statement "Jonathan Goodluck will contest the 2019 presidential election in Nigeria"; according to Lukasiewicz's system on the one hand, and which we can reduce to determinism: it is impossible for this statement to be either true or false at the moment; and on the other hand, it is necessary for it to be undetermined. So the undetermined in Lukasiewicz was pre-determined.

Here, I shall discuss the universe of discourse to a variant of three-valued logic called Ezumezu,[1] and show that the traditional laws of thought are inadequate hence, I will discuss the three new supplementary laws of thought which were introduced in Chap. 6. I have already formulated some of its syntactic and semantic rules in the previous chapters. I will then show that in logic, this system is comparable to systems developed by the likes of Lukasiewicz, Graham Priest, Stephen Read and other alternative logics. I will discuss two important theses namely, ontological and logi-

---

[1] I designate the system as Ezumezu with upper case E, and the third value from which the system derives its name as ezumezu with a lower case e.

cal theses that enable us further understand the three pillars of Ezumezu logic namely, nwa-nsa, nwa-nju and nwa-izugbe already discussed in the preceding chapter. Finally, I will demonstrate the formal structure of Ezumezu logic using its two argument types called arumaristic and ohakaristic to show how conclusions could be drawn from premises. Finally, I will contrast Ezumezu project with the projects of harmonious monism and complementary logic advanced by fellow elements of the Calabar School of Philosophy, Ijiomah and Asouzu respectively.

8.2 The Universe of Discourse in Ezumezu Logic

To clarify some issues of language or the syntax of Ezumezu, it is important that I define the universe of discourse in Ezumezu logic.

Definition of Universe of Discourse This is the domain consisting of sets of statements (TFC), the relations of variables and the formal treatments of statements can range over the parameters of the governing laws of thought in Ezumezu system. This universe of discourse contains the following types of statements:

1. The T-set {all statements that affirm}
2. The F-set {all statements that deny}
3. The C-set {some statements that affirm and some statements that deny}

While Figs. 6.2 and 6.5 in this book explain the T and F sets, Figs. 6.1 and 8.1 explain the C-set. The domain of all statements that affirm and those that deny are contextual modes while the domain of some statements that affirm and some statements that deny is a complementary mode. This universe of discourse is upheld by the three supplementary laws of thought in ways that preserve the consistency of systems in African logic and recognise the consistency of systems in other logic traditions.

There are three primary goals I wish to outline for any logic tradition: (1) the first is to avoid inconsistency of its statements. (2) The second is to avoid contradiction of its statements. (3) And the third is to avoid making its principles absolute. While goal 1 makes logical statements in a logic tradition intelligible, goal 3 limits the expressive power of a logic system or tradition such that statements of all logic traditions are 'context-specific' which means that they may apply only in 'relevant contexts' globally. This is also what the 'universalness' of a system of logic means. A scenario in which statements of all logic traditions apply in 'all contexts' globally or is 'context-non-specific' is what I mean by a logic system or tradition being absolute. Without this limitation, goal 2 cannot be achieved and statements of all logic

Fig. 8.1 Showing the Ezumezu three-valued thought model. (Source: Chimakonam 2014)

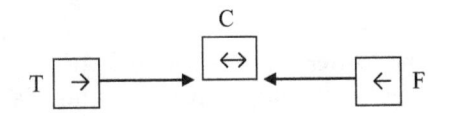

traditions would be absolute, i.e. they would apply in all contexts globally which is anathema because, systems of logic are supposed to be universal not absolute.

Being universal allows room for the determination of truth and false statements, valid, invalid and sound arguments, it enables us to separate the consistent from the inconsistent, the contradictory from the non-contradictory propositions, and most importantly, it enables us distinguish correct reasoning from incorrect reasoning. These aims of logic are set in light of the laws that govern each system. Such laws of thought make prescriptions that discriminate between what is legal and what is not within any system of logic. If we built our systems to be absolute and thereby overlooked this important discrimination, we would have scored a petty victory over thought but one which would destroy our purpose completely and render to noughts the human intelligence. For this, it is imperative that our systems of logic be universal but limited in their scopes to relevant contexts. A situation in which a statement of formal logic can apply in all contexts globally, such a statement would have gone beyond being universal and has become absolute. I am able to come to this point of understanding as a result of the important place which my system of Ezumezu allocates to contexts or contextualisation. The above is consistent with the prescriptions of the three traditional laws of thought. For example, if we say that Peter Obi is the running mate to Atiku Abubakar in Nigeria's 2019 presidential election, then it cannot be the case that Peter Obi is the running mate to Muhammadu Buhari in the same election. The laws of identity, contradiction and excluded middle impose a limitation to the claim and truthvalue of the first statement. If we simulate this election anywhere in the world, we would observe that candidate B cannot be a running mate to A and C at the same time; that candidate B can only be a running mate to A or to C; and that if candidate B is a running mate to A, then it is a running mate to A.

It is also because of the three goals enunciated above that the universality of systems of any properly formulated logic tradition is preserved. This is necessary because different logic traditions operate with a set of laws or supplementary laws obtained by relaxing or tightening the three traditional laws of thought. These supplementary laws like the ones I formulated for African logic are not strictly opposed to the three traditional laws such that may make systems in different logic traditions irreconcilable. What the additional laws warrant are nuances to the legal parameters that make statements in each tradition consistent or inconsistent, contradictory or non-contradictory, universal or absolute. But since statements of formal logic are supposed to be consistent, non-contradictory and above all, universal and not absolute, I formulate herewith, what can be called 1st and 2nd universalness theorems in logic.

1st Universalness Theorem
'Any system of logic S is universal U if and only if its elementary formal statements F are context-specific X,'

$$U s iff X f$$

2nd Universalness Theorem
'If the elementary formal statements of a system of logic Sf are context-non-specific $\sim Xf$, then the system is absolute As,'

$$(Sf \wedge \sim Xf\,) \mid \to As$$

Thus the first and second universalness theorems show that universal systems are consistent and if a system is universal and consistent then it cannot be absolute. This is because, every universal system obeys either the traditional laws of thought which includes the law of contradiction and depending on the expanse of its expressive power may also have to be governed by a set of supplementary laws of thought. In Ezumezu system, this would include the law of nmekoka.

8.3 Elementary Syntactic and Semantic Mappings in Ezumezu Logic

Ezumezu is an African logic that is three-valued, arumaristic and value-complementary. The basic differences between this and say the Lukasiewicz's model is as expected in the third value which lies in-between two extremes. In Lukasiewicz, it is called the undetermined read as neither true nor false (truth-value gap) whereas in my system, it is called ezumezu meaning the contingent and interpreted as both true and false (truth-value glut).

Again, the two principal values Truth and Falsity are treated as contradictories in Lukasiewicz hence in a truth table definition of the conditional $P \supset Q$, T, U will yield U; U, F will yield U, the undetermined from this reading is understood to mean it might be true or false though it is not known which (Jacquette 2000: 116; Lukasiewicz 1970a, b, c: 87–88). This is the semantic effect of the contradictory status of the two standard values which are supposed to jointly necessitate the third value. The interesting thing is found in the conditional definition where both the antecedent and the consequent in the truth table are undetermined. Lukasiewicz reads it as U, U will yield T given the traditional truth table definition of the conditional. Kleene (1952) would rather read it as U, U = U in the strict observation of the semantic content of the two undetermined values thus ignoring the truth table definition of the conditional as false only when the antecedent is true and the consequent false. Lukasiewicz on his part did not ignore this and the fall-out can be seen in their different interpretations above. But why would Lukasiewicz hold this position? Why would he jump from a supposedly three-valued reading back to a two-valued reading of the undetermined much like from a possible truth-value glut back to truth-value gap? He must have noticed that a consistent truth-glut reading obviously would be implausible because his two standard values are contradictories as a result it makes no sense to expect U, U (two unknowns) to yield any other value besides T given the traditional definition of conditional. Thus Lukasiewicz never really left bivalence and never truly escaped determinism. Some have criticised the undetermined and correctly so as not being a distinct value in itself. Michael Glanzberg for example, argues that truth-gaps are poorly motivated and that it is mysterious how they can be compatible with some attractive general principles and that they are useless any way you look at it (Glanzberg 2004). Simply put, if you wanted a three-valued system, then the intermediate value had better be a proper value and not some hanging undetermined thing that runs into a brick wall.

In Ezumezu model where the two standard values are treated as sub-contraries rather than contradictories, the Lukasiewicz's reading of the conditional would become obviously implausible. This is because the ezumezu is a distinct value in itself, even if tentatively, where the two standard values converge and complement. Hans Reichenbach (1944) clearly endorsed the idea of complementarity of logical values when he employed Bohr's complementary principle to describe the functionality of three-valued logic showing how two seemingly opposed variables complement.[2] Its interpretation is 'it is known that it could be both true and false'. It is strictly true or false when ezumezu is disintegrated once more into contextual modes. One readily questions the realist status of ezumezu that could be both true and false. Semantic evaluations as earlier mentioned in African thought are read contextually similar to situation semantics where statements of formal systems are interpreted as true or false relative to situations. In contextual semantics, that which is true, is true only in a context, it could be false in another. This is a realist rather than an epistemic reading of the three-valued thought model.

However, in Ezumezu logic, we do not talk about truth table definition of the conditional $P \supset Q$, we talk about truth table definition of the complement[3] $P \mid \supset Q$. It must be clarified at this point that our use of 'complement' in Ezumezu logic is not the same as its use in set theory. In set theory, A^c or A' is a complement and is read as 'all the objects that do not belong to set A.' In Ezumezu logic, $P \mid \supset Q$ is read as 'P complements Q' or 'P and Q complement each other.' Usually, when two variables complement in Ezumezu logic a third but tentative variable symbolised as 'C' is formed.

Under this reading, the truth table definitions of $P \mid \supset Q$ would be T, T = T; T, F = C; F, T = C where C replaces U and stands for the contingent or complemented value; F, F = F.

Another basic demarcating point is with recourse to the principle of ex falso quadlibet. This is a rule that permits the inference of any formula whatsoever from a contradiction (that is, from a formula and its negation) (Cook 2009: 110). It could be symbolised as A, ~A therefore B. In Lukasiewicz and strongly in Kleene, there are obvious ways in which ex falso quadlibet could be valid in that from the annihilation which proceeds from A and ~A, any formula could easily be inferred given the internal bivalence. But in Ezumezu model which is trivalent it is not a valid rule of inference because from A, ~A, one can easily infer (A $\mid \supset$ ~A) which is an impossible contingent. We may therefore produce the structure of Ezumezu three-values as follows:

The diagram above simply shows two standard values of truth and falsity labeled conventionally as T and F above which necessarily complement each other in the

---

[2] Hans Reichenbach in his magnum Opus *The philosophic foundations of quantum mechanics*. (1944, 22 & pp.139–165) showed the inadequacy of two-valued logic in axiomatising quantum theory and opted instead for three-valued logic as a viable option.

[3] It must be clarified that our use of 'complement' in Ezumezu logic is not the same as its use in set theory. In set theory A^c or A' is a complement and is read as 'all the objects that do not belong to set A.'

third value called ezumezu or the contingent labeled C above. The arrows in the boxes show the movement of the values or variables as the case may be from a contextual mode to a central platform where they achieve complementation. This is against the principle of bivalence which entrenches the place of contradiction in Western logic. What this means however is that the reasoning pattern in Ezumezu is non-bivalent or trivalent. The traditional laws of thought (identity, contradiction and excluded-middle) for example are insufficient in Ezumezu system and in their complement are the three supplementary laws of thought namely; Njikọka, Nmekọka and Ọnọna-etiti.

8.4 Discussion of the Three Supplementary Laws of Thought

I have already stated these three supplementary laws in an earlier chapter. What I want to do here is provide further discussion on them. It is easy to see with the study of Western systems that the main problem it has with African thought system is that it regards it as non-existent or at best a collection of mystical and pre-logical traditions lacking in rationality. This is because the principles of reasoning in the Western logic i.e. the laws of thought do not sufficiently cover the gamut of human reasoning as a whole. Unsure of what to make of this discovery, the French Anthropologist Lucien Levy-Bruhl (1947) declares that primitive societies which includes traditional Africa are governed by an inferior type of logic he describes as the "logic of mystical participation." Thus in light of Aristotelian logic, such peoples for him, are prelogical. When the question is asked: What does Levy-Bruhl mean when he claimed that primitive cultures are pre-logical and how did he arrive at such a conclusion?" Gordon Hunnings explains the answer provided by Robin Horton thus:

> One quite specific reason is because Aristotle's Laws of Thought are not formulated and do not appear to be observed in African languages. According to Western logic, these laws are the supreme principles of logical truth and any system of ideas expressed in a language in which these principles are not observed can only be described as pre-logical. Furthermore, as these logical principles represent the Laws of *Thought* their absence is not only a defect of language but of the mentality of the users of the language. (Hunnings 1975: 4)

On this ground, Hunnings replies:

> It was by reasoning along these lines that Levy-Bruhl felt entitled to draw far-reaching conclusions about the mind and even the soul of African peoples. It has often been observed that whereas the truths of philosophy turn out to be trivial tautologies, it is the errors of philosophy that are intrusive. This particular thesis seems to me not only to be an error, but a particularly intrusive one. Most of Levy-Bruhl's critics have contented themselves with a general refutation of his thesis on the ground that he exaggerated the difference between African and Western cultures. This is certainly true, but the philosophical errors involved in Levy-Bruhl's thesis are far more subtle than that. (Hunnings 1975: 4)

It is in this light that I here discuss the three laws of thought as supplementary principles undergirding the variant of three-valued logic I am formulating. It is probably full of contradictions when assessed with Western system but so are the Aristotelian and the Russellian systems when viewed in light of the Ezumezu system here formulated. It is not that the three traditional laws of thought do not hold in Ezumezu system or that the supplementary laws cannot hold in Western system but that they do not consistently hold in each system. To the extent they can hold in the opposite system defines their complementarity.[4]

The traditional laws are identity, contradiction and excluded-middle. Identity states that a thing is always equal to itself (A equals A); contradiction which is a negative formulation of identity states that a thing cannot be unequal to or different from itself (A is not non-A); and excluded middle which is the combination of the two above states that if a thing is equal to itself it cannot be unequal to or different from itself (if A equals A it cannot equal non-A). In line with their structures, these laws imply absolute difference and absolute identity in which things are mutually exclusive (Sogolo 1993). This means that a thing cannot be two different and mutually exclusive things at the same time. In the extended reasoning frameworks like the case of future contingents, this deterministic property becomes a telling weakness for the two-valued system.

I add three new laws to the above namely, njikoka, nmekoka and onona-etiti in lieu of the fact that the ideas of absolute identity, absolute difference and mutual exclusivity which the three traditional laws project in addition to serving a purpose of consistency in reasoning, actually undermine dynamism and short-change other facets of human reasoning by being overtly deterministic.

While identity and contradiction imply absolute identity in which things are mutually exclusive, excluded-middle imply absolute difference. In the same vein, njikoka and onona-etiti mitigate absolute identity in which things are mutually exclusive by implying relative identity in which things are mutually inclusive instead. Nmekoka on the other hand mitigate absolute difference by implying relative difference in which things are mutually inclusive.

This sort of thinking that recognises the intermediate value, eschews absolutism/exclusivity and promotes relativity/inclusivity is not covered in the mappings of two-valued logic. It is this sort of reasoning (complementary inference, theory of quanta and future contingents, etc.,) observed in different places in the universe including Africa when it comes to complementary reasoning that Ezumezu logic covers. By these three additional laws, Ezumezu gears up to surpass the efficacy of two-valued logic. The mathematical precision and consistency of two-valued logic means that dynamism is lost entirely and that makes it a logic for robots. Because humans are both emotive and rational entities, they are dynamic, and a better reasoning algorithm would be a logic that recognises this human plasticity. A strict adherence to the Western logic has turned men into machines without hearts that feel, or, to borrow the words of Franz Fanon (Fanon 1963), Europe has become morally sterile.

In the supplementary laws, njikoka maintains that because things exist in a network, every existence forms a necessary link of reality and nothing that exists, stands alone. Yet this is not a form of synthesis because everything in the network retains its identity despite being in a relationship with other things. Nmekoka on its part

---

[4] Further research is required to fully exploit this possibility.

maintains that things exist in a complementary network where things complement themselves. For this, everything serves a missing link of reality. Complementation in this regard is brought about by arumaristic reasoning and not dialectic reasoning, and as such a synthesis is not expected because things do not lose their individual identities, they only join to create the new complemented but tentative identity. For onona-etiti, everything that exists serves different functions from context to context. Through it, Ezumezu logic seeks to form the third value called nwa-izugbe from the interaction of nwa-nju and nwa-nsa. Arumaristics is different from Marxist and Hegelian dialectics because thesis and anti-thesis are not contradictories but subcontraries and as such do not yield a synthesis in Ezumezu logic.

8.4.1 The Law of Njikọka

Integrativity is a near equivalence of the Igbo concept Njikọka which means universal value or meaning is derived from variables when they come together. The emphasis of the law of Njikọka is on universal identity rather than on individual identity. The human society for example is communitarian which means the individual does not exist in isolation, he exists in a group (Menkiti 1984). It is the group that gives identity, as for example, an individual citizen of Nigeria is a Nigerian, an African and a member of the human race. On its own, the individual is capable of pursuing its own ideal although highly limited but in a group its potentialities are increased to fullness. In the law of Njikọka, the individuals are not subsumed or lost in the group because they are autonomous, but they come together to create a more powerful centre. Through the combined efforts of members of the set, the group forges a stronger identity.

This law which has been stated earlier reads as A is true if and only if A is true wedge-implies A and B is true. Here, the variable A is said to be true only in the company of another or other variables. The argument is that A primarily holds because it has a group to which it belongs. The emphasis here is not that A cannot hold outside the group but that within the group, the identity of A is secondary to that of the group. This is the law that upholds ohakaristic as a reasoning procedure.

8.4.2 Law of Nmekọka

The term complementarity comes nearest to explaining the concept of Nmekọka. Literally, Nmekọka means that individual strength or power is enhance in the group. The difference between the law of Nmekọka and that of Njikọka is that while the former centres on the enhanced group power or identity made possible by the combination of individual identities, the latter focuses on the enhanced individual identity within the group. In the metatheoretic formulation of Nmekọka, the variable C is said to be contingent or in a complementary mode of thought.

Further, let us note the value attached to C in the meta-theoretic formulation which is (T | ⊃ F), this is different from (T) ∧ (F) or (T) ∧ ~ (T) because the conjunction which is present in the latter formulae suggests admission or inclusion, (T) includes (F) or ~ (T) admits (T). In "C" we say that the two values (T) (F) are mutually complementary as Fig. 6.1 Shows. In "C" the individual (T) or (F) have come together to produce "C" but it is this coming together that enhances the identities of T and F, hence (T | ⊃ F) = C. This is the law that upholds arumaristic as a reasoning procedure.

8.4.3 Law of Ọnọna-etiti

If we say as the traditional law of excluded middle posits that either a thing is or it is not, we have as the name goes excluded the middle position which is the possibility of a thing being and not being at the same time. What is excluded by the traditional law of excluded middle is what onona-etiti includes hence, included-middle. The difference markers in the two laws are their operators. While excluded middle goes with disjunction "∨" Ọnọna-etiti or if you like included middle goes with conjunction "∧". Thus, as disjunction polarises and bifurcates in mutually exclusive absolute difference, conjunction unifies and centralises in mutually inclusive relative difference. Included middle therefore becomes a term which, closely interprets the Igbo concept Ọnọna-etiti meaning "between others, that which comes to the middle."

As a result, when some people for example, reason, they do not reason solely and strictly that either a thing is or it is not or neither this nor that in mutually exclusive absolute difference within a given contextual mode of interpretation but also that a thing could be and not be at the same time within a mutually inclusive relative difference in an integrated mode of interpretation. We can see another difference between African logic and Western logic. While Ezumezu logic admits of modes of interpretation of variables namely contextual, contingent or complementary and integrated, Western logic does not admit of the complementary and the integrated. In meta-theoretic formulation we symbolise the expression of Ọnọna-etiti as follows:

$$(T)A \wedge (T) \sim A \text{ or} (T)A \wedge (F)A$$

This can be expressed literally as A could be both true and false or if a thing is equal to itself it can be unequal to or different from itself depending on context. This idea of trivalence in African thought is also corroborated by Chris Ijiomah (2006) in his different account of an African variant of three-valued logic. This law alone summarises everything which Asouzu puts forward in his theory of complementary logic even though he did not attempt to formulate any law. But I still find his system inadequate as I shall show later because a system of logic requires more than a single law to stand.

8.5 The Two Theses in Ezumezu Logic

Ezumezu has two prominent theses namely; the ontological thesis and the logical thesis. It is from the spectra of these two that the methods of African philosophy can be understood.

Briefly, the ontological thesis states that:

> *realities exist not only as independent units at the periphery of the circle of existents but also as entities capable of coming together to the centre of the circle of existents, in a network for an interdependent relationship.*

Conceived in this way, African philosophers of diverse persuasions think of reality as one big network of variables some of which are opposed to some others, yet, they are interconnected. This accounts for why in the conversational curve which is an apparatus that explains how diverse variables relate in African ontology, even opposed variables that are in a disjunctive motion apart from each other come to discover the necessity of mutual interaction and enter the path of conjunctive motion once again.[5] So, there is a limit to how far apart the disjunctive motion could take the opposed variables—that limit is known as the complementary bar.

However, despite the possibility of binary complementation, there is also a limit to how close the opposed variables can relate—that limit is called the *benoke* point. This concept is derived from a collection of Igbo words: *Bere* which means 'reaching' and *n'oke* which means 'the limit or terminal point'. Put together '*berenoke*' or '*benoke*' for short means 'reaching the limit or terminal point'. This is the point beyond which opposed variables cannot achieve closer relationship due to their ontological variance which ensures the absence of synthesis in Ezumezu logic.

One could therefore see that despite their similarity, there is a difference between relationship of the types called arumaristics and ohakaristics and Hegelian dialectical relationship. Below is the diagram of conversational curve that can enable us measure the relationships of seemingly opposed variables in African ontology (See Fig. 8.2 below).

Definition Conversational Curve is a graphic representation of the arumaristic and ohakaristic relationship between opposed variables, call them *nwa-nsa* and its nemesis *nwa-nju*. It is drawn with the motions of conversation on vertical axis and the conversationalists or the variables themselves on horizontal axis.

In the diagram above, one can observe the dotted disjunctive v-shaped lines which demonstrate how variables move apart and diminish their contact and interaction (ohakaristics); and the conjunctive lines which demonstrate how seemingly opposed variables come close to interact (arumaristics). One can also observe concessional bridge defined as a mechanism for determining when complementation

---

[5] Disjunctive motion symbolised with the constant 'V' refers to the conversational track that leads to the differentiation of opinions as opposed variables diverge while conjunctive motion symbolised with the constant 'Λ' refers to the conversational track that leads to the homogenisation of opinions as opposed variables converge.

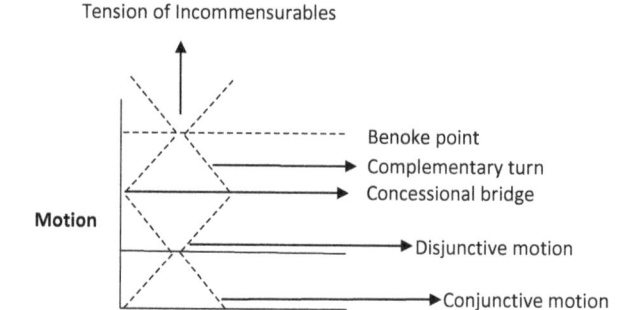

Fig. 8.2 Diagram of Conversational Curve. (Source: Chimakonam 2017, p19)

has become necessary; and complementary turn defined as a mechanism for determining when actual complementation has begun to take place. On top is the *benoke* point where the conjunctive lines could not meet and which is a point beyond which opposed variables cannot achieve closer relationship. Finally, there is one called tension of incommensurables defined as a mechanism for determining when complementary relationship has collapsed.

On the whole, ontological thesis enables us to understand the three pillars of Ezumezu logic namely, nwa-nsa, nwa-nju and nwa-izugbe. While nwa-nsa and nwa-nju are independent variables at the periphery or contextual mode, nwa-izugbe is the centre where they converge, the complementary mode.

The second is the logical thesis and it states that:

values are to be allocated to propositions not on the bases of the facts such propositions assert but on the bases of the contexts in which those propositions are asserted.

In this regard, one can see that context upsets fact as earlier explained. It is from this logical thesis that I articulate the principle of Context-dependence of Values (CdV) already discussed in the previous chapter. What can immediately be gleaned from this thesis is that in Ezumezu logic, we look at truth as something somewhat less rigid as the Aristotelian logical formulation as well as the Boolean algebraic equation would rather have us believe. The condensed idea is: 'truth value of propositions varies from context to context.'

Thus the methods of African philosophy like Afro-communitarianism, Complementary reflection and Conversational thinking which are grounded in Ezumezu logic aim at a non-synthetic outcome i.e. they do not broach the transculturality of truth; they are rather, arumaristic. What the logical thesis does is the affirmation of what can be called the 'intercommunication of truth' which means that truths emanating from different contexts can recognise and confirm one another, but that is how much we can expect. Thus at contextual levels, truths have a life of their own but somehow connected. One truth may confirm the other even though they may carry different values for the same set of facts—a practical solidarity of truths, if you will. For example, the proposition 'one needs water to stay alive' when contextualised in the Sahara desert where one is dehydrating and in the River Niger where one is drowning, respectively; they will carry different values even though they contain the same set of facts as demonstrated in the previous chapter. However, despite the difference in values, one confirms the other. Water could save your life in the desert but the same water could kill you in the river. These truths are in solidarity, each enables one to understand the other better and I think this is supposed to be the drive behind all genuine efforts geared towards intercultural philosophy. Conversational thinking epitomises this mechanism through a process known as creative struggle—a continuous arumaristics without synthesis. This method is a perpetual process and a critical-creative continuum by which the African philosopher or any philosopher for that matter can assess the relationships of diverse but interconnected entities, cultures and peoples, etc. The reshuffling of nwa-nsa and nwa-nju is a revision of some sort in which each set manifests a higher level of discourse called nwa-izugbe.

On the whole, Ezumezu logic through its fundamental notion of nmeko points to the idea of logical relationships among interdependent, interrelated and interconnected realities existing in a network whose peculiar truth conditions can more accurately and broadly be determined within specific contexts. This relationship exists even between opposed variables propelled and regulated by the conjunctive and the disjunctive mechanisms that seek to preserve diversity while enhancing inclusion and focusing on the progress of thought.

8.6 The Formal Structure of Ezumezu Logic

Formal reasoning in Ezumezu has two main procedures namely, arumaristics and ohakaristics which can be employed in drawing conclusions from sets of premises. There are elementary definitions that are necessary for us to proceed:

Centre and Peripheries In Ezumezu logic, we conceive universal and particular propositions or statements as centre and peripheries. This is due to the Afro-communitarian idea of coming together or communion. Communion presupposes relationship and relationship involves different variables coming together from different corners to form a unity at the centre. These variables therefore stand individually at the periphery which is an imaginary circle. The different points at the periphery represent diverse contexts or the contextual modes while the centre where the variables converge is the complementary mode.

Peripheral and Central Claims In arumaristic and ohakaristic arguments, there are three main propositions, the first premise is called a peripheral claim because, it is a particular statement in a contextual mode. The second premise is called the context of the claim because, it gives justification to the peripheral claim. The third which is the conclusion is also called the central claim because, it is a universal statement with complementary value. A standard form argument in African logic is called categorical arumaristicism or categorical ohakaristicism. So there are two types of categorical arguments in African logic each consisting of three propositions known as categorical propositions or two premises and one conclusion. The analysis of terms, moods and figures are quite the same as in Western logic except that as explained before, the universal proposition contains what is called the central claim while the particular propositions contain what are called the peripheral claims.

Example of an arumaristic argument:

Premise 1:   Momoh is immortal
Premise 2:   Momoh is an African
Conclusion: Therefore, all Africans are immortal

The mood and figure of the above argument is IIA-3 which is invalid in Western logic because that Momoh is immortal and an African do not constitute sufficient ground to infer that all Africans are immortal. The property of immortality seems in this case to be something peculiar to one individual named Momoh. It would be unreasonable to make such an inductive leap and generalise that property. There is no sufficient cause for such an effect.

In African logic however, the argument of the structure IIA-3 would be valid because of the permissibility principle introduced in Chap. 6. This principle allows one to infer a conclusion through a relevant context. The context through which the universal conclusion could be inferred from two particular premises is that of African ontology where being is transcendent and time is cyclical.

On the one hand, being for the African is not only spatio-temporal, it is transcendental. It is both physical and non-physical or has both physical and non-physical dimensions. So, even when humans for example, pass on, they are not dead and finished; they have only unrobed their physical aspect and begun another journey in the afterlife with their non-physical aspect.[6]

Time on the other hand, is cyclical[7] and not linear. Those who are said to have journeyed into afterlife descend to the land of the ancestors or the spirit world from where they either maintain contact, participate in the activities of the living or their non-physical aspects are recycled and sent back to the world through re-incarnation that their journey in life may begin anew. Now, if all Africans are said to be immortal, it is the context of re-incarnation[8] that warrant such a categorical proposition. It matters very little that such a universal conclusion was arrived at from two particular premises. The traditional law of contradiction has limitation in this context where the law of nmekoka is active. Re-incarnation and the cyclic nature of time apply to all in African world-view, it does not matter if one case is reported.

In Western logic, there are about 256 categorical syllogisms which going by the permutation of terms, moods and figures, only 24 are valid. Out of the 24, only 15 are unconditionally valid while 9 are conditionally valid. The study that will map

---

[6] See Ifeanyi Menkiti (1984) for a rich discussion of afterlife.
[7] See John Mbiti (1969).
[8] See discussions on re-incarnation in Innocent Onyewuenyi (1996) and Mesembe Edet (2016).

8.6 The Formal Structure of Ezumezu Logic

out all possible argument structures in both arumaristic and ohakaristic arguments is yet to be carried out in African logic and I here throw the challenge to the feet of the young African logicians.

I come now to the ohakaristic argument. Like the arumaristic version, it also has three statements. But more like the deductive argument of Western logic, its inference moves from the centre to the periphery much like from universal to particular. This similarity can be explained on the basis of the applicability of the traditional laws of thought in African world-view. Ezumezu does not reject or doubt that the three old or traditional laws apply in African thought. What Ezumezu emphasises is that they are limited to spheres of experiences where the traditional laws are upheld. For example, in African thought, there is left and right, a moving object can only occupy one space at a time. There is also up and down, when an object is tossed up under certain physical conditions, it can only occupy one of the two spaces at a time.

Ezumezu simply recognises the limitation of the three traditional laws of thought. My father is my father and I cannot have any other father biologically, no doubt, but I can have several other fathers in an Afro-communitarian sense. It is when inferences move from such universally known biological conditions to specific Afro-communitarian contextual conditions that Ezumezu logic begins to take over from Western logic.

An example of ohakaristic argument would be:

Premise 1:   All Africans are immortal
Premise 2:   Momoh is an African
Conclusion: Therefore, Momoh is immortal

The above example looks very much like a deductive argument except that there are some nuances in interpretation. The movement of inferences in ohakaristic argument is not thought of as from universal to particular propositions but from the centre to the peripheries. This is in keeping with the Afro-communitarian orientation of communion or relationship of variables. Again, while premise 1 is a central claim, premise 2 is the context that justifies the claim in premise 1. The conclusion then becomes a peripheral claim. So, more than the deductive argument, ohakaristic is the opposite of arumaristic. One of the main significances of ohakaristic argument is being able to contrast arumaristic argument with another type of argument in Ezumezu logic. Another significance is that it proves that the traditional laws of thought namely identity, contradiction and excluded middle apply in African language even though it has certain limitations. On the whole, it is important to note that Ezumezu is not the only system developed in African philosophy so far. There are two other systems called harmonious monism and complementary logic by Ijiomah and Asouzu respectively. Summarising their basic tenets, harmonious monism is three-valued and based on the notion of relationship inherent in African world-view. In it, the two extreme values are contraries designated as quasi truth and quasi false. The intermediate value which represents the combination of the two fragmented values is the region of complete truth. For complementary logic, it is many-valued, recognises each value as missing link and views the combination of all values as the truth. Inferences in this logic are governed by two principles namely; the conjunctive and the disjunctive principles. Of the two, the system sanctions the former and rejects the latter as the correct way to reason. On a positive note, these two systems of logic by Ijiomah and Asouzu do well in modelling African worldview or tapping from some of its viable id to design algorithms capable of mediating conflicts of interest. The problem they have are, for harmonious monism, there is no room for the value of falsehood, only quasi falsehood and the implication of such a model for the society can be scary. Further, it treats the two standard values as contraries but by the square of opposition, two contraries cannot both hold. So, it is mind-boggling how Ijiomah's intermediate value is possible in the first place. For complementary logic, the negation of truth is not an ideal worth pursuing, so is the disjuctive inference. It is only the conjuctive inference that is accepted in complementary logic. On the whole, both systems also negate in various degrees, the three traditional laws of thought but fail to promulgate alternatives. While not dismissing them outright, it may be rewarding to suggest further work on the systems.

8.7 Conclusion: Insights and Controversies

African scholars like C. S. Momoh, Godwin Sogolo, Leopold Senghor, Joseph Omoregbe, Meinrad Hebga, Hunnings Gordon, Udo Etuk and the present author to name a few have been concerned and have variously mooted the idea of a logic that can interpret a mapping of sections of human system of thought not covered in the traditional Aristotelian system. The challenge which has confronted this noble idea and of course, projects, over the last 30 or 40 years is the confusion with regard to location and the crises of the thought patterns not covered. Some African scholars like Udo Etuk, (2002)[9] and Chris Ijiomah, (2006)[10] take the radical but easily misunderstood or misplaced ambition. Either they make claim for a logic that is uniquely African or they emphasise a unique thought system upon which they erect the edifice of a peculiar African logic. This sort of logical radicalism was heralded by Leopold Senghor (1964) who differentiated between Western and African reasoning—the one being rational and the other being chiefly emotive.[11] Others like Hebga and Hunnings pointed to the lacuna in Western logic which needs to be filled. Momoh and Omoregbe affirmed this need and speculated on a possible logical construction of cultural orientation. This is the sort of orientation which has led to the

---

[9] Etuk argues for the possibility of a logic that could be called African.

[10] Ijiomah envisages a logic called harmonious monism which is a direct reflection of a peculiar African thought system. I have clarified that this sort of thinking is misplaced even though it is original.

[11] Senghor may have been misunderstood. His emphasis on emotions can be more accurately read as a claim for relevance in the logical reflections of Africans much more like the claim in the Australian tradition. Not being a professional logician, he could not finely articulate this in line with logical standards but he made a strong point which I believe is vital in developing the African tradition in Logic.

8.7 Conclusion: Insights and Controversies

talk about Indian and Chinese logics i.e. cultural location of logics which implies universal dislocation of the instrument of logic is, in itself, a great error.

I believe that the contributions which the Indian, Chinese, Western, Polish and African logics bring to the logical discourse are extensional rather than genetic. No logic is truly genetic even though the Western writers from the ancient time have commented on logic as if it were a pride collection of the Western mind (See Horton 1993; Hegel 1975; Levy-Brhul 1947).[12] This cultural location has sparked off a nostalgic force in other minds of the twentieth century down to label any further logical development from their horizon with cultural bias. To condone this would be to upturn the character of topic-neutrality and universal instrumentality of logic. To dismiss further logical developments from other traditions as nonsensical, irrational, anti-rational or inadmissible; or to treat historicity of logic as exclusive or preclusive is also a monumental error. It is another way of cultural location of logic. To tie the goat with the rope and to tie the rope with the goat as the Igbo would say, translate to the same activity but with nuances.

Logic would continue to grow. What we witness as the edifice of logic is chiefly the contributions from the Western traditions namely, Greek, German, British, American, Polish, Australian, etc. The contributions from the Chinese and the Indian traditions are beginning to be acknowledged while the contributions from the African tradition are being worked out since the twentieth century, some of them though from an erroneous precipice—one we have explained its cause. The two errors which resulted in cultural location and universal dislocation of the instrument of logic are to be abandoned. Logic is to be one principle of intelligibility with various traditions. The culturally ethnicised predicates as Western, Chinese, Indian, African, etc., which are exclusivist alter and bastardise the meaning of the subject if read outside the proper context. Logic can only be qualified within itself or with such predicates to reflect the various traditions e.g. polish logic, Igbo logic, American logic and to reflect the various orientations such as propositional logic, relevance logic, ezumezu logic, etc. The predicates Western, Chinese, Indian, African etc., must strictly be used to categorise various bigger umbrella traditions and not to differentiate or racialise various unique types of logic that are culturally exclusive.

Another gauntlet has to do with system of thought which is viewed by some as the metaphysical foundation of logic. Promoters of a unique African logic for instance take cue from this to agitate that Africa has a unique thought system which engenders unique African logic. Thought system has been defined as the aggregate of a people's basic beliefs which determine their norms, laws and judgments on what is acceptable and unacceptable within their society in accordance with established order (Chimakonam 2012, 2013). However, thought system is something that evolves with the development of human intellect. The intellectual development of all humanity and all societies are not at par and as such the evolution of human thought system in different environments cannot be at par or even channeled towards the same direction. But one central factor that undergirds them all is rationality

---

[12] This idea is strongly suggested by the much criticised French Anthropologist Lucien Levy-Bruhl, The German Idealist philosopher Georg Hegel and much later Robin Horton.

driven by circumstance. In this way, the circumstances of people in Europe may engender rational progress in one direction and lack of progress in another where Africa may have thrived given her circumstances. The inclination to reason following certain patterns and not another which is seamlessly due to circumstance has been erroneously described by the promoters of unique cultural logics as variegated or extremist relative thought systems. The acceptance of this inexorably leads to the enthronement of relative logics in the sense of exclusive cultural variations.

When we talk about say African logic we mean it as a tradition in the overall edifice of logic. Here, I call my system Ezumezu logic. Such logic could only be an extension of the conventional landscape of logic. So in essence, it is not a new or unique logic different from logic as it is conventionally known. Just as different traditions such as relevance, para-consistent, three-valued, four-valued, multi-valued logics etc., have come to be developed as extensions of the big umbrella of logic whose main differences are in the expansion or loosening of the laws which guide reasoning within them, Ezumezu joins that league as a variant of three-valued logic. As has been observed, any shift in the three traditional laws of thought constitutes an alternative system of logic. So, the question does African logic exist as a border-sensitive structure does not arise. This question alone is capable of generating academic controversies that might last a century or more but as it is said, "without arguments and clarifications, there is strictly no philosophy" (Wiredu 1980: 47). The importance of the project on Ezumezu logic is accounted for in the insights that could be derived from it as demonstrating the viability of African logic as a tradition. Whether it comes hidden in the critical denials or as an obvious outright acknowledgment of its merits, there must be something that engages the academic by threatening orthodoxy or by exposing his ignorance. There is always a difference between what we know for sure to be incorrect and what we merely presume should be incorrect based on our earlier assumptions and biases which are more likely to be faulty than valid. In the face of the latter, we are admonished to give some chance to our little controversies! The developments in the theory of quanta where the two-valued logic could not suffice and where J. Bochenski believes that the Lukasiewicz's three-valued logic suffices is a strong case in point. The issues of complementary inferences and future contingents which defy the Aristotelian system beckon for an alternative logic. Where the Lukasiewicz's three-valued logic is thought to be insufficient, Ezumezu might therefore, suffice. Since the growth of logic has been continuous, the development of Ezumezu as a formal system sustains the momentum.

References

Betti, Arianna. 2001. The Incomplete Story of Łukasiewicz and Bivalence', in T. Childers & O. Majer (eds.), *The Logica Yearbook,* (Filosofia, Prague, 2002): 21–36.

Chimakonam, O. Jonathan. 2012. *Building African logic as an algorithm for Africa's development.* Paper presented at The University of Georgia, USA, African Studies Institute Conference, November 8–10.

References

———. 2013. *Metric system in Igbo thought long before the arrival of theEuropeans: A systematization*. Paper presented at The 11th Annual Conference of the Igbo Studies Association on "Ohaka: The community is supreme" Held at Modotel, Enugu, Nigeria June 27–29.

———. 2014. *Ezumezu: A variant of three-valued logic*. Paper presented at the philosophical society of the Southern Africa PSSA. Free State University, Bloemfontein, January 20–22.

———. 2017. Conversationalism as an emerging method of thinking in and beyond African philosophy. *Acta Academica* 47 (2): 11–33.

Cook, Roy. 2009. *A dictionary of philosophical logic*. Edinburgh: Edinburgh University Press.

Edet, I. Mesembe. 2016. Innocent Onyewuenyi's "philosophical re-appraisal of the African belief in reincarnation": A conversational study. *Filosofia Theoretica: Journal of African Philosophy, Culture and Religions* 5 (1): 76–99. https://doi.org/10.4314/ft.v5i1.6.

Etuk, Udo. 2002. The possibility of African logic. In *The third way in African philosophy*, ed. Olusegun Oladipo, 98–116. Ibadan: Hope Publications.

Fanon, Franz. 1963. *Wretched of the earth*. New York: Grove Press.

Glanzberg, Michael. 2004. Against truth-value gaps. In *Liar and heaps: New essays on paradox*, ed. J.C. Beall, 151–193. New York: Oxford University Press.

Hegel, W.F. Georg. 1975. *Lectures on the Philosophy of World History*. Trans. H.B. Nisbet. Cambridge: Cambridge University Press.

Horton, Robin. 1993. *Patterns of thought in Africa and the West: Essays on magic, religion and science*. Cambridge: Cambridge University Press.

Hunnings, Gordon. 1975. Logic, language and culture. *Second Order: An African Journal of Philosophy* 4 (1): 3–13.

Ijiomah, Chris. 2006. An excavation of a logic in African world-view. *African Journal of Religion, Culture and Society* 1 (1): 29–35.

Jacquette, Dale. 2000. An internal determinacy metatheorem for Lukasiewicz's Aussagenkalkuls. *Bulletin of the Section of Logic* 29 (3): 115–124.

Kachi, Diasuke. 1996. *Was Lukasiewicz wrong? Three-valued logic and determinism*. Paper presented at Lukasiewicz in Dublin – An international conference on the works of Jan Lukasiewicz, July 7.

Kleene, C. Stephen. 1952. *Introduction to metamathematics*. Amsterdam: North Holland.

Levy-Bruhl, Lucien. 1947. *Primitive mentality*. Paris: University of France Press.

Łukasiewicz, Jan. 1970a. On three-valued logic. In *Selected works by Jan Łukasiewicz*, ed. L. Borkowski, 87–88. Amsterdam: North–Holland.

———. 1970b. On determinism. In *Selected works by Jan Łukasiewicz*, ed. L. Borkowski, 110–128. Amsterdam: North–Holland.

———. 1970c. Farewell lecture by Professor Jan Lukasiewcz delivered in the Warsaw University Lecture Hall on March 7, 1918. In *Selected works by Jan Łukasiewicz*, ed. L. Borkowski, 84–86. Amsterdam: North–Holland.

Mbiti, John. 1969. *African religions and philosophy*. London: Heinemann.

Menkiti, Ifeanyi. 1984. Person and community in African traditional thought. In *African philosophy: An introduction*, ed. Richard Wright, 3rd ed., 41–55. Lanham: University Press of America.

Onyewuenyi, C. Innocent. 1996. *African belief in reincarnation: A philosophical reappraisal*. Enugu: Snaap Press.

Reichenbach, Hans. 1944. *The philosophic foundations of quantum mechanics*. Berkeley: University of California Press.

Senghor, S. Leopold. 1964. *Liberte I: Negritude et humanisme*. Paris: Editions du Seuil.

Sogolo, S. Godwin. 1993. *Foundations of African philosophy: A definitive analysis of conceptual issues in African thought*. Ibadan: University of Ibadan Press.

Wiredu, Kwasi. 1980. *Philosophy and an African culture*. New York: Cambridge University Press.

Chapter 9
How Ezumezu Logic Grounds Some Theories in African Philosophy with a Special Focus on Afro-Communitarianism

Abstract With the structure of Ezumezu laid out in preceding chapters, I want to now demonstrate how Ezumezu logic actually grounds theories in African philosophy and studies. I argue that some theories in African philosophy can be grounded in an Africa-developed system of logic to demonstrate their originality and Africanness and deflate the accusation in some quarters that African philosophers copy their Western counterparts or that African philosophy is not original. I explain what it might look like to ground a theory in African logic. I briefly highlight this with examples of some currents like conversational philosophy, ubuntu, complementary reflection, consolation philosophy and Afro-communitarianism. I pay special attention to Afro-communitarianism which shares a lot in common with the first three by considering the perennial problem of 'priority' that exists in the relationship between the individual and the community. I use the twin issues of individual autonomy and rights to demonstrate how Afro-communitarianism can be grounded in (an) African logic.

9.1 Introduction: How Logic Grounds Theories

With the structure of Ezumezu laid out in preceding chapters, I want to now demonstrate how Ezumezu logic actually grounds theories in African philosophy and studies. I argue that some theories in African philosophy can be grounded in an Africa-developed system of logic to demonstrate their originality and Africanness and deflate the accusation in some quarters that African philosophers copy their Western counterparts or that African philosophy is not original. I explain what it might look like to ground a theory in African logic. I briefly highlight this with examples of some currents like conversational philosophy, ubuntu, complementary reflection, consolation philosophy and Afro-communitarianism. I pay special attention to Afro-communitarianism which shares a lot in common with the first three by considering the perennial problem of 'priority' that exists in the relationship between the individual and the community. I use the twin issues of individual autonomy and rights to demonstrate how Afro-communitarianism can be grounded in (an) African logic.

Every system must have a background logic, declares C. B. Okolo (1993: 13). It is its background logic that defines its structure and gives footing to its principles. We say for example that the version of communitarianism discussed in Western scholarship has the Aristotelian bivalent system as its background logic in that, in such a system, the communal values are said to be prior to individual endowments. Thus, for anyone to argue in the same communitarian system that individual endowments are prior to communal values would amount to a contradiction. So, one could say that the Aristotelian two-valued logic grounds the version of communitarianism discussed in Western scholarship.

Similarly, according to utilitarian ethics, an action is right if it leads to the happiness of the greater number, otherwise it is wrong. From the preceding, it is also clear that utilitarian ethical theory is grounded in the Aristotelian bivalent logic because; it states without equivocation that the logical condition for the rightness and the wrongness of any action is based on the number of beneficiaries. What this logically implies is that if an action fails to account for the happiness of the greater number of sentient agents, it would be deemed as a wrong action and there is no middle way to appeal to. It involves an 'either or' framework otherwise referred to as logical bivalence. It also involves 'truth-value gap' as well as determinism justified by the three traditional laws of thought. In all, once the logical condition of a theory such as utilitarian ethics is not met, then the opposite will be the case, inevitably.

The background logic of a theory is what determines how that theory functions in application. All the principles in a theory are insured by its background logic. For example, theory X makes certain stipulations Y and on the bases of those stipulations makes a range of claims Z. It is its background logic L which makes those stipulations and claims intelligible that makes the violation of those stipulations apparent on the one hand, and justifies the observance of those stipulations on the other hand. The background logic thus provides the conditions under which a theory is said to have been violated or upheld. The viability or otherwise of a theory can only be tested within the parameters of its background logic.

Different theories may have different background logics depending on the tradition of philosophy in which they are created. Sometimes, different traditions of philosophy are driven by different systems of logic as part of the paraphernalia that distinguish them. In this chapter, I will discuss the substance of Ezumezu logic as an African culture-inspired. My aim will be to show how Ezumezu, an African system of three-valued logic developed within the African philosophy tradition grounds some selected theories in African philosophy in order to establish not only the status of African philosophy as a full-fledged tradition but to deflate the accusation that it is a transliteration of Western philosophy. I will briefly highlight examples of some currents like conversational philosophy, ubuntu, consolation philosophy and complementary reflection before I provide a detailed demonstration with Afro-communitarianism.

Finally, I will argue on the basis of my demonstrations that African philosophy is not as Heinz Kimmerle and Jurgen Hengelbrock would suggest, a copycat philosophy or a transliteration of Western philosophy but a tradition in its own right grounded in an African culture-inspired system of logic where its practitioners demonstrate originality and creativity.

9.2 How Ezumezu Logic Grounds Some Theories in African Philosophy

In this section, I will briefly present five notable theories in African philosophy namely, conversational philosophy, ubuntu, complementary reflection, consolation philosophy and Afro-communitarianism and then show that they could be grounded in Ezumezu logic.

Conversational philosophy is a strictly formal intellectual engagement between or among proponents (called *nwa nsa*) and opponents (called *nwa nju*) who engage through the mechanism of arumaristics on a specific thought in which critical and rigorous questioning and answering are employed to creatively unveil new concepts and open up new vistas for thought. Conversational philosophy is a way of philosophising that brings two or more extreme points together to engage each other following a pattern known as arumaristics that allows room for contextual considerations and encourages creative struggle. In other words, the individual identities of the variables are maintained, the encounter is rule-governed and the purpose includes forging fruitful relationship and sustaining the engagement or conversation. Thus, conversational philosophy focuses on the nature, objectives and implications of the relationships between variables. This is why the notion of 'nmeko' or relationship is cardinal to conversational philosophy. It is therefore a way of philosophising that prioritises the relationships between and among variables.

One easy way to understand the nature of variables in conversational thinking is through what is called ontological thesis. This thesis as earlier mentioned in this book states that 'independent realities exist not as isolated units but as interconnected entities in a network'. "Conceived in this way, conversationalists think of reality as one big network of variables some of which are opposed to some others, yet, they are interconnected" (Chimakonam 2017: 18; 2018). There are two types of motions in what is called the conversational curve presented in the preceding chapter which the variables enter that characterise their relationships namely; disjunctive and conjunctive motions. While disjunctive motion symbolised with the constant 'V' refers to the conversational track that leads to the differentiation of opinions as opposed variables diverge, the conjunctive motion symbolised with the constant 'Λ' refers to the conversational track that leads to the homogenisation of opinions or complementarity of views as opposed variables converge.

Conversational philosophy from the foregoing is grounded in Ezumezu logic in that the two epistemic agents nwa-nsa and nwa-nju engage in a third mode called nwa-izugbe, where there is creative struggle to unveil new concepts and thoughts while maintaining their individual identities within nwa-izugbe. This process is a manifestation of arumaristics and ohakaristics and the three supplementary laws of thought. Nwa-izugbe as the name goes is a representation of complementation and mutual cooperation. The relationship between nwa-nsa and nwa-nju occurs in nwa-izugbe but nwa-izugbe is not only a dynamic of coming together, it also involves a dynamic of going apart. While the former dynamic is marshalled by the conjunctive motion, the latter is marshalled by disjunctive motion. The essence of the conversation between epistemic agents is to arrive at a certain station called nwa-izugbe and create certain outputs without the expectation of synthesis. Some of the notable figures in conversational philosophy include Jonathan Chimakonam, Victor Nweke, Uchenna Ogbonnaya, Aribiah Attoe, Uti Egbai, Fainos Mangena, to name just a few.

Ubuntu as a theory in African philosophy speaks to the ideas of caring, interdependence and solidarity amongst humans. It does not necessarily prioritise the agency of human beings as humanism does, it rather places premium on those special and most times, emotional attributes or the 'raw feels' that make people humans and distinguish them from brutes. So, it is a humanness of a sort which highlights the presence of nmeko. Ubuntu is best expressed in the classic, "umuntu ngumuntu nga bantu" which roughly translates to 'a person is a person through other persons' and highlights the values of communion and solidarity (Ramose 2005: 37; Praeg 2017: 299). This is a reflection of the law of nmekoka which enhances the identity of the individual in the collective. Those who promote this theory wish to demonstrate that a tragedy has occurred in our world, a tragedy of sacking emotion out of the circle of human relationship. They do not really stand opposed to rationality but they believe that emotions can moderate the fire of human reason. They believe that it may be important for our brave new world riding on the decisive chariot of reason to sustain the demands of logic but very vital to leave room for exceptions. Ubuntu teaches that we must look at reality twice before we draw conclusions; first, as rational entities and second, as emotional entities. Advocates of ubuntu, a philosophic doctrine that originated from the world-views of southern African cultures, seem to suggest that whilst the goal of humanity is to constantly aspire to alter, advance and make our civilisation more sophisticated, part of that goal is to do so without altering who we are. We want an advanced world but we do not want an 'advanced' humanity, whatever that means. Attempts to alter who we are especially those aimed at challenging our concept of humanity and thus advance the human entity are taking place in the laboratory of the genetic engineer particularly since the later part of the twentieth century. But a good number of his colleagues and by extension other informed intellectuals are battling him ferociously,[1] for it is the conviction of many that humans should remain humans.

Now if ubuntu does not oppose reason but advocates emotion, where does it actually stand? It is important to observe that ubuntu recognises that the human entity has two components; the rational and the emotional. But unlike in Western metaphysics where reason is prioritised over emotion, ubuntu as a representation of the African mind does not necessarily prioritise emotion over reason as Leopold Sedar Senghor (1962) claimed rather too excitedly. What ubuntu as an Africa-developed philosophic construct does is (i) highlight the important place of human emotions even in our modern or if you like, postmodern world, and (ii) show that emotion is there to moderate reason when it begins to overcharge and reason can uphold emotion when it begins to decay. This is guaranteed by the law of onona-etiti. One strat-

---

[1] See. Jonathan O. Chimakonam. 2013. Terminator technology: Appraising biotechnologists' claim to feed the world. *Online Journal of Health Ethics,* 9:1 1–14. Retrieved from http://aquila.usm.edu/ojhe/vol9/iss1/11. This paper outlines some strong ethical concerns in genetic engineering and criticisms of the technology with specific focus on genetic modification of crops.

egy for understanding ubuntu is to view humanity as an entity with two components, independent with distinct identities but which attains self-realisation only when these two seemingly opposed components symbiotically relate. In Ezumezu logic, this represents the inferential pattern from the peripheries to the centre. The reason it seems ubuntu theorists tend to emphasis the emotional component more than the rational component is because, the Western civilisation which is the dominant civilisation in our world today has artfully cordoned off emotion from its epistemology. But discussing ubuntu as if it is in itself opposed to reason is erroneous. Not highlighting reason may be pardoned but denying it is unforgivable because then, it destroys the project of ubuntu from foundation. Some of the contemporary exponents of ubuntu include: Mogobe Ramose, Fainos Mangena, Thaddeus Metz, Michael Eze, Leonhard Praeg and so forth. Ubuntu as a theory can be grounded in Ezumezu logic when we observe the triadic nature of its variables and the complementary relationship that exists between the two extremes, reason and emotion. It is in this relationship, otherwise called nmeko in Ezumezu logic that a humanity with ubuntu is forged. The basic statement of ubuntu which is, 'a person is a person through other persons' is a reflection of arumaristic reasoning upheld by the law of njikoka. Also, the internal dynamic of mutual interdependence found in ubuntu is guaranteed by both the ontological thesis and the law of onona-etiti.

I turn to the theory of complementary reflection propounded by Innocent Asouzu. It is a metaphysical theory also called ibuanyidanda ontology. The concept *Ibuanyidanda* comes from the Igbo language and maxim "ibu anyi danda" which can be translated to, "no load or burden is beyond the capacity of danda, a certain species of gregarious ants to bear". Asouzu's inspiration comes from the complementary way this species of ant lead their lives to construct a philosophy of humanness. This shows the central role of the logical concept of nmeko in this theory. Asouzu draws a distinction between *ibu anyi danda* as a descriptive hypothetical injunction from his system *Ibuanyidanda*—written as one word—which he elevates to a categorical imperative. This for him, rivals Aristotle's conception of being, which is divisive. As he put it:

> Since our tension-laden ambivalent existential experience and *ihe mkpuchi-anya* (phenomenon of concealment) often mislead us into assuming that life is a struggle involving irreconcilable opposites, *Ibuanyidanda* ontology seeks ways of reconciling the apparent ontological tension between being and its attributes. This type of tension found its way into Metaphysics by certain specifics of Aristotle's doctrine of being. (Asouzu 2013: 60)

Ibuanydanda or complementary reflection is therefore a theory of being from an African perspective which weaves its basic tenets around the idea that "being is that on account of which anything that exists serves a missing link of reality" (Asouzu 2004). It harps on the idea of missing link to present reality as many, interdependent and interconnected. To put it succinctly, complementary reflection sees reality as made up of different variables with unique identities. This uniqueness somehow makes them seem opposed to each other but being is not fully realised until these variables interact by complementing themselves. In this way, each variable, no matter how big or small is as important as the other in the network hence, the idea of being as missing link of reality. No variable is useless. The system of reality is like a network in which each variable has an important role to play i.e. it complements and is in return complemented because no variable is self sufficient. This can be explained by what is called the ontological thesis in Ezumezu system. Other scholars who follow Asouzu in this line of thinking include Mesembe Edet, Uchenna Ogbonnaya, Ada Agada, and a host of others.

Again, we can see the pattern of Ezumezu trivalent logic and the three supplementary laws of thought here. Realities may have distinct identities but they complement which is why they are viewed as missing links. Both nwa-nsa and nwa-nju are missing links that find constructive complementation in nwa-izugbe. The method of complementary reflection clearly exemplifies the application of njikoka, nmekoka and onona-etiti showing that opposed variables are sub-contraries rather than contradictions. This is why it is possible for variables to serve as missing links in the collective consciousness or nwa-izugbe.

Also, consolation philosophy or consolationism propounded by Ada Agada is another bourgeoning metaphysical theory in African philosophy founded on the idea of mood in which the interplay of joy and sadness characterises existence and human life. According to Agada:

> Consolationism has put forward its claim as a coherent philosophical system hatched in the image of Africa and therefore rooted in the African universe. It is not beholden to the West since its inspiration is African. Consolationism is a 21st century idealistic-cum-existentialist system... It insists that it is the completion of universal idealism. By positing *mood* at the base of a universe that unfolds not mechanically (and not wholly teleologically) but fatalistically, consolationism announces itself as an African idealism. As the doctrine of *mood*—the primordiality of joy and sadness and their origin in an irreducible silence of eternity—consolationism completes the task of idealism. (2018: 236)

There is therefore the idea of complementarity of the moods of joy and sadness and Ezumezu is the logic of complementarity in which arumaristic inference can be conducted from the peripheries to the centre. Thus consolationism as a metaphysical system is grounded in this logic. The laws or principles of the Ezumezu system, namely, the laws of njikoka, nmekoka and onona-etiti logically ground the arumaristics that undergirds consolation philosophy, which particularly focuses on the reconciliation of opposites and binaries in ever expanding fields where propositions and states of affairs increasingly find a common basis and existential rationale. The dynamism noticeable in the ezumezu (complemented value) where truth and falsity converge is reflected in the dynamism of consolationist philosophy of nature which regards events, objects, and state of affairs as evolving out of a basic given, the unity called *mood* or the proto-mind. This process also reflects the type of inference called ohakaristics in Ezumezu logic, i.e. from centre to peripheries. A concept like fatalism, for instance, which is fuzzy in what Ezumezu will call the complemented value (value-glut) and included middle mode gains clarity in the integration state as an epistemic challenge to the claim of the inviolability of the concept of determinism. Consolation philosophy challenges the straight cause-effect sequence by asserting that in a world whose origin and fundamental nature remains a matter of speculation, laws of nature themselves cannot be sacrosanct. Consequently, consolation philosophy augments the concept of determinism with the concept of fatalism deemed the mother of all necessities.[2] Such a claim finds validity in the laws of nmekoka and onona-etiti explicated in Ezumezu logic. The trivalent logic of Ezumezu which exhibits the conditions of an interconnected, interdependent universe grounds the pansychist framework of consolation philosophy, which seeks to account for an interconnected, interdependent universe by positing the fundamentality and ubiquity of *mood* throughout the universe.

Finally, I come to Afro-communitarianism, a theory that shares much in common with the first three theories already highlighted except that while conversational philosophy and complementary reflection are also methodological, ubuntu and Afro-communitarianism are doctrinal and are anthropocentric. All however emphasis the ideas of engagement, interaction and relationship of seemingly opposed variables in different ways which highlight the presence of the three supplementary laws of thought and the notion of nmeko. The classic expression of Afro-communitarianism is that which is credited to John Mbiti, "I am because we are, since we are, therefore I am" (1970: 141), or as Ifeanyi Menkiti (2004) suggested, a person is a person through the community. Mbiti's maxim specifically reflects both arumaristic and ohakaristic reasoning framework.

Menkiti's radical communitarianism follows the pattern of ohakaristic reasoning in Ezumezu logic in that the community is said to determine the individual. In Kwame Gyekye's moderate communitarianism where there is a balance in the relationship between the individual and the community, both arumaristics and ohakaristics can be found. In Bernard Matolino's limited communitarianism, it would be arumaristics, i.e. from the peripheries to the centre because the individual is said to determine the community. Michael Eze's realist perspectivism in which the relationship between the individual and the community is said to be contemporaneous is guaranteed in the complementary mode by the law of onona-etiti.

On the whole, promoters of Afro-communitarianism as a theory wish to demonstrate the necessity of the idea of mutual interdependence of humans which is explained by the laws of nmekoka and njikoka in Ezumezu logic. You find the communitarian orientation most prominent in the works of researchers working in African philosophy, literature, religions and cultures, etc. Some of them include; John Mbiti, Ifeanyi Menkiti, Kwasi Wiredu, Kwame Gyekye, Michael Eze and Bernard Matolino, OA Oyowe, Motsamai Molefe, Rianna Oelofsen, Thaddeus Metz, Polycarp Ikuenobe, to name just a few.

The centre-piece of the discourses in Afro-communitarianism is the nature and structure of the relationship between the individual and the community. This makes nmeko very important in any Afro-communitarian theory. While those called radical communitarians hold that the community values have primacy over individual endowments, those called moderate communitarians hold that there is a balance;

---

[2] Fatalism claims that the occurrence of events is to be understood in terms of inevitability rather than a rigid cause-effect sequence. An event is not rigidly determined beforehand but once it happens it becomes rigidly determined, and this is only because it could not have happened otherwise after it had occurred. For an event to happen it must first attain the fatalistic threshold or existence-point at which things become actual.

that is, in some ways, individual endowments like rights take preeminence and in some other ways, the community values take primacy. The position of the moderate communitarians is variously modified by those called the realist perspectivists and the limited communitarians respectively. In this chapter, I subscribe to the views of the later that individual autonomy and rights can be defended in Afro-communitariansim but I go beyond that to show how Afro-communitarianism could be grounded in an African logic of Ezumezu. I will proceed now to use the notions of individual autonomy and rights to demonstrate how this can be done.

The question whether there are such things as individual autonomy and inalienable rights in African communitarianism appears now to be one of the serious consequences of the individual-community relationship debate in African philosophy. Majority of African philosophers today may comfortably be grouped under radical communitarianism. These scholars like Menkiti do not subscribe to the possibility of individual rights within a communitarian set-up. Menkiti clearly denies autonomy and rights to individuals within his communitarian vision known as radical communitarianism,[3] while Gyekye in his moderate communitarianism struggles to uphold individual autonomy and rights.[4] Eze and Matolino in their own systems avoided the errors of focus and approach[5] by Menkiti and Gyekye respectively in stating their own proposals that is, realist perspectivism[6] and limited communitariansim[7] but somehow, came short of proper logical clarification sorely needed to justify their claims. Thus, the question still beckons; can individual autonomy and rights be defended within the African communitarian framework? My burden here is to provide the logical clarification needed to successfully defend individual autonomy and rights in African communitarianism and thus ground the later in Ezumezu logic.

At the centre of the individual-community imbroglio is a challenge to 'Aristotelian intellectual hegemony' either to uphold it or undermine it. Menkiti upheld Aristotelian logic to deny individual autonomy and rights; Gyekye upheld and undermined it as he attempted desperately to defend both the individual autonomy and rights and the primacy of the community; Eze and Matolino both undermined it in their various programmes but failed variously to clarify their alternative logical system. At the foundation of Aristotelian thought is his logic, and two principles in our context stand out in the Aristotelian logic; contradiction and bivalence. These are the logical principles that undergird the unqualified communitarianism[8] dis-

---

[3] For a detailed statement of this denial, see Ifeanyi Menkiti (1984, 2004).

[4] See Kwame Gyekye (1992).

[5] Menkiti set out to describe what was the case in pristine African traditional setting instead of what is or what ought to be the case in modern Africa. This constitutes what I describe as error of focus. For Gyekye, he employs a version of communitarianism whose internal logic opposes the position he defends, this constitutes what I describe as error of approach.

[6] For a statement of this theory, see Michael Eze (2008).

[7] For a detailed statement of this theory, see Bernard Matolino (2014).

[8] I use the notions of unqualified and qualified to distinguish the versions of communitarianism discussed in Western scholarship and the one discussed more often in African scholarship.

cussed in Western scholarship which makes it impossible for individual endowments like autonomy and rights to be prioritised over those of the community. For example, if one grants by this logic that the community component is primary in communitarianism, then he cannot negate the primacy of the community over the individual or uphold the primacy of the individual or even the contemporaneity of the two. Some Western communitarians like Michael Walzer (1983), Michael Sandel (1983) Charles Taylor (1992) Amitai Etzioni (1998), etc., might grant individual autonomy and rights but only as derivative or secondary to communal values. The problem with Gyekye and indeed, with most of the African legion who debate the individual-community relationship within the field of African philosophy is failure to first, draw a correct distinction between communitarianism in Western philosophy and communitarianism in African philosophy. Exception must be made of scholars like Eze (2008) Rianna Oelofsen (2015) and Molefe (2017) and some others who dutifully use the term Afro or African communitarianism to sign-post the African intellectual territory.

Masolo (2004) attempted unsuccessfully to distinguish Western and African versions of communitarianism. His failure was due to his assumption on where the difference lies. As he put it, the difference between African and Western communitarianism "lies in the fact they [*Africans*] could appeal to African traditional social and political orders as backing for their claims" (2004, 488 emphasis mine). This view is not only incorrect, it is acutely misleading. The Western communitarians were also influenced by the communal outlook of ancient peoples. The fact that Senghor, Nyerere and others tried to describe the pristine African traditional society in formulating their ideologies and their Western counterparts did not, makes no great difference. The former excavates and repackages the traditional order while the latter uses inspiration from the traditional order to create a new order. The Western communitarians do not have to tell stories of how the idea of common good shaped life in small communities 10,000 years ago in mainland Europe before one could tell that their inspiration was in history, from socialist to Christian thoughts and as far back as the early times. If we take Masolo seriously, then he is saying that besides cultural and historical origins, there is nothing substantially different between communitarianism in both Western and African scholarship. If this is true, then there would be no need to qualify the two and why draw the distinction in the first place following my preceding clarification?

African philosophers who are engaged in the business of defending the African version of communitarianism know that they intend it to be different. The problem is where do we place this difference? It is a correct answer to this question that will determine whether we can find a justification for denying individual endowments as Menkitians do or for affirming them as Gyekye and Matolino do or for affirming the contemporaneity of both as Eze does. A good number of African philosophers are uncomfortable with Menkiti's position; first, his theory describes the pristine African communal setting whereas what is needed is a theory that can account for the current postcolonial setting; second, his theory brazenly denies individual endowments such as autonomy and rights in a modern world where respect for these endowments are cardinal. Most people know about these disagreeable features in

Menkiti's theory but when they criticise him, they do so without addressing the wrong choice of communitarian framework that created the problem of focus. Also, most people may admire Gyekye's attempt to uphold individual autonomy and rights but by ignoring the error in his logic, they end up with conflicting ideas. The question is why? It is because we have not asked the right questions.

To begin with, we must find the answer to the question, what is it that makes a doctrine of communitarianism qualified as African such that it becomes distinguishable from a version that is not qualified? Since African philosophers are the ones that have chosen to develop a different version because they find the one discussed in Western scholarship inadequate, it is their burden to draw this distinction. The Western scholars are not bothered by this problem. From Mbiti to Menkiti to Gyekye to Eze and Matolino, and from Matolino to the current legion working on this theory, no one to my knowledge has seriously attempted this question besides the unsuccessful attempt by Masolo as discussed above.

I locate and place this distinction on logic. It is background logic that supplies the condition under which one version of communitarianism could be said to be qualified as African and another as Western. In the first, there is the presence of an African logic that eschews the strict polarity of contradiction and bivalence, and in the second, there is the presence of Western logic that imposes the burden of contradiction and bivalence. In what follows, I will attempt to use the concepts of individual autonomy and rights to home in on my submission that Afro-communitarianism can be grounded in an African logic.

Thus I ask: can individual autonomy and rights be defended within the communitarian framework? My bold answer is yes, but with a caveat, it would have to be a specific version of communitarianism—the African version—that is based on a system of logic other than that of Aristotle. An example of such a system would be Ezumezu logic. As against contradiction and bivalence in Aristotelian logic earlier highlighted, Ezumezu rides on the principles of complementarity and trivalence. While the principle of complementarity can be stated as saying 'given two seemingly opposed statements, there may be a context in which both may hold to complement each other,' the principle of trivalence can be stated as saying 'for any two polar truth values, there is an intermediate point at which they may come together to form the third truth value.'

Ezumezu logic is an African logic and a variant of three valued logic that is context-dependent which unlike the variants by Jan Lukasiewicz and Stephen Kleene, prioritises complementarity rather than contradiction. It does not deny the principle of contradiction; it only gives pre-eminence to the principle of complementarity. Its mechanism is governed by a type of inference called arumaristics rather than dialectics. In arumaristics, two independent epistemic variables, nwa-nju and nwa-nsa engage in a creative struggle aimed at spinning out new concepts, ideas and thoughts. As highlighted earlier, this creative struggle is characterised by two motions namely; conjunctive by which seemingly opposed variables complement and disjunctive by which they disintegrate. A new intermediate variable or truth value called nwa-izugbe may be created from the interaction of the two cardinal variables or truth values but it is not a synthesis as it is in Hegelian dialectics. This is because, what happens in an arumaristic process is not a dissolution of opposed variables into a synthesis or the harmonising of their identities into a new one, it is rather a complementarity or integration of two independent identities in what is called nwa-izugbe marshalled by the laws of nmekoka, njikoka and onona-etiti. The new thing that is created is tentative and as a result of mutual complementation of identities rather than mutual dissolution of identities into a new one.

African communitarianism is undergirded by this type of logic. In it, the community is viewed from two ends; the anthropological and the sociological. When viewed from the anthropological end, the community is nothing but individual identities and when viewed from the sociological end, it is an assembly, a network or a social affirmation of different individual identities. What is implied is that individuals come together to form communities and a community is what defines the individuals. There is a form of mutual independence and a form of mutual inter-dependence. In the former, the identity, autonomy and rights of individuals can be affirmed and in the latter, the identity of the community can be affirmed as well. Put together, and depending on context, one can defend the priority of individual endowments or community values or even their contemporaneity as Eze had attempted. It is important to highlight above all else, the important place of context in Ezumezu logic. It is because of it being context-dependent that the principle of complementarity is prioritised over the principle of contradiction. Thus the inherent logic of African communitarianism does not place the community first and the individual second as it is the case in the unqualified version discussed in the West, it rather upholds the independent identity of each. African communitarianism thus is not about the community alone, it is about the individuals that form the community and the community that defines the individuals.

The version of communitarianism discussed by Western scholars and indeed, by other scholars, insofar as it is not qualified with the prefix 'African' or 'Afro' has its foundation in Western or Aristotelian logic. In such a system, the best that can be hoped for is a scenario where individual autonomy and rights are dependent on the community. In other words, individual autonomy and rights would be derivatives, that is, they are mere entitlements that are due to the individual by virtue of his membership of the community. Thus if the individual autonomy and rights cannot be defended as stand-alone features of a communitarian set-up, they cannot be so defended in such a system. Individual autonomy and rights must be able to stand on their own or as inalienable before one can say that they are defensible in a system that is communitarian. What Taylor did was to show that in a communitarian system, a measure of individual autonomy and rights can be derived. As constituent parts of the community, it is only reasonable to assume a measure of autonomy and rights for the individual for its full functioning. In other words, the full functioning of the individuals that make up the community translates to the full functioning of the community itself. This is what Sandel (1983) describes as the limit of rights. He suggests that there is room for individual autonomy and rights in a communitarian setting, but that such a room is limited. For Taylor (1992), individual autonomy and rights are possible in a communitarian set-up except that they can only flourish in a community where they are derived from. This simply means that individual autonomy and rights are dependent on the community that awards them in such a system.

Gyekye's position is similar to Sandel's and Taylor's except that at some point, he purports to be defending individual rights as inalienable. Even when Walzer (1983) discusses individual rights as membership rights, that is, that membership of a community is a right; Gyekye seems to object to this limitation. According to him, "the natural membership of the individual person in a community cannot rob him of his dignity or worth, a fundamental and inalienable attribute he possesses as a person" (Gyekye 1992: 114). The problem with Gyekye is that on the one hand, he defends individual autonomy and rights as inalienable, and on the other hand, he grants communal values priority and subsumes the individual under the community. One gets the feeling that he throttles between two world-views, Western and African; and two doctrines, libertarianism and communitarianism. This dips his position in a contradiction.

In his study of African lifeworld, Gyekye feels convinced that there has always been place for the construal of inalienable rights for the individuals despite constituting the community but he seems to go about the defence of this position in an incorrect way. He imported the version of communitarianism geared-up with the Aristotelian logic to mount a defence of an idea that might be peculiar to the African world-view. But it is impossible to defend stand-alone individual autonomy and rights in a system of communitarianism that is not qualified, that is, the version undergirded by the Aristotelian logic. It does not actually matter that Gyekye nicknamed his proposal moderate communitarianism, Famakinwa and Matolino show that there is nothing different between it and the version discussed in Western scholarship, and between the conclusion reached in it and in Menkiti's proposal. What Gyekye should have done which he did not do, would have been to construct his programme of inalienable rights on a different version of communitarianism, but this would warrant a definition of the logic of such a system. Like I indicated earlier, the failure to differentiate African communitarianism from a version discussed in Western scholarship which is a task on logic has been an obstacle for the subject in African philosophy. It was what marred Gyekye's programme.

On the whole, my main task here is to show how some theories in African philosophy like conversational philosophy, ubuntu, complementary reflection, consolation philosophy and Afro-communitarianism could be grounded in an African logic that is African culture-inspired called Ezumezu logic in order to show not only the originality and creativity of the African philosophy tradition, but to establish the falsehood inherent in the claim by some Western iconoclasts that African philosophy is nothing but a transliteration of Western philosophy.

9.3 On the Accusation of Transliteration and Copycat Philosophy

There is an accusation or insinuation mostly by Western philosophers that African philosophy is a "copycat philosophy" and that African philosophers are stealing European and Western ideas (Asouzu 2007). Some Western scholars like Jurgen Hengelbrock and Heinz Kimmerle have clearly suggested this and argued that African philosophy was not yet mature to be regarded as a tradition in world philosophy. Both Hengelbrock and Kimmerle doubt its creativity and originality. It is because of this accusation that I undertake to map out the logic on which theories in African philosophy could be grounded and I showed that this logic could be African culture-inspired thus quashing the suggestion of lack of originality and creativity in African philosophy.

In a debate of 2002 between Kimmerle and Hengelbrock on the topic "The Stranger between Oppression and Superiority," Hengelbrock claimed that the philosophical ideas in African thought are similar to those in what he calls the Westfalian country.[9] This implies that the so-called African philosophy is not true philosophy or philosophy in the 'A' sense of the term. It is a collection of African wisdom. He goes on to show that the attempts to create African philosophy are fraught with lack of originality. He suggests that its creators merely ape and copy their Western counterparts when he bemoans the absence of originality and the receding African culture. As he put it:

> Indeed, arriving in Africa for the first time you feel a disappointment or even a certain shock. You are looking for African culture and you don't find anything but western life style in its worst form, and on the other hand terrible poverty and social disintegration. Speaking with African intellectuals you notice their European education and formation. (Hengelbrock 2002)[10]

Hengelbrock in the above suggests that African intellectuals and philosophers have lost connection with their cultures and are more focused with copying Western cultures and life styles in their worst forms. This shows lack of creativity and originality. Under this type of assessment, it is difficult to talk of a thorough-going tradition of African philosophy especially where African cultures which are to serve as the bedrock for the system of African philosophy are receding, abandoned and neglected. Having observed the immense cultural dislocation, Hengelbrock claimed he was pressurised to ask Paulin Hontoundji, a popular African philosopher: "where is Africa?" and the latter replied, "in our hearts".[11] Disappointed, Helgebrock exclaimed that "indeed, you must go very far in order to find the genuine Africa, far

---

[9] For this discussion, see Jurgen Hengelbrock (2002). You cannot free yourself from Hegel: An encounter with Heinz Kimmerle. Intercultural communication. http://www.galerie-inter.de/kimmerle

[10] Ibid.

[11] Ibid.

not only in a geographical sense but first of all in a mental one."[12] Thus he suggests that the project of African philosophy is a sham with a receding native cultural backbone and a dysfunctional imitation of Western culture.

Kimmerle also shows doubt in the authenticity or even existence of African philosophy tradition. In the preface he wrote to Sophie Oluwole's book, according to Asouzu, "Kimmerle hardly resists the temptation of pointing to the fact that the issues being raised by Oluwole have already been raised in European philosophy. In other words, he appears to be claiming that there is practically nothing new in Oluwole's contribution" (Asouzu 2007: 32).

Kimmerle further drew the implication of Hengelbrock's assertions especially his suggestion that African philosophy can be equated with that of his Westfalian country. Kimmerle (2002) argues that Hengelbrock means to say that the so-called African philosophy is at best cultural wisdom and at worst, poor imitation of Western philosophy. The latter possibility is an accusation that African philosophers are merely transliterating Western philosophy. Godfrey Ozumba in engaging with this accusation of transliteration of Western philosophy explains it as a scenario in which "…the so-called philosophical works in Africa are not about African philosophy, but just European or Western philosophy performed by Africans" (2015: 181). Ozumba goes on to note that:

> To say that Africans merely copy or transliterate, or translate or repackage Western philosophy into African containers is to accuse African philosophers of plagiarism and this opens up another scandal on another stolen legacy. This counter accusation will be the most uncharitable way of redressing the first "Stolen Legacy" Saga. However, it cannot be doubted that Western imperialism has negatively affected the colonized Africa especially in terms of willful erosion of African native culture and thought system which could hamper creativity and originality. (2015: 181)

The above suggests that the inclination to copy or transliterate Western philosophy by practitioners of African philosophy was caused by colonialism and imperialism that destroyed African cultures. Ozumba however claims that the suggestion that African philosophers transliterate their Western counterpart due to the evils of colonialism and imperialism which have eroded confidence in African cultures is to admit a crime that has not truly been committed. According to Ozumba "…inasmuch as I concur that colonialism did untold evil to the thought system and culture of the African peoples, I beg to disagree that what the immense population of African philosophers do amount to copying Western episteme" (2015: 182). Ozumba points that the fact that African philosophers employ Western languages and concepts does not imply that those concepts cannot be unrobed in order for the African original interpretation of reality to be shown. He dismisses the Western accusers as lazy and condemns them for not taking the time to study the corpus by African thinkers in order to understand the message of African philosophy.

Asouzu is another African philosopher who has addressed the accusation that Africans are imitating their Western counterparts. He draws attention to the works of Hengelbrock, Kimmerle and Stegmüller whom he accused of painting philoso-

---

[12] Ibid.

phers in the South as copying Western ideas. He says that this amounts to an accusation that Africans for example are doing copycat philosophy. But he cautions that "[T]his protectionist type of reasoning is a remnant of our natural instinct of self preservation in the course of which we seek to be considered as special types of human beings, along with our cultural heritages" (Asouzu 2007: 32). Asouzu goes on to explain that this type of superior mindset often leads to misleading reports and conclusions about the world and can easily lead to "fallacies that could have very serious implications for coexistence of peoples" (2007: 32). He calls this mindset unintended ethnocentric commitment and claims that it was what has misled Kimmerle and Hengelbrock to "see African philosophy mostly from the optics of African thinking or African thought and African philosophers as native "Westfallian country" thinker [SIC]; "originell" [SIC] or eccentrics" (2007: 32).

9.4 Conclusion

Finally, with all said, my aim in this chapter was to show how Ezumezu, a system of three-valued logic developed within the African philosophy tradition grounds some selected theories in African philosophy such as conversational philosophy, ubuntu, complementary reflection, consolation philosophy and Afro-communitarianism, in order to establish not only the status of African philosophy as a full-fledged tradition but to deflate the accusation that it is a transliteration of Western philosophy. It is, therefore, difficult for anyone to deny the Africanness of these theories and indeed, of any theory whatsoever whose methods are clearly shown to be grounded in African logic as the examples I have used in this chapter show. Part of the importance of this exercise is to show that African philosophy is now a full-fledged tradition like other established ones.

References

Agada, Ada. 2018. In *Ka-Osi-SQ-Onye: African philosophy in the postmodern era*, ed. O. Chimakonam Jonathan and Edwin Etieyibo, 231–252. Delaware: Vernon Press.
Asouzu, I. Innocent. 2004. *The method and principles of complementary reflection in and beyond African philosophy*. Calabar: University of Calabar Press.
———. 2007. *Ibuaru: The heavy burden of philosophy beyond African philosophy*. Münster: Litverlag.
———. 2013. *Ibuanyidanda (complementary reflection) and some basic philosophical problems in Africa today: Sense experience, "ihe mkpuchi anya" and the supermaxim*. Zurich: Lit Verlag GmbH and Co. Kg Wien.
Chimakonam, O. Jonathan. 2013. Terminator technology: Appraising biotechnologists' claim to feed the world. *Online Journal of Health Ethics* 9 (1): 1–14. Retrieved from http://aquila.usm.edu/ojhe/vol9/iss1/11.
———. 2017. Conversationalism as an emerging method of thinking in and beyond African philosophy. *Acta Academica* 47 (2): 11–33.

———. 2018. Ezumezu as a methodological reconstruction in African philosophy. In *Ka-Osi-SQ-Onye: African philosophy in the postmodern era*, ed. O. Chimakonam Jonathan and Edwin Etieyibo, 125–148. Delaware: Vernon Press.

Etzioni, Amitai. 1998. *The essential communitarian reader*. New York: Rowman & Littlefield.

Eze, Michael. 2008. What is African communitarianism? Against consensus as a regulative ideal. *South African Journal of Philosophy* 27 (4): 386–399.

Gyekye, Kwame. 1992. Person and community in African thought. In *Person and community: Ghanaian philosophical studies, 1*, ed. Kwasi Wiredu and Kwame Gyekye, 101–122. Washington, DC: Council for Research in Values and Philosophy.

Hengelbrock, Jurgen. 2002. You cannot free yourself from Hegel: An encounter with Heinz Kimmerle. In *The stranger between oppression and superiority: Close encounter with Heinz Kimmerle*. Intercultural communication. www.galerie-inter.de/kimmerle. Retrieved May 3, 2017.

Kimmerle, Heinz. 2002. Response to Jurgen Hengelbrock. In *The stranger between oppression and superiority: Close encounter with Heinz Kimmerle*. Intercultural communication. www.galerie-inter.de/kimmerle. Retrieved May 3, 2017.

Masolo, Dismass. 2004. Western and African communitarianism: A comparison. In *Companion to African philosophy*, ed. Wiredu Kwasi, 483–498. Oxford: Blackwell Publishing.

Matolino, Bernard. 2014. *Personhood in African philosophy*. Pietermaritzburg: Cluster Publications.

Mbiti, John. 1970. *African religions and philosophies*. New York: Doubleday and Company.

Menkiti, Ifeanyi. 1984. Person and community in African traditional thought. In *African philosophy: An introduction*, ed. Richard Wright, 3rd ed., 41–55. Lanham: University Press of America.

———. 2004. On the normative conception of a person. In *Companion to African philosophy*, ed. Kwasi Wiredu, 324–331. Oxford: Blackwell Publishing.

Molefe, Motsamai. 2017. Critical comments on Afro-communitarianism: The community versus individual. *Filosofia Theoretica: Journal of African Philosophy, Culture and Religions* 6 (1): 1–22.

Oelofsen, Rianna. 2015. Afro-communitarian forgiveness and the concept of reconciliation. *South African Journal of Philosophy* 34 (3): 368–378. https://doi.org/10.1080/02580136.2015.1077306.

Okolo, B. Chukwudum. 1993. What is African philosophy? A short introduction. Enugu: Cecta.

Ozumba, Godfrey. 2015. The transliteration question in African philosophy. In *Atuolu omalu: Some unanswered questions in contemporary African philosophy*, ed. Jonathan O. Chimakonam, 171–185. Lanham: University Press of America.

Praeg, Leonhard. 2017. Essential building blocks of the Ubuntu debate; or: I write what I must. *South African Journal of Philosophy* 36 (2): 292–304. https://doi.org/10.1080/02580136.2016.1261442.

Ramose, B. Mogobe. 2005. *African philosophy through Ubuntu*. Harare: Mond Books.

Sandel, Michael. 1983. *Liberalism and the limits of justice*. Cambridge: Cambridge University Press.

Senghor, S. Leopold. 1962. On negrohood: Psychology of the African negro. *Diogenes* 10 (37): 1–15.

Taylor, Charles. 1992. Atomism. In *Communitarianism and individualism*, ed. Avinery Shlomo and Avner De-Shalit, 29–50. New York: Oxford University Press.

Walzer, Michael. 1983. *Spheres of justice: A defence of pluralism and equality*. Oxford: Basil Blackwell.

Chapter 10
Justifying the System of Ezumezu Logic: An Analysis of the Problematic Structure of 'q na abughi q'

Abstract Here, I hold conversations with the Nigerian philosopher Udo Etuk and the American philosopher W. V. O. Quine whose respective essays "The Possibility of African Logic" and "Carnap and Logical Truth" have stoked the fire of exciting conversations among some philosophers on the nature of logic within African intellectual landscape. I will demonstrate the potency of Etuk's stimulation as an African philosopher of African origin and transcend the possibility question in African logic. I will further clarify the concept of African logic in order to answer the questions some colleagues and students have put across to me in the recent time. Some peers have continued to confront me with the question, is there any justification for the African logic project? I will attempt to provide them with some justifications. Thereafter, as part of the justifications, I will undertake a more rigorously committed exercise of investigating the structure: 'q na abughi q' which I suppose to be the hub of all controversies surrounding the logic question in African philosophy in this contemporary time. I will conclude following the insight of W. V. O. Quine that bad translators are responsible for the creation of what may be called the 'pre-logicality' thesis and adduce that 'q complements not q' which Africans accept as true is the correct translation of 'q na abughi q' rather than the contradiction 'q and not q'.

10.1 Introduction

I will hold conversations with the Nigerian philosopher Udo Etuk and the American philosopher W. V. O. Quine whose respective essays "The Possibility of African Logic" and "Carnap and Logical Truth" have stoked the fire of exciting conversations among some philosophers on the nature of logic within African intellectual landscape. These two conversations will ultimately be to justify Ezumezu as a system in African logic. In the first conversation with Etuk, I revisit the lingering consternation about the status of logic in African philosophy; is it possible? Is it not? If it is possible, what might such a system of alternative logic be like? And in the second conversation with Quine, I will investigate a particularly troublesome structure 'q na abughi q' highlighted in Quine (1960) which I will identify as the central problem of African logic. I will offer linguistic clarifications with Ezumezu system and correct the bad translations in order to emerge with 'q complements not q' as against 'q and not q' as the correct translation of the structure: 'q na abughi q' which is accepted as true in African thought.

In his momentous essay Udo Etuk (2002) extrapolates on what the idea of African logic might be like. I call it momentous because, it was published at a time when the Great Debate on the existence or otherwise of African philosophy has just waned following the disillusionment that trailed the project of deconstruction which crystallised in the works of V. Y. Mudimbe (1988) and Lucius Outlaw (2003) to name just a few. A new wave of consciousness was beginning to manifest in the later period of the history of African philosophy as a result. This consciousness was a drive for reconstruction. In the architecture of philosophy, logic is the central tool. So, it becomes not only needful but timely to ask the question of logic in African philosophy. Etuk's (2002) investigation of this concern thus becomes momentous. Although C. S. Momoh (2000) before him had raised this question and some others like Meinrad Hebga (1958), as well as C. B. Okolo (1993) have all expressed insightful opinions on the subject, it was Etuk that stirred the hornet's nest.

He begins by saying that his foremost goal is to "stimulate the thinking of *African* philosophers (by which I mean philosophers of African origin, rather than scholars who specialise on [sic] African philosophy) along the lines of whether or not there is African logic"(2002: 98). The heart-beat of Etuk's argument in the work is that the implication of the affirmation of the existence of African philosophy is that African logic can also exist after all every philosophy should have a logic. Etuk goes on to investigate a host of concerns including whether such a logic has any distinguishing characteristics or not, whether the project amounts to regionalising what otherwise should be a universal discipline and whether African logic needs to be discovered, invented or created. His conclusion is that the idea of African logic ought not to be dismissed without discussion.

Etuk gives examples of similar credible projects in other cultures such as the Polish, Indian and the Chinese logics and tends to suggest that just like the Poles, a resurgence by African born philosophers might be taken as African contributions to logic as a universal discipline. Etuk is also somewhat proudly opinionated that the appurtenances of African logic which he calls Affective Logic[1] are embedded in African cultures and languages and thus may just require simple discovery.

On another score, one must take a very long look at Etuk's choice of "philosophers of African origin" as best qualified for his proposed project on African logic. This position is not to be taken on its face value. Indeed, it may have some far-reaching implications. For example, why would Etuk want to exclude non-African scholars of African philosophy from this building project? Is he in any way inclined to thinking that logic is of a special stuff which only those connected to the ontological fibre of a given culture can explore? Already, he has suggested that the materials of African logic are embedded in African cultures and languages, should one

---

[1] Etuk most likely got this inspiration from Leopold Senghor (1962) who employed the concept 'affective' in his articulation of the doctrine of black emotional reason.

therefore conclude that it was for this that he has assigned the task of unbundling them to only those ontologically tied to such cultures and languages? If this is what Etuk gestures at, then he would have some of the die-hard universalists who would not place any limitations in *personale* whether in application or formulation of principles of logic to contend with.[2] This is a very exciting controversy which Etuk's essay stylishly birthed, something I am now inclined to name 'Etuk's Natural Selection' principle.[3]

On the whole, the importance of Etuk's work spans beyond a contribution to an ongoing debate. It was a work properly timed and which raises several issues the determination of which will be central to the resolution of the logic question in African philosophy. In this chapter, I will demonstrate the potency of Etuk's stimulation as an African philosopher of African origin and transcend the possibility question in African logic. I have already formulated the principles and linguistic rules of Ezumezu logic in the chapters above. Here, in order to provide justification for African logic project, I will further clarify the concept of African logic just to answer the questions some colleagues and students have put across to me in the recent time. Some peers have continued to confront me with the question, is there any justification for the African logic project? I will attempt to provide them with some justifications. Thereafter, as part of the justifications, I will undertake a more rigorously committed exercise of investigating the structure: 'q na abughi q' which I suppose to be the hub of all controversies surrounding the logic question in African philosophy in this contemporary time. I will conclude following the insight of W. V. O. Quine that bad translators are responsible for the creation of what may be called the 'pre-logicality' thesis and adduce that 'q complements not q' which Africans accept as true is the correct translation of 'q na abughi q' rather than the contradiction 'q and not q'.

10.2 Clarification of the Concept of African Logic

I have in chapter six given a conception of African logic. Here, I wish to clarify that conception by answering some critical questions concerning logic in a generic sense and African logic in a regional sense which have been posed to me by peers. These are no doubt loaded issues which I shall attempt to address in this section. To begin with, I shall first revisit the question "what is logic?" and thereafter take up the question "what is African logic?" Logic can broadly be defined as the procedure for reasoning. In this way, it means everything from arrangement of thoughts to evaluation of the same following specific rules.

---

[2] See specifically Odera Oruka (1975: 50).

[3] The principle of 'Etuk's Natural Selection' or ENS for short which is inspired by the thoughts of Charles Darwin on evolution may be conceived as an intellectual strategy to affirm or discredit a scholar's submission in African logic based on his/her ontological ties to the cultural roots of the continent.

The word logic comes from a highly dynamic Greek word "logos" which in the context of this usage means "reason". But logic is concerned with "reason" in quite extended way such that instead of "reason" logicians identify their trade with "reasoning", the art or science of. The word reason could elementarily be identified with excuse or explanation why something happened or failed to happen, or justification why something is so. Logic makes use of "reason" in that for every statement that is evaluated true or false and for every argument evaluated valid, invalid or sound, there are reasons. Reasoning on the other hand (colloquially) has to do with the process of establishing connection or disconnection among a set of explanations. In the former, we traditionally ask: what is your reason? …why did you do that?…why is it so?…why do you think so?…indeed, every explanation seeking why question is prompted by some "reason." Whereas in the latter, we ask: have you reasoned it out? Is it reasonable?… can you prove it?… we also make demands such as; convince me that…defend your claim that…show us that…etc., these are justification seeking questions and demands that are not so much interested in why something happened or failed to happen but on the connection or disconnection that exists in a set of explanations.

Leila Haaparanta (2009: 3) is of the view that "when we state in everyday language that a person's logic fails, we normally mean that the rules of valid reasoning, which ought to guide our thinking, are not in action for some reason." This is why it is fair to conceive it as a procedure for distinguishing correct reasoning from incorrect reasoning. This is also why Elliott Mendelson (1997) indicates that one of the popular definitions of logic is that it is the analysis of methods of reasoning. He goes on to suggest that in studying these methods, logic is interested in the form rather than the content of the argument. It is for this that Irving Copi (1982) says that a standard valid argument is valid by virtue of its form alone. This is not to suggest that content or subject matter has no place in logic. In fact, since the modern time logic has evolved towards not only greater exactness and precision in formal terms but towards evaluation of content in terms of subject matter. There is now a bridge between the syntactic and the semantic components of logic. As early as the nineteenth century, George Boole (1854) writes that to enable us deduce correct inferences from given premises is no longer the only object of logic. Just as Richard Kaye clarifies:

> The principal feature of logic is that it should be about reasoning or deduction, and should attempt to provide rules for valid inferences. If these rules are sufficiently precisely defined (and they should be), they became rules for manipulating strings of symbols on a page. The next stage is to attach meaning to these strings of symbols and try to present mathematical justification for the inference rules. (2007: viii)

In this way logic as Chris Ijiomah (1995) notes is about relations among statements and the realities which the symbols represent. This position obviously corroborates the assertion of Kaye above. But it was Jean van Heijenoort (1967: vi) who writes that "a great epoch in the history of logic did open in 1879, when Gottlob Frege's *Begriffsschrift* was published". Frege's contributions to modern logic are many but we are here concerned with the extent to which his emphasis on semantic content could influence the development of alternative logics. Dale Jacquette explains that:

> Logic is no longer the monolithic edifice to which Russell could point in 1914, when in our *Knowledge of the External World* he made his famous observation that, "[E]very philosophical problem, when it is subjected to the necessary analysis and purification, is found either to be not really philosophical at all, or else to be, in the sense in which we are using the word, logical" .... When contemporary philosophers speak of logic, they generally mean to refer to any of a variety of alternative formal symbolisms that can be used to formulate particular aspects of the formal inferential structures of language, including but not limited to languages in which philosophical ideas are conveyed... .to define the concept of logic, to understand the diverse kinds of systems that have been considered logics, and to arrive at a satisfactory definition of the concept of logic that applies alike to Aristotelian syllogisms, Boolean algebras, Frege's *Begriffsschrift*, Whitehead and Russell's *Principia Mathematica*, and unlimitedly many non standard formal systems, and informal logic in several traditions, grading off into rhetoric, argumentation theory, and discourse analysis, is a formidable task. (2006: 1)

My concern here is not to attempt this formidable task but to offer clarifications on logic as a discipline with different traditions. Thus from the thoughts of Jacquette above, we can also see the extent to which the original absolutistic conception of logic may be watered down chiefly because of the place of content analysis which Frege harped on in the history of modern logic. What constitutes correct reasoning may now vary from one logical tradition to another depending on contexts which could now determine applications of the same rules. The admission of semantic content also meant that logical expressions could be relativised according to contextual demands. This automatically entrenches the idea of logical relativity which endorses the existence of various logic traditions.

10.3 Justifying the System of Ezumezu Logic

Ezumezu is a system of three-valued logic, but the three-valued thought model has had its critics all along. What might the intermediate value be called? How can it be assessed? Some logicians have been worried over its structure and lack of definiteness. The demanding question has always been: how do the opposites converge in the middle value? Also, the idea of a harmony of opposites has mounted the greatest stumbling block on the path of three-valued thought model. How one can justify the project of Ezumezu logic amidst these concerns seems to be the difficult task. My intention here is not to answer these questions clearly and satisfactorily because no one really can engage with such polemical queries. My aim and hope is to say a few things which I believe should persuade those who need persuading, convince those who are doubtful and enlighten those who are already optimistic. The debate on African logic cannot be expected to end in this generation or even in the next but a continuous effort to develop its systems will one day, I believe put the polemicists out of job.

I wish to revisit the three clarifying positions which I put forward elsewhere[4] concerning my idea of African Logic. This is because, if I have to provide a justification for African logic, it is imperative to state what I mean and what I do not mean by African logic.

1. By African logic I do not mean a border-sensitive, culture-bound exclusive system that holds only in African thought and is not universally applicable.
2. By logic tradition in Africa I do not mean in its simplistic form, the applicability or observance of two-valued logic in African thought as the only universal logic.
3. By African logic or logic tradition in Africa, two terms I use synonymously, I mean the system of logic formulated from the world-view of African cultures based elementarily on the extension of the traditional laws of thought. A prototype of this logic is a variant of three-valued system I call Ezumezu logic complete with three supplementary laws of thought.

My first justification is based on the fact that there are different logic traditions for different philosophical traditions and not a one-standard Western particular imposed on all philosophical traditions. It is in this light that Okolo (1993) declares that every philosophical system must have its own background logic. My idea of African logic can correctly be understood as one of those traditions. It is a three-valued logic that prioritises the law of onona-etiti over the law of excluded middle; njikoka over identity and nmekoka over contradiction. It is my claim that logic is what determines a philosophy tradition by grounding its methodology. The idea of universality of logic is not about universalising the particulars in a dominant culture or about sweeping generalisations of a universal principle, it is about principles and systems that have widespread applicability. But having a widespread applicability does not mean having an unlimited sphere or what can be called an absolute applicability. Universal principles and systems should have limitations. As I expressed it in the first and second universalness theorems earlier in this book, universal systems are consistent and their formal statements are context-specific and if a system is universal and consistent then it cannot be absolute nor can its formal statements be context-non-specific. So, my justification for African logic stems partly from the supposition that every philosophical tradition requires a logic tradition to rest on, and partly from the argument that properly formulated systems of different logic traditions would all be universal and consistent with reference to the first and second universalness theorems.

The problem of most philosophical traditions from the global south is that they readily adopt the Aristotelian two-valued logic in developing their philosophical traditions but this has its lapses. It amounts to sometimes, in keeping the bath water and throwing the baby away. This is because the theories they mold in their philosophical traditions end up having the same logical structure as Western philosophy. This has led to the accusations of transliteration and copy-cat philosophy. Some assessors of other philosophical traditions like the African philosophy have suggested that there is nothing in African philosophy that was not already in Western

---

[4] See Jonathan O. Chimakonam (2015: 115–116).

10.3 Justifying the System of Ezumezu Logic

philosophy thereby insinuating that African philosophers copy Western philosophy and simply tag it African philosophy.[5] Recall that Paulin Hountondji in his criterion states that African philosophy is that text produced by Africans and described as philosophical by their authors themselves. This creates Paul Feyerabend's infamous impression of "anything goes"[6] including, if possible, copycat philosophy. To avoid this type of scenario, it becomes necessary for various philosophical traditions to formulate the logic system that undergird their tradition. This is what the project on African logic I subscribe to is about.

Unfortunately, Sceptics and nihilists have categorised me as a cultural jingoist and irredentist,[7] I hope by these clarifications I have escaped from such molds of thought. I particularly refer to the Nigerian logician Uduma Oji Uduma and my undergraduate teacher who has given laser-guided criticisms to my thoughts more than anyone else. I must therefore appreciate him and all my critics here as Hountondji would say "for prompting me to clarify certain ambiguities, refine some notions, and occasionally, deepen the analysis" (1996: viii). I have also criticised Uduma especially his polemicism against the possibility of African logic which from the language of his response[8] was not well-received. But it is not proper for a scholar to think that some others should not criticise their thoughts or for him to expect a pious veneration from former students, for as the erudite Nigerian philosopher Peter Bodunrin (1985, xii–xiv) points out, real scholarship consists in "freedom of enquiry, openness to criticism…and non-veneration of authorities." Further, Bodunrin states that "[P]hilosophy thrives on mutual criticism, and criticism is best when it is directed at those who are in a position to reply." This is the main purpose of my 2011[9] publication where I criticised Uduma's work and not "a *gustation* for easy shine" as he sarcastically interpreted it.[10]

A story is told about the ancient Babylonia: while some men trained as architects and building engineers to design and build, others equally trained to be critics of such designs and building. In this way, better and stronger structures like the hanging gardens were built and more builders escaped the punitive draconian edict that punished anyone whose project collapsed and killed people or was found to be substandard. Like the fabled architect and building engineer, I highlight the importance of the peer-critics to my system and state that their contributions have been immensely invaluable.

---

[5] See Innocent Asouzu (2007:.30–32).

[6] See Paul Feyerabend (1975).

[7] See Uduma Oji Uduma (2015).

[8] See Uduma (2015: 89–93).

[9] See Jonathan Chimakonam (2011). In 2011, I was in the final year of my PhD programme and undoubtedly unrenowned and uninfluential in the field but it would be unfair to dismiss one's publication as "a *gustation* for easy shine" simply because he was a student. Not all criticism are correct of course, but sometimes, not all writers express their ideas clearly and without vagueness and ambiguity. The essence of criticism is not limited to making authors correct a presumed error but more importantly, to make them clarify their ideas.

[10] See Uduma (2015: 92).

Here, I have promoted the position that every well-formulated logic tradition like every philosophy tradition participates in the universal idea of logic and has a universal applicability which is nonetheless, limited. This limitation applies to various logic traditions.

It is, therefore intellectually harmful to underrate or ignore the importance of the idea of logical relativity which is what the second universalness theorem demonstrates in the ever evolving world civilisation. According to Bochenski (1965:78), the assessment of the relative merits of systems of logic has become a problem for methodology. This is so because, champions of one universal logic or prototype for civilisation presume in error that it is unthinkable to have more than one logical system with nuances in their rules and principles. This presumption is wrong! There is more than one logical system but their rules and principles are not explicitly different, there are places of intersection despite the differences in the degrees at which the rules are tightened or relaxed. They have a lot in common, in fact, more in common than they have setting them apart.

The relativity of logical systems does not point to boundary-sensitive and exclusive ontologies as in the traditional sense of culture relativity but in a technically refined sense of each system, despite being a part of the universal structure has a relative merit consisting of adjusted principles that mark it from one or two other systems.

This is also the sense we talk of African philosophy as one of the philosophical traditions within the canopy of universal philosophy. It behoves me with wonder why some African philosophers accept the existence of African philosophy as a designate tradition and deny African logic.[11] The error of this group of scholars is much more fundamental because they treat African philosophy as an exclusive entity set apart from universal idea of philosophy. Not knowing how to construct an equally exclusive logic to match, they decided to appropriate Western logic which borrowing a leaf from Aristotle they declare as absolute instrument of philosophising. 'There is no African logic but there is African philosophy' is the most inconsistent assertion of the professional school in African philosophy. Their inconsistency is made further manifest by the sort of criterion they provided for African philosophy namely; it must be produced by an African and the producer must describe it as philosophical.

Yai Babalola (1977) makes a strong suggestion that the foundation upon which the position of the professional or the modernist school rests is faulty which is why he accuses them of avoiding the debate on what constitutes the content of African philosophy. In his response, Hountondji (1996: xii) on behalf of the school states that they were not avoiding but merely postponing the content debate. One however, wonders where the difference lies.

To state that there is African philosophy and at the same time fail to describe the content that forms its structure and the substance that makes it African and marks it out from other philosophies is the pontification of this grand failure. The project of

---

[11] See Makinde (2010), Fayemi (2010), Uduma (2015).

the professional school can, therefore, be likened to the fabled city of Royalux—rich in promises but empty in content and is unsustainable.

On the whole, a dispassionate assessment of my theory of logic articulated in this book is welcome but a fair grasp of African system of thought as Oruka recommends is imperative for understanding it. Non-Africans and certified African born Évoléus are likely to fall into the error of assessing Ezumezu from the spectacle of Aristotelian logic. This would amount to a great error for if Ezumezu complies with Aristotelian standard and principles, what then would make it different from the Aristotelian system? In the next section, I will further shed light on the originality of African logic by address a particularly problematic structure, 'q na abughi q.'

10.4 Investigating the Structure 'q na abughi q'

In sum, the whole fuss about African logic can be reduced to one structural problem namely; 'q na abughi q'. This is an Igbo expression which in English is oversimplified as 'p and not p'. Almost all actors in the troubled field of African logic conceive it as the inevitable contradiction that arises in a three-valued system; an intelligent re-arrangement of bivalence into trivalence that just happens to meet a brick wall. We are already familiar with the idea of three-valuedness from the works of the Polish logician Jan Lukasiewicz and others in the West. So, it does not sound quite strange when some scholars talk of a version of a three-valued system in African tradition let alone novel. What is strange if not downright controversial is the supposition that in the so-called African logic the intermediate value is formed by a seamless complementarity of the two standard values in which contradiction is also vanquished. A classic rendering of this in Igbo language as already stated is 'q na abughi q' which in English appears to translate to 'p and not p'.[12] However, I have observed that this translation is over-simplified because neither 'na abughi' nor 'ka bu' translates to 'and not'. It is on the basis of this type of over-simplification that some Western ignoramuses have dismissed African thought as "pre-logical" or inherently contradictory.

The American logician W. V. O. Quine has taken on Lucien Levy-Bruhl on this error. He accuses Levy-Bruhl of falling into the pit dug by "bad translators" of the heathen form "q ka bu q" who produced the English rendering of the Igbo language expression "ka bu" as "and not". As W. V. O. Quine put it:

> Much the same point can be brought out by a caricature of a doctrine of Levy-Bruhl, according to which there are pre-logical peoples who accept certain simple self-contradictions as true. Oversimplifying, no doubt, let us suppose it claimed that these natives accept as true a certain sentence of the form 'p and not p'. Or—not to over-simplify too much—that they accept as true a certain heathen sentence of the form 'q ka bu q' the English translation of which is the form 'p and not p'. But now just how good a translation

---

[12] This particular structure was erroneously rendered as 'q ka bu. q' by Quine's bad translator. See W. V. O. Quine (1960: 352).

is this, and what may the lexicographer's method have been? If any evidence can count against a lexicographer's adoption of 'and' and 'not' as translations of 'ka' and 'bu', certainly the natives' acceptance of 'q ka bu q' as true counts overwhelmingly. We are left with the meaninglessness of the doctrine of there being pre-logical peoples; prelogicality is a trait injected by bad translators. This is one more illustration of the inseparability of the truths of logic from the meanings of the logical vocabulary. (1960: 352)

Quine in the above tries to show that the truths of logic depend to a large extent on the meanings of the language employed in expressing them. Translations very often and bad translators most especially tend to mislead us. If the natives as Quine calls them accepted as true the logical form 'q ka bu q' as rendered in their own language, it suggests if somewhat intelligently that 'p and not p' may not be the proper translation of 'q ka bu q'. And for Quine, this is enough to demonstrate that Levy-Bruhl's pre-logicality thesis is false.

Quine's analysis in the above is insightful although not completely informing. Quine comes short of telling us which language the expression 'ka bu' is derived from. His description of such a language or its speakers as 'heathen' which means uncultured or uncivilised is no less misleading as Levy-Bruhl's use of the word 'primitive'. For how can uncultured or uncivilised people be masters of logic, a tool only the cultured could be familiar with? We must recall that the word 'heathen' is a cognate for the word 'primitive' which has been used in the mainstream anthropological studies to describe the uncultured or the uncivilised peoples.[13] In philosophy, it has been used to describe a form of thinking pattern that is again uncultured and below Western civilisation.[14] Some African scholars have not minced words in condemning the use of such a term in qualifying African peoples and cultures. Quine's use of a cognate term 'heathen' is no less despicable and uncharitable.

However, the substance of Quine's criticism of Levy-Bruhl is worth further analysis. As Quine did not specify which African language the expression 'q ka bu q' is derived from, I am inclined to think it is the Igbo language, one of the Niger-Congo family of languages spoken by over 40 million people in West Africa. In it, the expression 'ka bu' means 'is still or remains'. Thus 'q ka bu q' translates in English to 'q is still q'. One could see Quine's suspicion that a certain bad translator may have done some injustice to the expression on the basis of which scholars like Levy-Bruhl reached their off-handed conclusions. The Igbo logical expression 'q ka bu q' does not translate to the contradiction 'p and not p' or 'q and not q' as erroneously supposed, rather it translates to 'p is still p' or 'q is still q' which is a sort of identity.

The Igbo expression for 'q and not q' is something like 'q na abughi q' where 'na abughi' could easily be translated somewhat clumsily as 'and not'. The reason why I used the expression 'something like' is because even though the English translation is what appears to be said, it is not exactly what is meant. 'Na abughi' does not translate exactly to 'and not' as understood in the formulation of a logical

---

[13] See: Francis L. K. Hsu (1964). Hsu did a wonderful survey of the use and meaning of the concept 'primitive' in the field of anthropological studies.

[14] See: William V. Brelsford (1935).

contradiction. For lack of a better English translation, it can be said to translate more closely to 'complements' as in 'q complements not q'. There is recognition of their structural difference as well as their similarity—difference in terms of quality (affirmation and negation) and similarity in terms of quantity. It is however the latter that is prioritised. Quantities though different in quality may complement—the particular can complement the universal and vice versa. The correct idea then is complementation rather than conjunction plus negation. We can employ the analogy of husband and wife or men and women to explain this. It is this that the Igbo mean when they use the symbolism 'q na abughi q' which they accept as true rather than the misleading English translation 'q and not q'.

My formulation of Ezumezu logic is based on this idea of complementation rather than conjunction plus negation of seemingly opposed variables. In no way does it amount to the denial of contradiction. What is achieved in reasoning in this fashion is another, equally intrusive way of looking at realities and their relationships thereof. We can analyse the relationship between two realities in terms of identity (q ka bu q), contradiction (q na abughi q) and excluded-middle (p ma obu q) but so also can we analyse such relationships in terms of complementation (q na-abuighi q). I have hyphenated the second occurrence of 'na-abughi' to differentiate it from the first.

10.5 Conclusion

In this chapter, I have focused on one of Etuk's papers on African logic. A number of scholars including Uduma Oji, Chris Ijiomah and the present author to name just a few have variously reacted to the work. Its contribution to the shaping of the field of African logic is immense. But the work has its low points. One that I must mention was its limitation to meta-discourse. Etuk did not attempt to create a system of African logic. He restricted the work to discussions on the possibility of such a system as the title suggests. My aim here is to demonstrate how in heeding the calls by Etuk and others like Momoh, I have been able to go beyond the possibility debate to in the words of Kwasi Wiredu (1980: xi) get down to actually creating such a system.

My system called Ezumezu articulated in the previous chapters with elementary principles and linguistic rules receives further clarifications here. Above all, I moved to investigate a particularly troublesome structure 'q na abughi q' that I identified as the central problem of the African logic debate which has tended to make sense of the so-called 'pre-logicality' thesis associated with the purported acceptance as true of a contradictory structure 'p and not p' by Africans. My conclusion was a proof that this supposition was mistaken as it was based on bad translations and translators of African languages. I offered linguistic clarifications and corrected the bad translations in order to emerge with 'q complements not q' which Africans accept as true as against 'q and not q' which is a bad translation of the structure: 'q na abughi q' or indeed, its mis-rendering 'q ka bu q.'

References

Asouzu, I. Innocent. 2007. *Ibuaru: The heavy burden of philosophy beyond African philosophy*. Münster: Litverlag.
Bochenski, M. Jozef. 1965. *The methods of contemporary thought*. Dordrecht-Holland: Reidel Publishing.
Bodunrin, Peter, ed. 1985. *Philosophy in Africa: Trends and perspectives*. Ile-Ife: Obafemi Awolowo University Press.
Boole, George. 1854. *An investigation of the laws of thought on which, are founded the mathematical theories of logic and probabilities*. London: Walton and Maberly.
Brelsford, V. William. 1935. *Primitive philosophy*. London: J. Bale and Co.
Chimakonam, O. Jonathan. 2011. Why can't there be an African logic? *Integrative Humanism Journal* 1 (2): 141–152.
———. 2015. The criteria question in African philosophy: Escape from the horns of jingoism and Afrocentrism. In *Atuolu omalu: Some unanswered questions in contemporary African philosophy*, ed. Jonathan O. Chimakonam, 101–123. Lanham: University Press of America.
Etuk, Udo. 2002. The possibility of African logic. In *The third way in African philosophy*, ed. Olusegun Oladipo, 98–116. Ibadan: Hope Publications.
Fayemi, K. Ademola. 2010. Logic in Yoruba Proverbs. *Itupale: Online Journal of African Studies* 2: 1–14.
Feyerabend, Paul. 1975. *Against method: Outline of an anarchistic theory of knowledge*. London: New Left Books.
Haaparanta, Leila, ed. 2009. *The development of modern logic*. Oxford: Oxford University press.
Hebga, Meinrad. 1958. Logic in Africa. *Philosophy Today* 11 (4): 221–229.
Hountondji, Paulin. 1996. *African philosophy: Myth and reality,*. 2nd revised edn. Bloomington: University Press.
Hsu, L.K. Francis. 1964. Rethinking the concept "primitive". *Current Anthropology* 5 (3): 169–178.
Ijiomah, O. Chris. 1995. *Modern logic: A systematic approach*. Owerri: A. P. Publishers.
Irving, Copi M. 1982. *Introduction to logic*. 6th ed. New York: Macmillan Publishing.
Jacquette, Dale. ed. 2006. Introduction. In *A companion to philosophical logic*. Malden: Blackwell publishing.
Kaye, Richard. 2007. *The mathematics of logic. A guide to completeness theorem and their applications*. Cambridge: Cambridge University Press.
Makinde, M. Akin. 2010. *African philosophy: The demise of a controversy*, Revised edn. Ile Ife: Obafemi Awolowo University Press.
Mendelson, Elliot. 1997. *Introduction to mathematical logic*. 4th ed. London: Chapman and Hall.
Momoh, S. Campbell. 2000. The logic question in African philosophy. In *The substance of African philosophy*, ed. Campbell Momoh, 2nd ed., 175–192. Auchi: APP Publications.
Mudimbe, Y. Valentin. 1988. *The invention of Africa: Gnosis, philosophy and the order of knowledge*. Bloomington: Indiana University Press.
Okolo, B. Chukwudum. 1993. *What is African philosophy? A short introduction*. Enugu: Cecta.
Oruka, Odera. 1975. The fundamental principles in the question of African philosophy. *Second Order* 4: 1 44–1 65.
Outlaw, Lucius. 1987/2003. African philosophy: Deconstructive and reconstructive challenges. In *The African philosophy reader*, ed. P.H. Coetzee and A.P.J. Roux, 2nd ed., 162–191. London: Routledge.
Quine, V.O. Willard. 1960. Carnap and logical truth. *Synthese* 12: 4 350–4 374.
Senghor, S. Leopold. 1962. On negrohood: Psychology of the African negro. *Diogenes* 10 (37): 1–15.
Uduma, O. Uduma. 2015. The logic question in African philosophy: Between the horns of irredentism and jingoism. In *Atuolu omalu: Some unanswered questions in contemporary African philosophy*, ed. Jonathan O. Chimakonam, 83–100. Lanham: University Press of America.

Van Heijenoort, Jean. 1967. In *From Frege to Godel: A source book in mathematical logic, (1879–1931)*, ed. Jean van Heijenoort. Cambridge: Harvard University Press.
Wiredu, Kwasi. 1980. *Philosophy and an African culture*. New York: Cambridge University Press.
Yai, Babalola. 1977. Theory and practice in African philosophy: The poverty of speculative philosophy. A review of the work of P. Hountondji, M. Towa, et al. *Second Order* 2:2.

Chapter 11
Decolonisation, Africanisation and Transformation: Why We Need 'That' African Contribution to World History and Civilisation

Abstract In this final chapter, I take up one of the most menacing problems confronting Africa in our time: the curriculum problem. The curriculum of education in Africa has two fundamental problems namely; it is colonial and thus stifles creative originality of a child, and it is fitted with alien background logic which estranges and condemns its victim to a life time of imitation. To transform this colonial curriculum and construct a new one on the basis of African logic thus becomes the most urgent task which is the focus of this chapter. I will formulate a theory of curriculum transformation in Africa based on Ezumezu logic that utilises the twin strategies of decolonisation and Africanisation. I will argue that it is only a transformed curriculum that can, among others, develop critical and creative thinking abilities in the African child. Further, I will identify some objections that have been levelled against the effort to transform curriculum in Africa and address them.

11.1 Introduction

In this final chapter, I take up one of the most menacing problems confronting Africa in our time: the curriculum problem. The curriculum of education in Africa has two fundamental problems namely; it is colonial and thus stifles creative originality of a child, and it is fitted with alien background logic which estranges and condemns its victim to a life time of imitation. To transform this colonial curriculum and construct a new one on the basis of African logic thus becomes the most urgent task which is the focus of this chapter.

In more than a century, a bad curriculum with unsuitable and alien background logic has been deployed to miseducated the African child. As a result, the intellectual history of Africa since the colonial times has been marred by lack of criticality, originality and creativity. As we take stock and step into the new millennium, the campaign to fix the continent ravaged by centuries of slave trade, colonialism and postcolonialism must get down to the foundation. A badly educated citizenry is the first enemy of the state. African intellectuals must therefore turn their searchlight within to correct the bad structure that eats the continent from within—that bad structure has to do with the education curriculum and its logic. In the preceding chapters, I have laid out principles of a new African logic called Ezumezu, here, I will seek to demonstrate how it can be applied in solving the curriculum problem in Africa.

In 2015, tertiary students in South Africa took to the streets in the famous Rhodes Must Fall protests in which among others, they demanded that universities in the country should stop honouring colonial figures especially the racist ones, should hire more African professors who would serve as role models to African students and include contents on African thought in various disciplines. Since then, ideas such as decolonisation and Africanisation of curriculum have become catchwords in academic discussions and research. These two ideas have become main strategies which African intellectuals are proposing for the actualisation of curriculum transformation.

The students consisting of majority African population claim that the tertiary curriculum in South Africa is too European and that very little of African ideas are taught in their schools. This campaign divided opinions both within and outside South Africa and still continues to do so to this day. Here, I will look at some of the matters arising from the Rhodes Must Fall campaign. This book, which is not only about the African content in education, but, fundamentally, about the African foundation to education, is in line with the demands of Rhodes Must Fall campaign. Beyond that, it seems also to answer some of the objections raised against the demand for curriculum transformation and the twin strategies of decolonisation and Africanisation. I will tap into the models of Africanisation (Chimakonam 2016; Chimakonam and Nweke 2018) earlier developed to formulate a theory of curriculum transformation in Africa that utilises the twin strategies of decolonisation and Africanisation. I will explain that decolonisation involves the removal of some colonial contents, i.e. those aspects of European education curriculum that denigrate and subordinate the African and his culture and replacing them with re-valorised African contents. I will also explain that Africanisation takes place only when decolonisation has occurred. Africanisation for me involves replacing the background Western logic with a prototype African logic, so that it would be African logic that drives the transformed curriculum which will make it truly African and suitable for the education of the African child. I will argue that it is only a transformed curriculum that can, among others, develop critical and creative thinking abilities in the African child. Further, I will identify some objections that have been levelled against the effort to transform curriculum in Africa and address them. Finally, I will show how slavery and colonialism destroyed African knowledges in order to provide further justification for this book.

11.2 A Theory of Curriculum Transformation in Africa: From Decolonisation to Africanisation

This theory states that decolonisation and Africanisation are twin strategies required to achieve curriculum transformation in various disciplines in African school systems. These strategies also represent the two main phases of curriculum transformation beginning with decolonisation and ending with Africanisation. While the phase of decolonisation focuses on content, the phase of Africansation focuses on background logic. What this entails is that there cannot be transformation without any of the two strategies or without the proper sequence of the two. In other words, transformation cannot be achieved if decolonisation occurs but Africanisation did not, or Africanisation occurs before decolonisation. So, transformation is what happens when a curriculum has been decolonised and then Africanised. I believe that this is where the so-called African renaissance should begin.

There cannot be a new beginning for the continent until it is able to identify the foundation of its post-independence crises and restructures its epistemic formation. Slavery, colonialism, imperialism and postcolonialism were and are still possible because Europe conquered Africa epistemologically. Usually in war, when a nation is conquered, its cities and villages are burnt down. This was what happened when Europe conquered Africa epistemologically, they burnt down the African epistemic formations, something Boaventura de Suosa Santos (2016) calls epistemicide. Now, if Africa wants to create a new beginning, it must raise a new structure. I am of the view that this structure need not be completely African, it should not! If the pristine African epistemic formations were good enough to mediate and satisfy the requirements of modern age, Europe would not have conquered Africa. So, a certain level of humility and honesty is required at this critical stage to harmonise and consolidate the new found intellectual audacity. This new beginning is a delicate project that must be executed with precision. We must humbly accept that Europe has made an appreciable level of advancement in knowledge. We should then take the relevant aspects of this knowledge system and do away with those that are not relevant or that are harmful. Also, we should be proud to assert that Africa before colonialism has a certain level of knowledge advancement in some areas that may still be relevant in this age. We should take these relevant aspects and do away with those that are not relevant or that are harmful. In merging the local content with the borrowed foreign content, we should be able to forge a new and formidable epistemic vision. To complete the process, we must then Africanise this new vision by rooting out Western logic and replacing it with African logic as the new driver of epistemic processes in Africa. In this consists my theory of curriculum transformation. I will get down to the specifics presently.

I would like to now define our main concepts and clarify our strategies beginning with decolonisation. To understand the concept of decolonisation, we have to understand the concept of colonisation under the context of usage, that is, curriculum transformation. A colonial education curriculum focuses on displacing the African content with the European content. It denigrates the African content and valorises the European content as *the* knowledge. The colonial curriculum which is primarily structured to keep the African below the European is deployed to (1) prepare the native for a life of service to the colonial power and her peoples whether as a house maid, errand boy, book keeper, etc., the native is prepared to submit both body and mind to the service of colonial authority with diligence and obedience and without questioning or rebelling against authority. (2) It is also structured to rupture the psychology of the native by subordinating his culture and world-view as barbaric, uncivilised and bush. Once this is accomplished, and the native loses self-confidence and a sense of cultural pride, it becomes easy to cut him off from his cultural roots and disidentify him. (3) Once the goal outlined in number 2 is achieved, the native enters a stage of struggle to mimic his colonial conqueror in order to become civilised and achieve a new identity, a self-delusional phase that entraps him in a mental slavery and embeds the feeling of inferiority of the self and the superiority of the colonialist permanently in his psyche. (4) The colonial curriculum is also structured to present colonial knowledge formation as *the* knowledge, residualise the native content and destroy permanently the possibility, veracity and viability of a native knowledge system. (5) Finally, the colonial curriculum is not structured to develop the critical and creative thinking abilities of the natives. If anything, it is structured to ensure that these abilities are destroyed as early as possible in the life of the African and make him a life time imitator of the European.

The above represents the goals of 'colonial' curriculum. But what are the goals of decolonisation of a curriculum? There are two goals namely; (a) to displace the aspects of European curriculum that negate the African and his culture, (b) and to replace them with aspects of African cultural ideas that valorise the African identity and are relevant to modern age. So, to decolonise a curriculum would mean to alter some of its contents such that the African content becomes valorised and comes to displace the negative aspects of European content or those aspects I describe as 'colonial.' This displacement is marginal because it is not every aspect of modern European intellectual accumulation that is colonial. There are aspects that are positive, progressive and relevant to modern age. We must retain and improve upon these aspects in ways that can bring advancement to African peoples. There is nothing shameful about borrowing from other cultures. Every culture borrows from others including the European culture which is in many ways indebted to African cultures.

Thus, decolonising a curriculum does not mean denigrating all of the European content or displacing established intellectual ideas that are progressive. The aspects of a curriculum that are 'colonial' in keeping with my explanation above are those that denigrate the African cultures, ideas and the gamut of the African epistemic formation and all those strategies that discount the African content, rupture the psychology of the African, destroy his self-confidence, his critical and creative thinking abilities, his sense of identity and cultural pride. It is to this collection that the concept of decolonisation applies. Because colonisation was systematic, decolonisation of curriculum should also become a systematic displacement of colonial content in the education systems and curricula of African countries.

Now I turn to the strategy of Africanisation. To understand this concept, we have to first understand what the concept of 'non-African' means under the context of curriculum transformation. If a curriculum is said to be non-African, it means it is foreign, could be European or Asian, etc., but it is not 'colonial.' A non-African curriculum represents the best ideas that drive the knowledge institutions in a foreign culture. Since much of Africa was colonised by European powers, it means that the foreign curriculum ideas that we have are mainly European. Now, if the strategy of decolonisation has enabled us to cut off aspects of the European curriculum that are inimical to the African culture and personality, it means that what is left are those adjudged to be positive, progressive and relevant. To the vacuum that is created when the negative aspects were displaced, African content is brought in to replace them. So we may now have what can be called a decolonised curriculum which comprises of harmless, positive and relevant aspects of European and African intellectual accumulations. But this is still not good enough for the proper education of the African child.

The African was first African before he became cosmopolitan. Similarly, the European, the Asian, the South American, the native American, etc., were first a citizen of his culture area before he became a citizen of the world. As appealing as cosmopolitanism and various forms of homogenisation might be, diversity and or differentiation is a beautiful aspect of humanity that should never be trivialised or allowed to disappear. The cultural identity of various peoples are retained and protected through education. In the past, this used to be done through indigenous systems of education. But with the advent of modernity, things have changed. It means that we can now retain and protect cultural identities through formal education system adapted to different cultural requirements. The problem is that those cultures like in Africa who passed through the unfortunate phase of colonialism found themselves in danger of losing their cultures and their identities. The insistence that everything African was diabolical, bush, barbaric, uncivilised and harmful as the colonialist has falsely claimed; that there are aspects of pristine African cultures that are healthy and relevant to modern age and that these good aspects should be integrated to those borrowed from foreign cultures in a bid to create Africa's new beginning, is the bastion of the call for curriculum transformation in Africa. And this process is not completed without the strategy of Africanisation.

Africanisation involves two stages; the first is rooting out Western background logic and planting African logic as its replacement to drive the new hybrid curriculum. The second is assembling relevant foreign contents from diverse cultures and combining them with relevant local content to form a formidable system. So, even though the new curriculum is a mixture of African and foreign contents which by the way should accommodate ideas from Asia, south America and other cultures, the logical framework that undergirds it would be African, and this is what would make such a curriculum African. Every borrowed idea is re-shaped and restructured to suit African needs with the tool of African logic. It is only when this second strategy of Africanisation is achieved that a curriculum could be said to have been transformed. Below is a figure of a transformed curriculum (See Fig. 11.1 below).

Fig. 11.1 Structure of a transformed curriculum

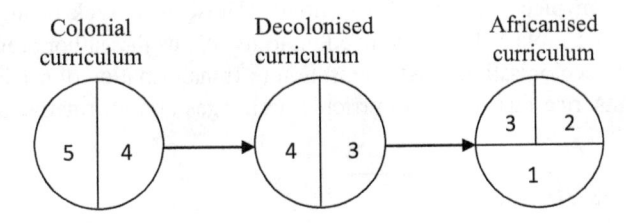

Colonial curriculum → Decolonised curriculum → Africanised curriculum

11.2.1 Interpretation

1. African Background Logic
2. Relevant Foreign Contents
3. Relevant African Content
4. Relevant Foreign Content and Logic
5. Irrelevant Foreign Content and Logic

I have a firm believe that a transformed curriculum in the African school systems is the first step towards ending postcolonialism—a continuation of colonialism in subtle ways—and entering the post-colonial era—the period after colonialism. It is in this era, which is yet to come, that African intellectuals, as products of a transformed curriculum would be able to go beyond adding or improving upon what Europeans and other peoples have done in world civilisation but most importantly, would be able to make 'that' African contribution to world's knowledge formation in the modern age.

Thus transformation or the T-model becomes a theory for Africanising a curriculum. I have arrived at this model-theory by tapping into the previous models, B, C, D which I first created (in 2016) as well as the P-model which Victor Nweke and I created (in 2018). From the B-model, I harnessed the idea of balancing different contents; from D-model I took the idea of displacement to bring in African background logic in place of Western logic and from the P-model, I took the idea of plurality to create a formidable and diverse curriculum content which promises exciting results in the classrooms.

11.3 Why We Need 'That' African Contribution to World History and Civilisation

In this section, I will address a number of objections which some Europeans and their African allies whom I have described as Évoléus in this book have raised against decolonisation, Africanisation and transformation of curriculum. It should be borne in mind that these strategies and campaigns to transform the African intellectual landscape are connected directly to the project of this book which is to recreate African culture and identity on the foundation of a systematised African logic.

Soon after a wave of Rhodes Must Fall protests gripped South African tertiary institutions in 2015, David Benatar of University of Cape Town published an opinion piece in *Cape Times* titled "Those who seek changes must show they are desirable."[1] The piece lived up to its title as the author argued point after point that decolonisation or Africanisation or transformation of academic landscape of South Africa that involves curriculum changes and affirmative action may not be desir-

---

[1] See David Benatar (2015).

11.3 Why We Need 'That' African Contribution to World History and Civilisation

able. In response, Xulela Mangcu also of University of Cape Town in a rejoinder titled "Racially offensive diatribe has no place"[2] articulated a six-point rejoinder with which he dismissed Benatar's submissions as racist and misinformed. However, Mansoor Jaffer of the University of the Free State waded in to douse the rising tension. In his piece titled "Mangcu has a point, Professor Benatar,"[3] Jaffer clarified the points in Mangcu's arguments in a less provocative tone. I have no intention of analysing each submission and passing personal judgements in order not to raise the tension further. But I believe as Jaffer pointed out is that a functional synergy of those at the two sides of this argument would be inspirational in leading the African intellectual heritage "to our halls of learning where they belong." This is because, it may not be the case that those who are opposed to Africanisation of our education system are racists. It could just be that they needed to be convinced of its necessity and viability. But those of them on the opposition side must also realise that the way they insist on the so-called proven European methods and standard sometimes, may come across as insensitivity to the African condition hence, the accusation of racism. I will leave this here and move over to another important scene in the Africanisation campaign.

By September 2015, Edwin Etieyibo of the University of the Witwatersrand invited some philosophers to discuss the boiling issue of Africanisation of curriculum in South Africa. I was not invited to this workshop but somehow, when they managed to reach a resolution at the end of it to write papers and bring out a special issue in the *South African Journal of Philosophy* dedicated to "Africanising the philosophy curriculum in universities in Africa," I was invited to contribute a paper. I accepted this invitation heartily because I had been working on a similar project to Africanise philosophy curriculum in the University of Calabar since 2013 when it had not acquired the flashy names of decolonisation and Africanisation. Some people in attendance at Etieyibo's workshop, I believe, were already aware of the project of setting up a Department of African Philosophy at my university which the likes of Innocent Asouzu and myself were spear-heading.[4] Thus inviting me to contribute a paper in the planned special issue on Africanising the philosophy curriculum appears well-informed.

The special issue was published timely in 2016 with fourteen articles from some of the most vocal philosophers on the continent at the time cutting across different races. Expectedly, opinions were divided with some contributions endorsing the project to Africanise, some opposing it and some others hanging on the fence. My

---

[2] See Xulela Mangcu (2015).
[3] See Mansoor Jaffer (2015).
[4] Unfortunately, internal politics has trapped the white paper generated by the committee at the faculty curriculum committee for nearly 5 years now. The committee that sits every month is yet to deliberate on the department of African philosophy proposal submitted to it in 2015 despite constant reminders from me. This programme was to be the first of its kind in the world to the best of knowledge and it was to serve as a model for others to copy from. A number of colleagues from elsewhere in Nigeria and beyond still ask me questions. This reminds us that colonialism may have done great evils to Africa but the havoc which the postcolonial mindset is doing to Africa might be worse.

contribution titled "Can the philosophy curriculum be Africanised? An examination of the prospects and challenges of some models of Africanisation" was among those that endorsed the project. In it, I proposed some models—B, C and D models—and the C-model was what I recommended for the University of Calabar project. I discussed these models and examined their prospects and challenges. In the end, I left the judgement as to which model is preferable open to the readers as I was unsure at that time.

Due to the internal conflict I experienced, I started another research with Victor Nweke almost immediately. He too was not comfortable that I had avoided taking a position which I tried to explain. What resulted eventually was a co-authored paper published in 2018 in *Dialogue: Canadian Philosophical Review*. In the paper titled "Why the 'Politics' against African Philosophy should be Discontinued," we went beyond the B, C and D models and proposed the P-model as something more cosmopolitan, progressive and viable. Chiseled out of the method of conversational thinking, the P-model was designed to be comprehensive by accommodating the best ideas from other cultures besides Europe, but African in outlook.

Over all, my continued endorsement of the Africanisation project is partly because I believe we need a system that can enable African intellectuals to make African contributions to world history and civilisation. A good number of objections have been raised against this project in the *Cape Times* conversations I reported above as well as in some contributions in Etieyibo's special issue and I turn now to address some of them.

(a) ***African intellectuals should seek to add something valuable to world's intellectual history rather than think of making African contributions:***

I think there is need for African contributions. The genesis of racism that motivated the transatlantic slave trade and subsequently colonialism can be traced to the idea that the African race is not intellectually endowed and as a result, has not, and may never make any original contributions to world history and civilisation. It, therefore, seemed at the time and to the insincere Europe that the best that can be made of the African was to fashion a labourer out of him. If the African is not intellectually endowed as the reasoning seems to go, then, he is not fully as human as the European stock. It means that the European is at liberty to do with him whatever that advances his interest such as slave labour. Immanuel Kant claimed that from the record of national histories, only those in Europe demonstrated regular progress which means Europe will eventually be the one to give law to the others.[5] In fact, it was even supposed by some that enslaving the African might not be morally wrong because slavery made him useful to 'humans.' In this way, Georg Hegel claimed that "slavery is still necessary: for it is a moment in the transition towards a higher stage of development" (1975: 184). When colonialism was eventually contrived some leading European scholars thought it was a great favour done to the African because it meant that Europeans might now civilise him and hope to turn him into some type of human.

---

[5] See *Kant on History*. Lewis White Beck ed. P. 24. Quoted in Tsenay Serequeberhan (1991: 6).

The African was never looked upon as a human. David Hume put the enlightenment view succinctly when he claimed that the Negroes and other races were naturally inferior to the European race.[6] Kant was more mannerless. He not only claimed that the difference between the African and the European was in terms of the former's mental incapacity, he declared in a sarcastic remark about an African that "this fellow was quite black from head to foot, a clear proof that what he said was stupid."[7] Here, Kant could not even bring himself to refer to the person he was antagonising as a human being. He referred to him as a 'fellow.' One also wonders the type of logical inference Kant employed to arrive at such a conclusion from the premise that the fellow was black.

Further, for Hegel, Africa proper, that is, Africa south of the Sahara has not made any contributions to world history and civilisation. He claimed that Africa was "a land of childhood, removed from the light of self-conscious history and wrapped in the dark mantle of night" (1975: 174). The African for him "is an example of animal man in all his savagery and lawlessness" (1975: 177). In this regard, the African is considered by ill-informed racists in Europe as a being in perpetual infancy who could not handle his affairs chiefly because he has not developed a logical mind.

It is this type of thinking that the African cannot do it for himself that licenses some Europeans to play God and legislate for Africa. The Belgian Priest Placide Tempels[8] who wrote what he called *Bantu Philosophy*—a book that has been shown to severely misrepresent African conception of reality[9]—claimed in the book that it was the responsibility of Europeans to write the philosophy of the Bantu for them. In this same way, as I hear, a certain European government has awarded funding to one of her citizens to produce volumes in the history of African philosophy. To suggest that a government board would approve such a proposal in the twenty-first century without at least, insisting that the European collaborates with some African philosophers shows you the mindset that makes the European think he is the one that can write an accurate history of Africa for Africans, and that he alone, has that responsibility. But the idea is motivated by a more evil colonial intent because they want to put Egypt as the birth place of African philosophy, and place the light-skinned Egyptian at the beginning of African philosophy. It is easy, Hegel (1975: 173) had already divided Africa into three parts, one of which is north Africa which he describes as European Africa and this is widely agreed to in literature. So, if our mystery European philosopher eventually publishes their volumes in the history of African philosophy and begins in Egypt where his characters would be Egyptians, it will further consolidate on the colonial agenda of making Europe the tutor of Africa if without them, Africans may never have learnt philosophy nor how to philosophise. This was how in the past, several European governments and presses commissioned their citizens to write histories of various African peoples. Nowadays, most of those history books have clouds of controversy hovering over them. But it

---

[6] See Richard Popkin. 1977–1978. Hume's racism. 213.
[7] See *Kant on History*. Lewis White Beck ed. P. 24. Quoted in Tsenay Serequeberhan (1991: 6).
[8] See Tempels Placid (1959).
[9] See Innocent Asouzu (2004).

does not matter to Europe that those literature might have misrepresented African histories because it had an agenda and it was actualised.

Similarly, in the present time, this colonial politics is still very much in effect. There are professional bodies for academics and researchers registered and managed by Westerners but with Africa as focus. Some of them are associations for professional African philosophers or scholars in the field of sundry African or postcolonial or Third World studies. When you hear the names, you would be deceived into thinking that these associations are registered in Africa and run by African intellectuals. The shocking reality however is that such is not the case. These mercenary associations get funding from Western governments, multi-national corporations and even from African governments that are usually ill-informed to carry out history-destroying, fact-suffocating programmes, research and publications on Africa. They establish journals where Europeans publish their lies and where few African Évoléus or unsuspecting scholars may have their papers published after serious mutilations of the original ideas they presented. By registering these associations, they deter African intellectuals from registering theirs because no government or corporation would want to work with a 'splinter group' or an unknown alternative association. To ensure that true African professional associations are not registered and did not come into existence, they invite prominent African intellectuals who may have what it takes to set up parallel bodies and put them in committees where they would have no impactful voice, give them mouth-watering allowances for virtually doing nothing and quarter them in exquisite luxurious hotels. In this way, they buy them over and prevent any form of intellectual rebellion.

What I have said in the above are serious accusations no doubt, but I invite any doubter to investigate for themselves. However, it must be clarified that Europe has this sinister agenda for Africa and that some Europeans are directly involved in working it out, does not mean that all European scholars represent this opprobrium in their scholarships. No, that would be an exaggeration. There have been some Westerners that have produced objective research on Africa and there are some Western contemporaries who produce objective research in different areas of African studies. But the point is that those who do the incorrect thing may outnumber those who do the correct thing. For all this, it should be clear now to anyone that truly cares to know why African intellectuals of this age should aim at making 'that' African contribution to the world's epistemic formation. The witch cried the other night and a child died in the morning. African intellectuals of this age must silence the witch so that it does not get to cry another night.

Returning to the objection, if the descendants of Kant, Hume and Hegel in today's world chastise the descendants of those Africans (criticised by their forefathers for having made no contributions to world history and civilisation), for thinking of how to make African contributions to world history and civilisation and instead, recommend that they should rather think of what to add to the advances already made by Europeans, then, it is either such persons making such a recommendation are naïve or insincere. It is possible that many Europeans today are ignorant of the sort of things their fore-fathers wrote about or did to the African and out of sheer naiveté might make pronouncements the implications of which they might not know. Such ignorant pronouncements should not always be interpreted as racist disposition.

Normally, there is a transfer of guilt from the European parents that enslaved and murdered Africans during the slave trade and subsequent colonialism to their descendants today. Even the blood of Christ cannot wash that enormous guilt away. For example, every citizen of Belgium today carries the guilty scar on their palms and foreheads of the murder of over 20 million Congolese in King Leopold's time. We do not expect these scars to fade away anytime soon in this or the tenth generation, but a conscientious restitution by Europeans of today is expected to lighten that burden of guilt. The African intellectual of today must be tolerant enough to understand that not too many Europeans are aware of the bad condition their fore-fathers have subjected the African. Slavery, colonialism and racialism are experiences which the African is familiar with because he lived and still live through them, those who have never and do not have these experiences may never understand the feeling. It is up to us to convince those who need to be convinced and explain to those who lack this understanding but show willingness to learn. I have met quite a number of Westerners a few of whom have mindlessly made what seemed like uncouth remarks towards me but upon closer conversations come to realise that what they said were offensive and apologised. We all err as humans, sometimes, from the point of ignorance, and so we must give our offenders the opportunity to make up for their mistakes, if they genuinely desire it because this type of ignorance can affect anyone, whether African or European. For example, many Westerners today do not know that 'black' which they use in referring to those believed to have dark skin is a racial slur. Many Africans today do not even know this and would proudly refer to themselves as blacks. There is no limit to the harm which ignorance can cause and we now know better that the European is not immuned to the problem of ignorance.

I am not saying that ignorance is an excuse especially when one that is afflicted by it shows unwillingness to be led to the light of reason and understanding. What I am saying is that we must be cautious and careful to clearly note the difference between a racist and one whose ignorance portrays as a racist. In this age and time, where we can boldly claim that we know better, racism is an act of foolishness and insensitivity to other peoples and a sign of decline to infantile way of thinking. All the reasons that justified the subordination of fellow human beings in the past were foolish then and even more so now. A twenty-first century racist is probably a fool forever. Most times, we cannot detect a racist by his actions because humans pretend a lot. But a racist knows in his heart that he is one just as a criminal knows himself. As the victims of a hidden racist's bitter machinations are shielded in the innocence of their ignorance, it is the quiet racist that burns himself away like a candle at the devil's altar. In the end, a racist, whether open or hidden, reaps doom, inevitably.

Further, the recommendation that African intellectuals of today should aim at adding to what Europeans have done is amusing to say the least. What would such persons seriously expect the African who is striving to catch up to what the European has done to add to such knowledge accumulation? Unless of course, such a recommendation is guarded by spikes of insincerity, to wryly put the African to a difficult challenge, to expose him to mockery and undermine him further. This recommendation is like Zeno's fabled race between Tortoise and Achilles in which Achilles starts at a distance behind Tortoise consisting of infinite number of points so that no matter how fast Achilles runs, he would never catch up with Tortoise let alone overtake him. It is important that Europeans who think this way and instrumentalise the pride in their history learn some lessons in humility. No one gave the Chinese any chances some 50 years ago, but look at where they are today. Not quite long ago in history, the Greeks regarded the present day Germans where the proud Kant and Hegel hailed from as barbarians, but look at where Greece is today, the country almost depends on Germany for its daily bread.

There is certainly nothing wrong if African intellectuals can add or better still improve upon what the Westerners have done but that should not be the primary target. There is need for 'that' African contribution. Europeans have earned their name as authors of modern civilisation not by adding to what they stole from Egypt but by utilising that inspiration to create new ideas, invent new methods and open new vistas for thought. This is exactly what the Chinese are doing at present. Why would Africans be given the lowly responsibility of adding to what others have done? It needs be reminded that the mindset that compels some Europeans to make this recommendation might not be so different from that which views the African as subordinated. Otherwise, why would some Europeans of today feel entitled to be the ones to tell Africans what to do and what not to do? Why should they see this as their responsibility? To this end, the first task of the African intellectual of this age is to emancipate themselves from mental slavery so that he can make that all important modern African contributions to world history and civilisation. Any other thing should be secondary.

(b) *The supposition that Africans are intellectually inferior:*

The main argument which racists used to justify slavery in those days and which formed part of official government policy in some countries in Europe was that "blacks were intrinsically, naturally, inferior to whites" (Fauvel and Gerdes 1990, 144; see also Barker 1978). Hume believed that there was no nation of the dark complexion that had any civilisation. In his words:

> I am apt to suspect the Negroes to be naturally inferior to the Whites. There scarcely ever was a civilized nation of that complexion, nor even any individual, eminent in either action or speculation. No ingenious manufactures amongst them, no arts, no sciences. ... Such a uniform and constant difference could not happen, in so many countries and ages, if nature had not made an original distinction between these breeds of men. Not to mention our colonies, there are Negro slaves dispersed all over Europe, of whom none ever discovered any symptoms of ingenuity, though low people, without education, will start up amongst us, and distinguish themselves in every profession. In Jamaica, indeed, they talk of one Negro as a man of parts and learning; but it is likely he is admired for slender accomplishments, like a parrot who speaks a few words plainly. (Hume 1741–1742, 123)

It is obvious from the above that Hume's racism was ingrained. He was even unwilling to accept testimonies of those who had interacted with a certain eminent African intellectual in Jamaica. He rather chose to denigrate the opinion of eye witnesses and ridicule such as misjudgement.

Writing in his *Observations on the feeling of the beautiful and sublime*, Kant re-echoes Hume's erroneous supposition. He believed that the difference between the African and the European was not just a matter of skin colour but fundamentally, that of mental incapacities. According to him:

> Mr. Hume challenges anyone to cite a simple example in which a Negro has shown talents, and asserts that among the hundreds of thousands of blacks who are transported elsewhere from their countries, although many of them have been set free, still not a single one was ever found who presented anything great in art or science or any other praiseworthy quality. (1960: 110–111)

All these erroneous suppositions crystallised in justifying slavery and the sort of destructive colonialism Africa suffered. The insistence that African intellectuals should aim at making original African contributions is targeted at challenging this type of corrugated mindset and falsified history by the likes of Hume and Kant. They ignored the well-known and well-reported mathematical genius of Thomas Fuller (1710–1790), possibly an Igbo slave (or one of other tribes along the coast of West Africa from Liberia to Benin to Nigeria) shipped away through the Niger River when he was barely 14 years of age and was used by the pro-abolitionists in their days to argue that Africans were not mentally inferior to Europeans. He was a contemporary of Hume (1711–1776) and Kant (1724–1804) who most likely knew of him because his extra-ordinary intellect was famous but chose to pretend otherwise. Fuller's genius was reported in Mathew Carey's *American Museum., Vol v* by Benjamin Rush (1789), and in his letter to the Royal Society of London about Thomas Fuller's incredible intellectual prowess in 1788. Hume was already late by this time and Kant had already published his most stereotypical work, *The Observations* in 1764 but Fuller's genius was already well-known before Hume and Kant became popular philosophers. And if they both claimed to have done thorough research about peoples and cultures of the world before publishing their works in which they denigrated the intellect of the African, then, it is most likely that they heard of Fuller. Assuming this was not the case, Kant, who continued to work actively beyond the 1780s when Fuller's fame became global through the pro-abolitionist campaigns, did not recant his initial uninformed view of the African showing that his original views were clearly motivated by racism.

Fuller was reputed for his uncommon and near divine mathematical abilities that befuddled and dusted the best European intellect in history (Carey 1789: 62–63). If Fuller had gone to school and had become a scientist or anything at all, history would have remembered him for what he truly was, the greatest genius of all time and he was a dark-skinned man from West African. It is unlikely there would ever be another human with his type of intellect. Fuller among many things, could perform complicated mathematical calculations in a time frame that is marginally second only to the speed of a twenty-first century supper computer, even though he had no formal education of any kind and could not read nor write. Mathew Carey, a nationally respected and renowned intellectual historian was a contemporary of Fuller. Similarly, Benjamin Rush whose reports were published in Carey's book was a respected man of remarkable energy, physician, psychiatrist, professor of chemistry, signatory to the Declaration of Independence, who knew Fuller personally having interacted with him describes the mathematical genius as extra-ordinary (Carey 1789: 62). Carey's work was so respected that President George Washington wrote him a personal letter in which he describes his work in the following words: "Sir, I believe the American museum has met with extensive, I may say, with universal approbation from competent judges: for I am of opinion, that the work is not only eminently calculated to disseminate political, agricultural, philosophical, and other valuable information—but that it has been uniformly conducted with taste, attention and propriety" (Carey 1789: iii). So I am quoting two sources that knew Fuller, that witnessed Fuller's genius and interviewed those that experienced it directly as well. Carey particularly, was a source that was impeccable that the list of noble men who subscribed to his volumes as printed in the volume v were as long as a lengthy book chapter. A source so revered and objective that the America's first president approved a state funding to circulate copies of the volumes in all American cities, towns and villages.

It turned out that in the prime of his youth, there was no human who could contrive a problem Fuller could not solve within minutes. For this, he was nicknamed the Virginia calculator after the state in the US where the plantation he worked in was located. Many spectacles were organised to test his genius during his life time and the consistent astounding successes made him a slave everyone wanted to buy. Rush reports one of such public spectacles: "In the presence of Thomas Wislar and Benjamin W. Morris, two respectable citizens of Philadelphia, he gave the amount of nine figures, multiplied by nine" (Carey 1789: 62). The above test is like asking someone to solve: 739,853, 593 times 9. Fuller gave the accurate answer in a few minutes. For his extra-ordinary genius, the type history has not recorded before, insane sums were offered to his owners, Presley and Elizabeth Cox of Alexandria, Virginia but they refused to sell for which Fuller was grateful.

As Rush reported, when Fuller was 70 years old and showing signs of senile decay as most people of that age coupled with the fact that he had lived a life of hard labour as a slave, two American intellectuals from Pennsylvania, William Hartshorne and Samuel Coates, whom Rush describes as "men of probity and respectable characters" (Carey 1789: 62), went to put him to what would be the final test in hope that his old and fatigued mind might fail him once. They went with an excellent mathematician and posed three carefully planned questions to him: "First, upon being asked, how many seconds there are in a year and a half, he answered in about two minutes, 47,304,000. Second. On being asked, how many seconds a man has lived, who is seventy years, seventeen days and twelve hours old, he answered, in a minute and a half, 2,210,500,800" (Carey 1789: 62). The mathematician present who was working out the problems on a paper later arrived at his own answer and told Fuller that he was wrong, because the answer he got on his paper was smaller. But Fuller hastily replied, "'Top, massa, you forget de leap year." When the mathematician added the seconds of the leap years to what he got originally, the result matched the one given by Fuller in less than 2 min.

Then came to the third and most complex question, "suppose a farmer has six cows, and each cow has six female pigs, the first year, and they all increase in the same proportion, to the end of 8 years, how many cows will the farmer then have? Initially as Rush reported, Fuller did not understand the question due to language barrier. The gentlemen had to take some time to rephrase the question in a simpler English and Fuller immediately computed the figures and answered correctly: 34,588,806. All of this including the wasted time in 10 min. The two gentlemen were flabbergasted and awe-struck of what a 70 year old man could do with his debilitating mind as Rush (Carey 1789: 63) reports: "One of the gentlemen (Mr. Coates) having remarked in his presence, that it was a pity he had not had an education equal to his genius: he said, 'no massa—it is best I got no learning; for many learned men be great fools." The truth of Fuller's declaration can be attested to by what is happening in different African countries in the postcolonial where miseducated leaders run their countries down. It can also be attested to by the way several Western leaders run the world and the type of believes held by many Western intellectuals about other cultures and their fellow human beings.

(c) *African intellectuals must prove themselves through quality research and publications in standard international journals and presses:*

I agree that quality research and publications are features of intellectual prowess and I agree that African intellectuals should strive to demonstrate these two requirements. But there are other things involved, racism for instance is not limited to the attacks in our public spaces, there is entrenched racism in the academic sphere which many gifted Africans face daily. Besides reported cases where many talented African sportsmen and women are under-promoted due to clear racism, there are many of such incidences in the academe.

In a recent paper (Chimakonam 2017), where I investigated the question: "who has the right to know?" something I described as the anthropological question in philosophy or the anthropology of philosophy as opposed to philosophy of anthropology, I explained that the West still dominate and control knowledge production, regulation and dissemination processes through their big presses and news media. With this monopolistic control, they determine what gets published, disseminated and promoted. I gave an example of a typical journal or press where editors and reviewers gate keep manuscripts from global south using two main strategies namely; rejection and conformation. They can reject a manuscript by a scholar for all kinds of reasons that are not connected with quality of the work. It could be for commercial purposes where they think that the unknown scholar from the global south cannot be a market hit, or "They may discriminate against manuscripts for carrying messages which they deem offensive to the Western mind, or which rival the Western truth/ epistemic perspective, or which is against the logic of the West, … or simply for the name and nativity of the author" (2017: 127). Just the same way some people think that African scholars are not good enough to hold a teaching and research positions in their universities, that is also how many an editor and reviewer think that publishing an African on their journal would constitute a dent on the image of their journals. So, it is not just about a demand for African intellectuals to publish their research in established and reputable international journals and presses, it needs be stressed that some of these so-called excellent international journals and presses have unstated racist policies that ensure that excellent manuscripts from talented African intellectuals are rejected.

The second strategy they employ is what I called "conformation" (2017: 127). Most times, reviewers and editors go extra mile to mutilate quality manuscripts from African scholars before publishing it. They accept to publish such manuscripts "on condition that such authors restructure the logic of their work to align with accepted Western epistemic perspective. In the end, the original epistemic value of such works are lost as they become at worst, a distortion of say, the African epistemic perspective, and at best, a poor mimicry of the Western perspective" (2017: 127). It is publications like this that some other Western colleagues criticise as unoriginal and lacking in creative ideas. Some go further to mock their African authors as transliterating or copying Western generated ideas. Others unsympathetically draw attention to the fact that ideas or topics which the African author investigated had already been exhausted in Western scholarship.[10] So much for those who recommend that African intellectuals of this age should focus on adding to what the Europeans have done rather than attempting to make African contributions, a point I have already discussed above. He who wears the shoe they say, knows where it pinches.

I have been a victim of the scenarios I painted above and so were many other African colleagues. In fact, I am yet to see anyone who has not. You take your time to ensure that your manuscript falls clearly within the scope of a journal before you submit. Sometimes, you do not even get the courtesy of an acknowledgement. At other occasions, you receive one which informs you that your submission cannot be considered further without reasons. When you do get reasons from the editor, they are usually a polite way of saying 'we are not interested in you nor in your paper.' In some cases, when you are lucky and your submission gets sent out to reviewers, the reports in most cases are appalling. Sometimes, you recognise that your manuscript probably needs more work but at some other times, you search out published papers from the journal that rejected your submission just to learn a few tricks and you are alarmed that some of the journal's published papers are not better than your rejected manuscript. Only in rare cases do you get objective review reports even if the paper in the end is rejected but you could see the reports were objective. In fewer cases, you get a report with acceptance on condition of changes that would affect the soul of the paper. Even when your paper is published, rarely do you come by a European working in the same areas that cites it. They may read and steal ideas from your paper which they go on to modify and use in their own work but would hardly

---

[10] See for example the debate between Heinz Kimmerle and Jurgen Hengelbrock where it was claimed that African philosophy lacked originality, www.galerie-inter.de/kimmerle. See also the preface Kimmerle wrote for Sophie Oluwole's book (1989) where according to Innocent Asouzu (2007: 32), Kimmerle could not resist the temptation of pointing out that all the issues raised by Oluwole were already exhausted in European philosophy.

cite you as an African except when they feel a burning desire to demonstrate the poverty of your scholarship.

In the face of all these discriminations by journal and presses, African intellectuals have learned to write five or ten papers before one is accepted. Sometimes, the one that is accepted is the same paper that has been rejected by three or four journals but you kept sending it to other journals until one accepted it. It is experiences like these that gradually begin to conquer your stubborn objective but delusional view that a certain uncanny standard truly guides the process and you begin to be convinced that there may be more to the much touted imaginary standard.

The proposal for this book was rejected by three different presses before it was eventually accepted by the present publishers. In fact, one review report from one of those presses says that "this proposal must be rejected…besides being untenable, the ideas the author claims to inaugurate are too dangerous for civilisation…" I welcome the reader to judge for himself if, indeed, the ideas in this book are "too dangerous for civilisation." But these are the sort of language used by some European editors and reviewers to slaughter manuscripts from African intellectuals and gate keep them from seeing the light of book shelves and book stores. So, yes, there are numerous African intellectuals out there doing everything required to prove themselves through quality research but racism, most times, stands in the door way and prevents the publication of such research in the so-called excellent international journals.

It is difficult for an average European out there to know about these experiences. What some tend to know is the prevailing mindset and stereotype that African scholars do not measure up to standard. In some cases, this can be true, but even in those cases where it is not true, how can an already biased European editor or reviewer prevent themselves from being influenced by this stereotype? And this is the *benoke* point where standard begins to give way to sentiments.

There are impeachable proofs nowadays that show that most times, this much touted standard are set for outsiders. In the 1990s Alan Sokal, a New York University physics professor wrote a fake nonsensical paper and sent it to *Social Text*, a respected journal, it was published. This created a shock-wave in Western academy and all sorts of reason were adduced to explain why the journal editors and their reviewers could not detect that the paper was utter nonsense. In 2011, John Bahannon, a journalist produced a fake paper in the field of the biological sciences which he submitted to 304 journals, surprisingly, 157 accepted the paper for publication which was more than half (King 2014). Recently, the trio of Lindsay et al. (2018) conducted the same experiments with twenty fake papers they produced. Seven of those twenty nonsensical papers have already been accepted mid-way into the experiment by the so-called reputable and excellent international peer-reviewed journals.

Like in the case of the Sokal hoax, all kinds of reasons are being adduced to explain away the error. But the fact is, if editors and reviewers do what they claim they do, which is to insist and uphold standard for everyone irrespective of race, then, the fake papers by Western hoaxers would not have passed through the so-called rigorous system of reviews. What this suggests is that there is another explanation: sentiment and stereotype. There is a sentiment that Westerners know what they are doing and there is a stereotype that Africans do not know what they are doing. Sentiment and stereotype therefore determine in most cases whose paper is accepted and whose paper is rejected without proper and objective assessment. There are of course, exceptions to these two cases, the point I want to make is that sentiment and stereotype play huge roles even if not exclusively, in academic publishing and while they favour the Westerner, they place the African at disadvantage. This highlights the strong influence of racism in academic publishing which makes it difficult for talented Africans to have their papers accepted and published by the so-called reputable journals. Would it not be unfair therefore to judge the African intellectual by the number of papers he has been able to publish in the so-called excellent international peer-reviewed journals and presses that would more than likely reject his submission without objective reviews? Sometime ago, an American friend asked me to recommend some important work in African philosophy which I would want him to read. When I gave him a list, he complained that most African intellectuals do not publish in recognised international journals and presses which makes it difficult to access their work. I quickly drew his attention to the salient problem of racism in academic publishing which discriminates against the manuscripts by African intellectuals. Usually, their other option would be to have their work printed by local printers who had neither influence nor the resources to compete with their western counterparts.

If the so-called international journals and presses subject submissions from any part of the world to the same level of rigour, it would be difficult for Western hoaxers to get at them. Take as another example, the nonsensical paper by Bruce Gilley which *Third World Quarterly* accepted and published in 2017. Gilley is a scholar known for his racist views against Africans. Some of his previous publications have advanced racist positions. His paper "A case for colonialism" was one of such papers where he recommended that Africa be re-colonised and made to pay European countries that would come to re-colonise them. He went on to make all sorts of incoherent arguments, contradicted himself in some places, committed series of factual errors, and so on. Yet, reviewers and journal editors approved it for publication and published it. It was a tremendous outcry from intellectuals that forced the journal to retract the really shameful and obviously racist paper. What can be gleaned from this case is that we have a journal dedicated to the Third World issues but registered, run and edited by intellectuals from the so-called First world countries who were so eager to publish a paper that undermined and insulted the Third World that they overlooked the tremendous errors in the paper. There are certainly a lot of implications that can be drawn from all these cases but I simply want to refute the claim that publishing in the so-called reputable, international, excellent peer-reviewed journals is a correct yardstick to measure anyone's intellectual capability and expertise in any field at all. There is more to the system that makes it difficult for one to regard it as unsullied.

(d) ***The university should be a place for merit rather than a place for affirmative action:***

To be honest, I could not agree more with the position that the university should be a place where merit counts rather than a place for affirmative action. But there should be a caveat: 'all things being equal' to this supposition. After all, the university primarily is supposed to be a universe for knowledge production. It should be a universe in the sense of gathering the very best from different corners of the world. A situation like the one reported by Olivia Goldhill (2018) in her opinion piece published in *Quartz,* in which departments in some universities in South Africa hired majority of their professors from the United States and United Kingdom not only defeats this goal of the university but is in itself a prognostic to something much more sinister. There is no logic that can establish that at least thirty per cent quality staff cannot be sourced from within the country, another forty per cent from the rest of the continent and the remaining thirty per cent from different corners of the world and not just from the US and the UK alone.

When a system is run in such a way that stereotype is used by one group whether consciously or unconsciously to sideline or deny opportunities to people of another group, and especially if there had been historical legacy of policies like apartheid, then reversal policies like affirmative action become necessary. The end of apartheid in the official policy papers of South Africa does not imply the end of such practice in the minds of all of its former practitioners. The human mind usually needs longer time to adjust its beliefs. The point is, the challenge and effect of epistemic marginalisation against some groups in our world today are probably more serious than those who are unaffected by it are willing or ready to recognise. In a recent work (Chimakonam 2018), I tried to show that epistemic marginalisation is the mother of all forms of marginalisations whether in race, gender or class. One is first discounted and cut off from the power to control knowledge production, regulation and dissemination before they are discounted or cut off from race, gender or class-based exigencies. If African countries and African intellectuals have no stake in over ninety-seven per cent of the dominant publishers and media outlets in the world, who control knowledge production, regulation and dissemination in our world, how can there be fair level playing field for Africans to compete?

Talk of merit makes sense only where there is fair competition. In the absence of fair competition, programmes like affirmative action become necessary. The idea behind affirmative action is however not to create room for quacks. If one uses affirmative action as a ploy to bring in quacks and misfits, then, that becomes an abuse of the programme. What affirmative action entail is that in a lopsided system where a good number of quality talents would never get deserved opportunities because of their group membership, a positive action is used to hand such opportunities to them. It is incorrect to suppose that affirmative action is a strategy that promotes mediocrity and undermines merit. What has to be guarded against is any attempt to abuse the programme and this concern must be taken seriously because, often, nationalist elements are blinded by vengeance or a skewed sense of patriotism that they fail to recognise that to take as much as you want is never as good as to know when to stop. I believe that in a society trying to heal and where there are well-meaning people on all sides, redressing past injustices including epistemic injustice might be a tortuous process but the good conscience of those involved, will almost always prevail. The intellectual is, in such a scenario, tasked to show rare example by aspiring to those values and moral standards which ordinarily, might be larger than himself.

(e) *The curriculum of some disciplines cannot be Africanised:*

The claim that the curriculum of some disciplines cannot be Africanised is quite uninformed. Those who hold this naïve view assume quite in error that Africanising a curriculum means creating an African version of that discipline. For example, they ask wryly, is it possible to have an African chemistry, physics, mathematics or even philosophy? No, no, no! To Africanise a curriculum simply means to alter the background logic. For example, Newtonian physics has a different background logic from Einsteinian physics, it does not discount any of them as implausible. Students of physics study both but are well aware of the variation in their approaches to the study of physical realities. Likewise, the curriculum of every discipline can be Africanised when their background logic is altered and replaced with African logic.

Expectedly, opponents of this vision would ask; is there such a thing as African logic? What is it like? Well, thankfully, that is the focus of this book as a whole. Having discussed the background to African logic in part one, I laid out the principles of a prototype African logic complete with its syntactic and semantic formulations in part two. Specifically, chapters six, seven and eight articulated Ezumezu as philosophy of logic, methodology and formal system respectively. This type of logic which is based on the world-view and ontological lifeworld of African cultures, when deployed as the foundation of curriculum, alters approach and methodology.

An Africanised curriculum is not the one in which African content completely displace Western content. It is not the one in which tried and tested principles and laws are jettisoned or abandoned because they were formulated by Westerners. It is also not the one in which an African version of every theory would be created just to prove a point that Africans can do as well. No, these are all myopic. The most important thing in the project to Africanise and which is what makes it desirable is that it introduces yet another model for studying the world which is capable of expanding our frontiers of knowledge in new directions, deepening our understanding of the world and broadening our epistemic horizon. What we now know through the epistemic framework driven by Western logic is not all there is and neither is it all that we can possibly know. Since the later part of the twentieth century, advances in knowledge, arguably has slowed in many fields. Even the Nobel prizes are now being awarded for trifling discoveries compared to astounding discoveries and inventions in the first and second quarters of the twentieth century. All this point to one simple truth, that we may have become too comfortable with the Western epistemic framework undergirded by the Aristotelian logic. Time has now come for us to make that needed paradigm shift, this time, not in science but in logic. The campaign to Africanise education in institutions in Africa is therefore a welcome development.

The second most important thing is that Africanising education curriculum would enable a hitherto, epistemologically marginalised peoples of Africa to restore their identity, self-confidence and pride in their cultures. It would enable them to re-discover themselves anew and shake off the chains of mental slavery. It would pave the way for a culture of education that trains critical and creative thinking abilities of Africans and put an end to a colonial caricature of education which from the beginning sets out to conform and negate the creative originality of the African. It is this type of curriculum and system of education designed to liberate and unleash the African genius that can empower Africa to regain its place in the comity of nations.

11.4 How Slavery and Colonialism Destroyed African Epistemologies and How Postcolonialism is Sustaining that Epistemic Destruction

It may seem that I was too harsh on Europe in the above discussions. Some may even argue that my accusations against the colonial conquerors of Africa were exaggerated. Let me make something clear: Africa probably would have inflicted similar damage on Europe were they the ones to enslave and colonise Europe. The trait of animality is in every human no matter where they come from. So, I am not constructing a moral high ground for Africans, I am only trying to show the cost of lack of moral and humane disposition of the conquering Europe to the epistemic heritage of Africa.

Before the arrival of Europe and the Portuguese specifically in the fifteenth century AD on the shores of Africa, there was a large epistemological accumulation in diverse areas from medicine to art and to complicated technologies you could think of. These knowledges had been passed on from several hundred years during which constant improvements and advancements were made on existing discoveries and inventions. One thing was lacking though, the presentation of such knowledges remained archaic, if not mystical. The doctor was at the same time a priest, a chief, a sorcerer, etc., the typical Jack of all trade but ironically, a master of all. It was also this attribute of being Jack of all trade in which scientific knowledge was professed by the priests of local deities that gave Europeans the cover to destroy African epistemic heritage as evil practices. When colonialism began, it also forged a profitable partnership with missionary campaigns. The latter which wasted no time in branding the traditional African religions fetish, pagan, heathen and diabolic, sought to destroy the scientific knowledges alongside the traditional religions.

Just as slavery took away tens of millions of young generation who were to receive the various knowledges from their fathers and elders, colonialism decimated what was left after the epistemic disruption of generational knowledge transfer caused by slavery. Many reports nowadays indict Africans for wilfully selling their kit and kin into slavery but only a few would begin by stressing the fact that the Europeans aligned with the bad apples in various African societies to commence the slave trade. In Africa of old, there were derelicts who were usually lazy and scorned by the society. It was this group of people that the Europeans struck business with to kidnap people in exchange for valuables. In today's Western world, such derelicts do all sorts of odd jobs including kidnapping for ransom, assassination for a fee, human trafficking, human organ trafficking, sex-trafficking, etc. So, it was not that Africans do not value their children and as a result, sold them for trifling goods. Those who actually engaged in this type of practice were mostly deceived. They were first impressed by the European technology and when they demanded to be taught, the European cunningly claimed the secret to his technology could only be learned in his country. So, if Africans agreed to put their children in his impeccable custody, he would graciously ferry them across the great sea to his own country where they would learn the ways of the European and return to their people afterwards.

Besides the tens of millions who were transported out of the continent and into slavery, tens of millions more, like the case of the Congo, were slaughtered during colonialism. The result was the decimation of African knowledges. Since African knowledges prior to slavery were based mainly on oral tradition transferred from one generation unto another, slave trade and colonialism that decimated the populations disrupted this age long process. The case of Thomas Fuller discussed earlier, the African slave who humbled the Europeans with his mathematical genius was a typical case of immense knowledges that were taken out of Africa during slavery and destroyed.

A serious charge against colonialism with regards to the destruction of African epistemologies can be built on the fact of colonial support of the evil missionary campaigns. As I stated earlier, the missionaries who were jealous of the pampered African gods branded them demons and taking inspiration from the bible story of the confrontation between Elijah and the prophets of Baal, destroyed both deities and priests from one village to the other while the colonial administration provided protection and support. A good case was the destruction of *Ibini Ukpabi*, what the British called Long Juju and the execution of its priests during the British Expedition in 1901–1902. As colonial soldiers destroyed local knowledge centres, they killed the specialists of diverse knowledge persuasions. The missionaries preached and condemned local knowledge formations as evil and demonic and in some cases, forcibly converted local peoples into Western Christian religion. The new converts were intimidated with the concepts of the Western God and heaven and terrorised with the concepts of hell and eternal damnation, taking advantage of the Africans' belief in afterlife.

In actuality, the missionary was a wing of the colonial programme tasked to provide mental brainwash, decimation of critical, creative and independent thinking, and subduing of rebellious spirit in the African peoples. The problem is that it has taken stronger root in African mind since then. It ensured that colonialism carefully transitioned into postcolonialism—the continuation of colonial evils in subtle ways. Nowadays, the average African whose relative is afflicted with one illness or the other would prefer to take him to church for the priests of European Christian religion to pray and restore his health. Even cases of mental relapse are now viewed as spiritual attacks which only the Christian God can ward away. There is wide spread addiction to the Christian God in Africa today, who actually offers nothing but continued self-delusion. It is a strong sign of postcolonialism. This destructive ideology planted into the African through miseducation and religious brainwash has now taken toll on the people and is perpetuating the will of colonial Europe which was then to keep Africa down, tractable and obedient. Well, they are now tractable and obedient, but Europe should stop complaining and open its borders to God's people who are jostling to migrate to 'Canaan'.

This is contrary to the scientific view in many places in Africa before the Europeans arrived. A very important online website archives video evidences of traditional African knowledges. Some of those videos are footage of traditional neurosurgeries and brain surgeries as performed by traditional African healers. In these videos shot decades ago, the British narrator who witnessed some of these sessions stated that the surgeries had ninety-six percent success rates, better than what the surgeons in the best hospitals in London could offer.[11] In the case of the brain surgery, it is said that when people observe signs of mental problem in their loved one, they take him to a witch doctor who specialised in brain surgery. The latter will examine the patient to determine whether he has a tumour or lump in the brain. Once he confirms this, a surgery is scheduled to remove or cleanse the brain. The video referred to above shows a live performance of one of such brain surgeries.

Overall, this video evidence confirms my thesis that different disciplines can be Africanised where the latter means altering the background logic to yield a different knowledge protocol. As can be seen in the footage of the brain surgery performed by the traditional African surgeon, the method and apparatuses he used in performing the brain surgeon are much simpler and different from the method and complicated equipments used by the European surgeon, yet, the success rates in the former, decades ago, may well still surpass the success rates in the latter in our twenty-first century world. What was needed in colonial times was not the destruction but modernisation of African knowledges.

Now, most of these knowledges and advancements are gone, destroyed by the activities of slavery that disrupted their transmission to the next generations, and by colonial/missionary campaigns that ended their practices. What the African was given in return by the treacherous colonialist/missionary was religion and endless prayers to the European God who of course, being light of skin and male, like the chauvinistic European racist, discriminates against prayers from his unwanted African children. As the rest of the world are making advances in knowledge, Africans are tearing down industries and building churches some of which can take about one thousand worshippers at a sitting. The future, with the subtle problem of postcolonialism, now looks bleak for the continent and it is for this reason, that the project of this book is further justified.

---

[11] See "Traditional Brain Surgeries." https://oddafrica.com/category/healing/ Retrieved October 15, 2018.

11.5 Conclusion

The project of curriculum transformation is a concern with logic. It is logic that shapes the way we think and look at reality. It is logic that determines the direction and even the extent of our epistemic expansions. A given logic model might tend to be conservative in approaching and studying realities. It puts them into clear and predictable perspectives which tend to mediate a certain level of order and organisation in an epistemic project. But this predictability might also have some shortcomings. For example, Einstein's relativity theory might not have the level of orderliness which characterises Newton's physics, but it proved to be more resourceful enabling us to unleash the power of nature many times over.

This is the benefit which a paradigm shift in background logic of educational curriculum might offer. We want to continue making new and more extensive discoveries. We want to be able to compel nature bear more revealing witnesses against itself. To achieve this, new logic models that allow us see nature in new light and are less conservative might be required. This is what is attempted in a theory of curriculum transformation. We want to change the way the African child is educated. For more than a century, the African child has been put through a curriculum that is largely 'colonial.' This curriculum has two prominent disadvantages: first, it was designed to suppress and stifle the critical and creative originality of the African, and second, it was too alien and its background logic does not speak to the realities of the African world. So, an African child may be put through several years of schooling where he learns a lot of things by imitation but nothing by way of understanding.

The project to transform curriculum in Africa is therefore urgent, not only because the system driven by Western logic is now known to slow our knowledge economy down, but also because that system has never suited the African. And at a time where our world needs to take that next giant step to get our knowledge machine running again, if Africa could step forward with a new idea, a new logic to drive the process, then, it would have made 'that' vital African contribution to world's intellectual history and civilisation.

In this final chapter, I bring together, a pressing problem, one that I consider the foundation of all problems facing Africa in the postcolonial, with our new logic called Ezumezu to demonstrate how the new tool can be deployed in solving problems for the continent.

References

Asouzu, I. Innocent. 2004. *The method and principles of complementary reflection in and beyond African philosophy*. Calabar: University of Calabar Press.
———. 2007. *Ibuaru: The heavy burden of philosophy beyond African philosophy*. Zurich: Lit Verlag GmbH/Co. Kg Wien.
Barker, J. Anthony. 1978. *The African link: British attitudes to the Negro in the era of the Atlantic slave trade, 1550–1807*. London: Cass.

References

Beck, W. Lewis, ed. *Kant on History*. Quoted in Serequeberhan, Tsenay. 1991. African philosophy: The point in question. In African philosophy: The essential reading, ed. Tsenay Serequeberhan, 3–28. New York: Paragon House.

Benatar, David. 2015. Those who seek changes must show they are desirable. *Cape Times* https://www.iol.co.za/capetimes/opinion/those-who-seek-changes-must-show-they-are-desirable-1886695. Retrieved 2 Sept 2018.

Chimakonam, Jonathan O. 2016. Can the philosophy curriculum be Africanised? An examination of the prospects and challenges of some models of Africanisation. *South African Journal of Philosophy* 35 (4): 513–522. https://doi.org/10.1080/02580136.2016.1245553.

———. 2017. African philosophy and global epistemic injustice. *Journal of Global Ethics* 13 (2): 120–137.

———. 2018. Addressing the epistemic marginalization of women in African philosophy and building a culture of conversations. In *African philosophy and the epistemic marginalization of women*, ed. Jonathan Chimakonam. London: Routledge.

Chimakonam, Jonathan O., and C.A. Victor Nweke. 2018. Why the 'Politics' against African philosophy should be discontinued. *Dialogue* 57 (2): 277–301. https://doi.org/10.1017/S0012217317000907.

Fauvel, John, and Paulus Gerdes. 1990. African slave and calculating prodigy: Bicentenary of the death of Thomas Fuller. *Historia Mathematica* 17: 141–151.

Gilley, Bruce. 2017. The case for colonialism. *Third World Quarterly*. https://doi.org/10.1080/01436597.2017.1369037. Retracted.

Goldhill, Olivia. 2018. Philosophy is the new battleground in South Africa's fight against colonialism. *Quartz*. https://qz.com/1332351/philosophy-is-the-new-battleground-in-south-africas-fight-against-colonialism/. Retrieved 2 Sept 2018.

Hegel, W. F. Georg. 1975. *Lectures on the philosophy of world history*. Trans. H. B. Nisbet. Cambridge: Cambridge University Press.

Hengelbrock, Jurgen. *You cannot free yourself from Hegel: An encounter with Heinz Kimmerle*. Intercultural communication. www.galerie-inter.de/kimmerle. Retrieved 3 May 2017.

Hume, David. 1741–1742. Of national characters, Essay XX. In *Essays, literary, moral, and political*. London: Ward, Locke and Tyler, n.d.

Jaffer, Mansoor. 2015. Mangcu has a point, Professor Benatar. *Cape Times*. https://www.iol.co.za/capetimes/opinion/mangcu-has-a-point-professor-benatar-1882510. Retrieved 2 Sept 2018.

Kant, Immanuel. 1960. *Observations on the feeling of the beautiful and sublime*. Trans. John T. Goldthwait, Berkely: University of California Press.

Kimmerle, Heinz. *The stranger between oppression and superiority*. www.galerie-inter.de/kimmerle. Retrieved 3 May 2017.

King, Ritchie. 2014. *It's surprisingly easy to get a fake study published in an academic journal*. https://www.theatlantic.com/national/archive/2014/01/its-surprisingly-easy-get-fake-study-published-academic-journal/357006/?utm_source=feed. Retrieved 6 Sept 2018.

Lindsay, James, Helen Pluckrose, and Peter Boghossian. 2018. *What an Audacious Hoax reveals about academia*. https://www.theatlantic.com/ideas/archive/2018/10/new-sokal-hoax/572212/. Retrieved 6 Sept 2018.

Oluwole, B. Sophie, ed. 1989. *Readings in African philosophy*. Lagos: Masstech Publications.

Popkin, Richard. 1978. Hume's racism. *The Philosophical Forum* 9 (2–3): 213–218.

Rush, Benjamin. 1789. Account of a wonderful talent for arithmetical calculation, in an African slave, living in Virginia. In *The American museum: Or repository of ancient and modern fugitive pieces, prose and poetical*, ed. Mathew Carey, vol. vol. v, 62–63. Philadelphia: Mathew Carey.

Santos, Boaventura de Sousa. 2016. *Epistemologies of the south: Justice against epistemicide*. New York: Routledge.

Tempels, Placid. 1959. Bantu Philosophy. Paris: Presence Africaine.

Xulela, Mangcu. 2015. Racially offensive diatribe has no place. *Cape Times*. https://www.iol.co.za/capetimes/opinion/racially-offensive-diatribe-has-no-place-1879582. Retrieved, 2 Sept 2018.

General Conclusion

Logic, it is safe to say, lies at the foundation of all thoughts. The way we look at realities is a function of the system of logic we subscribe to or the one we were raised with. Cultural diversity is a product of logic. Some of these models of logic have not been systematised and put into syntactic forms and semantic principles. Some are even used in certain cultures almost unconsciously. The intriguing thing is that there appears to be a sort of harmony of logics because despite the variations that exist in these systems, users tend to find ways to understand themselves across knowledge ecologies. It shows, at least, that all logics are artificial and can be taught or learned by anyone irrespective of their cultural background. The problem however seems to be that the ontology of one's cultural background is difficult to abandon. It can be corrupted but hardly abandoned. So, learning to reason with a foreign logic other than the one which underbellies one's native ontology almost always leads to the suffocation of mental critical and creative abilities. We can interact across different logical platforms but maintaining a logic and an ontology that are incompatible is difficult. This shows that the particular is just as serious as the universal and the latter is a product of the former. As Aime Cesaire succinctly captured it: "My conception of the universal is that of a universal enriched by all that is particular, a universal enriched by every particular: the deepening and coexistence of all particulars" (2010: 152). This shows that the African particular like other particulars in different cultural epistemologies, no matter the field, is necessary for creating a true universal epistemic vision.

As a result of the challenge identified in the preceding, different intellectual cultures thrive better on native logic and ontology. To cultivate any art or science, methodology is imperative and this is a question of logic. A formidable methodology, once created can lead to the opening of new vistas for thought and this is how civilisations are built. Africa, through the unfortunate experiences of slavery and colonialism lost touch with its culture and with it, its native logic and ontology. It has since become a laughing stock to its former colonialists who challenge it to contribute to world's history as a proof that it is intellectually equal to the West.

The above is a case well substantiated by Washington Williams when he wrote on the genius of Thomas Fuller, an African arithmetical prodigy:

> One of the standing arguments against the Negro was, that he lacked the faculty of solving mathematical problems. This charge was made without a disposition to allow him an opportunity to submit himself to a proper test. It was equivalent to putting out a man's eyes, and then asserting boldly that he cannot see; of manacling his ankles, and charging him with the inability to run. But notwithstanding all the prohibitions against instructing the Negro, and his far remove from intellectual stimulants, the subject to whom attention is now called [Thomas Fuller] had within his own untutored intellect the elements of a great mathematician. [...] That he was a prodigy, no one will question. He was the wonder of the age. (1883: 398–399).

From the foregoing, my claim in this book is that the African intellectual was born a stillbirth because colonialism decimated his culture and displaced its logic. An alien Western logic was then forced down his throat which continues to choke his creative originality even in the postcolonial. To restore his eyes so that he can regain his vision and to unbind the manacles at his ankles so that he can regain his freedom, is a task in logic and one that confronts Africa in the postcolonial. I envisage that this will be a long tortuous road but it is the only way to true African freedom, independence, emancipation and new beginning.

Unfortunately, Africa has the West which has laid all kinds of traps in his path to contend with. It is as if Europe is saying, 'to see far, you must see through me, to walk free, you must walk through me.' Colonialism may have ended but postcolonialism is in effect and motivated by racism. Racial discriminations and subordinations against Africa, has for the most part, driven a wedge between the West and Africa. There are many things that rupture the relationship between one group and another: one of it is the thinking that we know some things which others do not know or that what we know is superior to what they know or that they are incapable of knowing what we know. This mindset tends to make the side that perceives itself as dominant and superior was to dictate and legislate for the other side. This type of thinking is motivated by the remnant of the human animalistic disposition to carve territory. This disposition is animalistic not just because of its inclination to defend territory compelled by the instinct of self preservation, but because of the little known inclination to discount other territories and members of those territories as outsiders simply because it boosts our ego to do so. The joy created in the hearts of people who retain this mindset is similar to the one experienced by a lion that heads a pride when he successfully exiles some growing males whom he considers as future competition.

I know that since the tremendous successes of capitalism, the world tends to think that the sense of competition is an advanced form of human feeling but this is not always the case. They think that seeing life as competition means that we have outgrown a childish stage of human emotion that makes us feel compassion for others and restrain ourselves from doing anything that might harm or disadvantage them. To their understanding, an advanced humanity is one guided by individual interest alone. But this merely corroborates the old African wisdom that says that humans cannot outsmart nature. The more we try to purge the animal aspect of us, the more it finds expression in subtle ways. For example, we may have developed the technology that allows us to clothe ourselves while still restraining dogs and other animals with ropes tied around their necks, but somehow, we managed to create the tie which is a rope and put it around our own necks. No matter the reason we might give to justify this, it is a rope and it is tied around our necks. Is it not self abnegation that the European created the tie for himself after he has created something similar for animals and for the Africans he enslaved? It is the same animal instinct that drives the sense of competition. It is a sense of competition that makes a group of people want to carve territory in other to discount those they deem as competition unbeknownst to.

So most times, talks about standard, criteria, minimum acceptable bar, etc., in academics and other areas are motivated by innate sense of animal insecurity in a world adjudged to be about competition. Those who set the minimum acceptable bar place it at their level of tested proficiency. So they are the bar which outsiders may now struggle to approximate. Bars are not set for everyone and every group, it is set for outsiders alone. This is what the journals, presses and media run by Westerners do, they set bars for outsiders and pretend it was for everyone. A bar is a line that discounts outsiders and protects the interests of insiders.

Individuals bind together to form a group not necessarily because they have certain things in common—all humans share the most important features such as rationality and life in common—but because they would become more competitive in a group. Such persons may not even be comfortable with the group but because it promises the protection of their most cherished individual interests, they tend to endure and put up a smile. This is not different from what happens in the animal kingdom. Other lions and lionesses remain in the pride and endure the unjust and sometimes, brutish rule of the pride male not because they are completely pleased, but because their most cherished interests are protected within the pride. If anyone thinks the heightened sense of competition prevalent in the Western world today is advancement in humanity, he is wrong. It actually remarks a degradation of humanity. Humanity has two components, the animalistic and the humane. Unfortunately, the two aspects cannot advance simultaneously. They are like two buckets in a scale, if one goes up the other goes down. The best that can be achieved is equilibrium.

The contemporary Western world-view fails to hit this equilibrium in that the animal component has soared and the human component has dipped. Every industrial advancement that enhances luxury promotes the animal side of people; it does not as widely assumed in our time, promote the so-called quality of life. The quality of life is not something measured with luxury of the flesh, life is not flesh. Otherwise, majority of depressed, unhappy, insecure and unfree people would not be the ultra rich, yet they are. Quality of life is something internal like tranquillity, compassion, peace of the mind, freedom, internal sense of security, milk of human kindness, etc. A clear proof that the human component has plummeted and the animal component has soared in the West is the proliferation of debased crimes like school shootings, serial murders, suicides, and debased lifestyles such as gluttony, bestiality, etc. Why would societies that have made life easier and luxurious produce this level of depravity? It is because with luxury comes corruption, decadence, degeneracy and wickedness which are traits of animality not of humanity.

It is the pristine African communalism that came close to hitting the equilibrium of the animalistic and humane components. In it, there is the group concern in which the collective interest is protected. Yet, it carves territory that discounts others or the outsiders. This system may have lacked the luxuries afforded by a system like capitalism but it made humanity happier. Our world today may never hit the equilibrium, our animal component may continue to rule our human component as capitalism has come to stay, but let us not confuse the two and let us at least, give our sense of competition human face. The African intellectual or the African epistemic perspective will compete but let there be fair ground and let the rules not be those of the jungle. Ọgwụ go, now let the conversation begin!

References

Cesaire, Aime. 1956/2010. Letter to Maurice Thorez. Trans. Chike Jeffers. *Social Text* 103 (28): 2145–2152. https://doi.org/10.1215/01642472-2009-072.

Williams, G. Washington. 1883. *History of the Negro race in America from 1619 to 1880*. New York: Putnam's.

Index

A
Absolute, 5, 11, 17, 40, 49, 50, 55, 64, 80, 81, 83, 85, 87, 97, 111, 125, 133–135, 138, 140, 172, 174
Acholi logic, 63
Affective, 56, 57, 62, 110, 168
Affirmative action, 186, 199
Africa, 14, 24, 27, 29, 31, 33, 35, 36, 44, 55, 59, 60, 63, 81, 83, 94, 96, 103, 108, 110, 120, 137, 138, 147, 156, 163, 164, 172, 181–185, 187, 189, 190, 193, 198, 200–204, 208
African intellectuals, 26, 88, 159, 163, 167, 181, 182, 185–188, 193, 195, 199, 208, 210
Africanisation, 181–204
Africanised curriculum, 183, 188, 200
African logic, 5, 35, 36, 39–53, 55, 77, 93–96, 99–101, 104, 105, 108, 109, 111, 120, 123, 124, 133–135, 140, 143–148, 151, 158, 160, 162, 165, 167–169, 171–175, 177, 181–183, 185, 186, 200
Africanness, 22, 23, 33, 34, 151, 165
African philosophy, 3, 22, 56, 77, 94, 116, 141, 151, 167, 187
Afro-communitarianism, 6, 116, 123, 124, 142, 151–165
Agada, A., 57, 84, 156
Alternative logics, 4, 5, 18, 36, 40, 48, 60, 70, 71, 132, 158, 167, 171
Animalu, O.E.A., 98, 111
Apologists, 55, 56, 73
Aristotle, 6, 9, 10, 12–14, 40–42, 48, 52, 60, 78, 81, 83–85, 87, 88, 95, 115, 116, 127–129, 137, 155, 160, 174

Arumaristic complementarity, 126, 156
Arumaristic concession, 126
Arumaristicism, 144
Arumaristics, 34, 35, 95, 117–119, 125, 126, 132, 133, 135, 139, 141–145, 153, 156, 157, 160
Arumaruka unification principle, 104
Asouzu, I., 13, 63, 66, 68–70, 84, 104, 105, 110, 155, 163, 164, 173, 187, 189, 196
The Axiom of Re-generation, 123
The Axiom of Solidarity, 123
The Axiom of Truth, 123

B
Background logics, 58, 81, 82, 152, 160, 172, 181, 183, 185, 186, 200, 203, 204
Bantu Philosophy, 88, 189
Barnes, H., 45, 46, 61
Benoke point, 119, 141, 142, 197
Bivalence, 61, 97, 98, 108–111, 132, 135–137, 152, 158, 160, 175
Bochenski, M.J., 42, 46, 47, 61, 71, 95, 98, 148, 174
Bodunrin, P., 22, 28–30, 33, 83, 85, 173

C
The Calabar School of Philosophy, 68, 70, 105
Central claim, 143–146
Chimakonam, O.J., 24, 33, 65, 66, 81, 96–98, 101, 102, 105, 111, 122, 126, 147, 153, 154, 172, 173, 182, 195, 199
Civilisation, 7, 16, 41, 44, 45, 60, 83, 115, 154, 155, 174, 176, 181–204, 207

Colonial, 10, 31, 44–46, 57, 78, 84, 108,
 181–184, 186, 189, 190, 201–204
Colonial curriculum, 181, 183, 184
Colonialism, 11, 43, 85, 120, 121, 164,
 181–183, 185, 186, 188, 191, 193,
 198, 201, 207, 208
Communitarianism, 6, 32, 152, 153, 157–162
Communities, 15, 32, 33, 83, 103, 124, 151,
 157–159, 161, 162
Complementarity, 124, 126, 136, 138, 139,
 153, 156, 160, 161, 175
Complementary, 52, 61, 68–70, 84, 94,
 99–101, 105, 106, 110, 116–120,
 124, 133, 139–143, 151–153,
 155–157, 162, 165
Complementary reflection, 68, 116, 124, 142,
 151–153, 155–157, 162, 165
Complementary relationship, 118, 142
Complementary turn, 118, 142, 155
Complemented, 98–100, 106, 136, 139, 156,
 160, 177
Complemented value, 99, 106, 136, 156
Conceptual envelopment, 10–11
Congo, 202
Consolation philosophy, 116, 124, 151–153,
 156, 162, 165
Contemporaneity, 159, 161
Contextual modes, 99, 100, 106, 117, 119,
 133, 136, 137, 140, 142, 143
Contradictions, 45, 47, 49, 61, 63, 70, 72,
 96–98, 100, 101, 109, 116, 132,
 133, 135–138, 145, 152, 156, 158,
 160–162, 169, 172, 175–177
Conversational curve, 119, 141, 142, 153
Conversational philosophy, 66, 72, 105, 116,
 124, 151–153, 157, 162, 165
Conversational thinking, 17, 18, 34, 118, 119,
 122, 124, 125, 142, 153, 188
Criterion, 22–27, 29–35, 59, 69, 79, 104,
 173, 174
Critical re-othering, 127, 128
Cultural diversity, 207
Culture-bound systems, 3, 46, 57, 65, 172
Curriculum, 62, 181–188, 200, 201, 204

D

Decolonisation, 44, 181–204
Decolonised curriculum, 183, 185
Descartes, R., 8–10, 41, 83, 87, 127, 129
Determinism, 97, 101, 108, 109, 132, 135,
 152, 156
Disjunctive motion, 99, 118, 119,
 141, 153

E

Egypt, 41, 189, 192
Egyptians, 7, 189
Einstein, A., 41, 42, 120
Enlightenment, 5, 7, 8, 189
Epistemicides, 85, 86, 183
Epistemic marginalization, 199
Equilibrium, 209, 210
Essentialism, 13, 14, 88, 115
Ethnologicians, 40, 63
Ethnophilosophy, 24, 36
Ethocentricism, 35
Etuk, U., 35, 51, 59, 61–63, 65, 96, 104, 110,
 146, 167–169, 177
Eurocentricism, 41, 43, 44, 48, 56, 64
Eurocentric scholars, 43
Europe, 55, 138, 148, 159, 183, 188–190, 192,
 201, 203, 208
Evans-Pritchard, E.E., 44, 45, 58
Évoléus, 64, 108, 175, 186, 190
Excluded-middle, 49, 56, 72, 96, 100, 137,
 138, 177
Ezu, 99, 100, 104, 106
Ezumezu logic, 55, 73, 80, 94–98, 100–102,
 105–111, 116, 117, 122, 124, 126,
 128, 132, 133, 135–148, 151–165,
 167–177

F

Fayemi, A.K., 35, 59, 63, 96, 108, 174
Feyerabend, P., 80, 83, 173
1st Universalness Theorem, 134
Frege, G., 16, 107, 122, 170, 171
Frege, G. 'The Thought: A Logical Inquiry"
 Mind: A Quarterly Review of
 Psychology & Philosophy New
 Series, Vol. 65, No. 259, (July,
 1956) pp. 289-311., 59
Fuller, T., 193–195, 202, 208

G

Gap paradox, 108, 109
Global South, 81, 88, 172, 195
Goldenweiser, A., 45, 46
Greece, 7, 41, 192
Gyekye, K., 6, 123, 157–160, 162

H

Hengelbrock, J., 22, 36, 152, 163, 164, 196
Hegel, G., 10, 44, 46, 55, 83, 108, 147, 163,
 188–190, 192

History, 4, 6, 10, 11, 13–15, 32, 35, 41, 43, 44, 55, 78, 81, 83, 84, 88, 89, 96, 120, 121, 127, 129, 159, 168, 170, 171, 181–204, 207
Horton, R., 44, 60, 62–64, 89, 96, 137, 147
Hountondji, P., 22–25, 28–30, 32–34, 65, 81, 84, 85, 173, 174
Humanity, 6, 9, 13, 15, 17, 35, 43, 56, 57, 62, 65, 81–83, 85, 86, 120, 147, 154, 155, 185, 208–210
Hume, D., 7, 8, 10, 44, 189, 190, 192, 193
Hunnings, G., 49, 59, 60, 63, 111, 137, 146

I

Ibuanyidanda, 68, 69, 155
Identities, 10, 15, 21, 27, 43, 50, 64, 65, 72, 83, 86, 96, 97, 99, 100, 106, 117, 118, 120, 137–140, 145, 153–156, 161, 172, 176, 177, 184–186, 201
Igbo, 14, 16, 63, 87, 94, 102, 104, 109, 123, 125, 139–141, 147, 155, 175, 176, 193
Ijiomah, C., 35, 48, 59, 63, 65, 66, 70, 71, 96, 104, 105, 110, 111, 123, 140, 146, 170, 177
Ijiomah, C. *Modern Logic*. Owerri; A. P. Publications, 1995, 146
Intellectual hegemony, 78, 116, 158
Intellectual history, 10, 32, 83, 88, 89, 181, 188, 204
Intellectuals, 26, 88, 108, 154, 159, 163, 167, 181, 182, 185–199, 208, 210
Intercommunication of truth, 142
Iroegbu, P., 84, 103, 123
Izu, 72, 98–100, 106

J

Jacquette, D., 48, 95, 106, 135, 171
James, G., 41
Janz, B., 11

K

Kant, I., 6–10, 31, 44, 55, 81, 83, 87, 107, 123, 127, 129, 188–190, 192, 193
Kimmerle, H., 22, 36, 152, 163–165, 196
Kleene, S., 106, 109, 135, 136, 160

L

Law of Njikǫka, 96, 137, 139
Law of Nmekǫka, 96, 137

Law of Ǫnǫna-etiti, 96, 137, 140
Legitimation, 127, 128
Levy-Bruhl, L., 10, 44–46, 55, 58, 64, 96, 137, 147, 175, 176
Lifeworld, 32, 70, 73, 162, 200
Logic, 4, 22, 39, 55, 80, 93, 115, 131, 151, 167, 181, 207
Logica docens, 56, 63, 64, 96
Logical systems, 48, 49, 81, 82, 94, 96, 101, 174
Logical thesis, 119, 121, 122, 141, 142
Logica utens, 56, 63, 64
Logic criterion, 34
Logic relativism, 47, 48, 59, 61
Logic relativity, 47–49, 58, 61
Logic traditions, 26, 35, 41, 42, 48, 53, 65, 66, 93, 110, 111, 133, 134, 171, 172, 174
Logocentricism, 4, 5, 10–13, 17, 48, 78
Logomania, 5, 12, 13
Logophilia, 10–13
Logos, 5, 10–18, 44, 55, 87, 170
Lukasiewicz, J., 47, 56, 106, 110, 132, 135, 136, 148, 160, 175

M

Makinde, A., 49–52, 59, 60, 62, 64, 65, 174
Matolino, B., 157–160, 162
Mbiti, J., 22, 32–33, 103, 144, 157, 160
Menkiti, I., 6, 22, 32, 103, 139, 144, 157–160, 162
Methodology, 39, 50, 71–73, 78–80, 82–85, 88, 89, 95, 111, 115, 172, 174, 200, 207
Methods, 4, 8, 18, 22, 23, 25, 26, 28, 34–36, 46, 48, 50, 56, 60, 62, 71, 77, 80, 83, 85, 89, 95, 115–119, 122, 124–126, 128, 141–143, 156, 165, 170, 176, 187, 188, 192, 203
Metz, T., 82, 123, 155
Mindviews, 5–9, 11–13, 48, 78, 80, 81, 122, 126–129
Miseducation, 203
Mode context principle, 99–101
Modernism, 5–9, 12, 13, 83

N

Newton, I., 8, 41
Nietzsche, F., 9
Nigeria, 66, 84, 105, 109, 132, 139, 187
Nmeko, 116, 117, 119, 122–124, 128, 143, 153–155, 157

Nwa-izugbe, 100, 116, 119, 120, 133, 139, 142, 143, 153, 156, 160
Nwa-nju, 66, 72, 116–118, 120, 125, 133, 139, 141–143, 153, 156, 160
Nwa-nsa, 66, 72, 116–120, 125, 133, 139, 141–143, 153, 156, 160

O

Ohakarasi principle, 102, 103
Ohakaristicism, 144
Ohakaristic reasoning, 157
Okolo, B.C., 4, 22, 27, 28, 33, 45, 58, 62, 65, 79, 82, 152, 168, 172
Okoro, C.M., 44
Okwu, 13–18
Okwucentricism, 5, 17, 18
Oluwole, S., 22, 27, 33, 164
Omoregbe, J., 48, 59, 60, 62, 63, 96, 146
Ontological equality, 118
Ontological quadrant, 97
Ontological thesis, 120, 141, 142, 153, 156
Ontological variance, 118
Onyewuenyi, I., 22, 32–33, 144
Oriental, 24, 33, 34, 80
Oruka, O., 22, 25, 26, 29, 34, 59, 83, 89, 175
Othering, 82, 127, 128
Outlaw, L., 10, 13, 14, 78, 81, 84, 85, 168
Ozumba, G., 36, 104, 164

P

Peripheral claim, 143, 145
Peripheries, 99, 102, 103, 116–118, 143, 145, 155–157
Permissibility principle, 102, 144
Philosophizens, 86, 87
Plato, 9, 10, 12–14, 48, 78, 83–85, 87, 88, 115, 127–129
Polynesian, 13, 80, 81
Popper, K., 84, 129
Postcolonial, 78, 159, 187, 195, 204, 208
Postcolonialism, 181, 183, 186, 201–203, 208
Postmodern, 4–10, 17, 78, 80, 83, 85, 87, 124–128, 154
Postmodernism, 4–6, 9, 12, 13, 83, 126, 127
Prelogical, 50
Primitive mentality, 31, 44–46
Primitives, 44–46, 58, 59, 63, 64, 89, 137, 176
Principles of consent, 101–105
The principle of Context-Dependence of Value (CdV), 119, 142
Problematics, 39–53, 66, 105, 167–177

Q

Quine, V.O.W., 10, 128, 167, 169, 175, 176

R

Racism, 42, 86, 187–189, 191–193, 195, 197, 198, 208
Radical communitarianism, 32, 157, 158
Rationality, 15–17, 57–59, 64, 137, 147, 154, 209
Ratiosusuism, 16
Reiser, O., 40
Relationships, 6, 32, 51, 66, 96, 116–118, 120, 122–124, 138, 141–143, 145, 151, 153–155, 157–159, 177, 208
Re-othering, 82, 88, 127, 128
Rhodes Must Fall, 182, 186
Ritcher, M., 72

S

Santos, Boaventura de Suosa, 4, 82, 85, 183
2nd Universalsness Theorem, 134, 172, 174
Senghor, L., 33, 56–59, 62, 63, 96, 110, 146, 154, 159, 168
Serequeberhan, T., 11, 12, 78, 81, 84, 85, 188
Sogolo, G., 23, 58, 59, 138, 146
South Africa, 182, 186, 187, 199
Stebbing, S., 40
Sub-contraries, 61, 98–100, 106, 109, 126, 127, 132, 136, 139, 156
Subordinations, 42, 43, 191, 208

T

Tempels, P., 88, 89, 189
Tension of incommensurables, 118, 119, 142
The three supplementary laws of thought, 100, 117, 133, 137–140, 153, 156, 157, 172
Three-values, 40, 47, 56, 61, 70, 72, 97–99, 105, 106, 108–111, 132, 133, 135–137, 140, 148, 152, 165, 171, 172, 175
Traditions of logic, 96
Transformation, 181–204
Trivalence, 97, 98, 108, 132, 140, 160, 175
Truth-value-glut, 109

U

Ubuntu, 103, 116, 118, 123, 124, 151–155, 157, 162, 165

Uduma, O.U., 22, 23, 29, 33, 34, 50–52, 59, 64, 65, 96, 101, 108, 173, 174, 177
Undetermined, 106, 132, 135
Universalists, 3, 14, 24–26, 35, 40, 48, 49, 67, 83, 85, 96, 169
Universalist school, 3, 24, 83, 85
Universalness, 133–135, 172, 174
Universe of discourse, 58, 59, 132–135
University of Calabar, 105, 187, 188

V
Value-glut, 156
Verran, H., 63, 66–68, 82, 96, 105
Villagisation of knowledge, 5, 18, 77–89

W
Wedged-implication, 101, 102

Western, 4, 10, 22, 41, 56, 77, 94, 115, 132, 151, 182, 208
Western civilisation, 60, 155, 176
Westernism, 31
Western logics, 35, 42, 43, 47–49, 59–62, 65, 68, 72, 94, 95, 99, 102, 108, 132, 137, 138, 140, 144–146, 160, 174, 182, 183, 186, 200, 204, 208
Western philosophy, 4, 10–12, 22, 33, 35, 48, 77, 81, 82, 85, 86, 94, 115, 152, 159, 162, 164, 165, 172, 173
Whitehead, A.N., 13, 171
Wiredu, K., 22, 30–33, 35, 60, 64, 65, 79, 96, 121, 148, 157, 177

Y
Yoruba numeric system, 66–68

CPSIA information can be obtained
at www.ICGtesting.com
Printed in the USA
LVHW040839040122
707796LV00001B/3

9 783030 110741